INDIGENIZING ARCHAEOLOGY

UNIVERSITY PRESS OF FLORIDA

Florida A&M University, Tallahassee
Florida Atlantic University, Boca Raton
Florida Gulf Coast University, Ft. Myers
Florida International University, Miami
Florida State University, Tallahassee
New College of Florida, Sarasota
University of Central Florida, Orlando
University of Florida, Gainesville
University of North Florida, Jacksonville
University of South Florida, Tampa
University of West Florida, Pensacola

INDIGENIZING ARCHAEOLOGY

Putting Theory into Practice

Edited by Emily C. Van Alst
and Carlton Shield Chief Gover

Foreword by Roger Echo-Hawk

UNIVERSITY PRESS OF FLORIDA

Gainesville/Tallahassee/Tampa/Boca Raton
Pensacola/Orlando/Miami/Jacksonville/Ft. Myers/Sarasota

Copyright 2024 by Emily C. Van Alst and Carlton Shield Chief Gover
Some rights reserved

This work is licensed under a Creative Commons Attribution-NonCommercial-NoDerivatives 4.0 International License (CC BY-NC-ND 4.0) https://creativecommons.org/licenses/by-nc-nd/4.0/.

Note to users: A Creative Commons license is only valid when it is applied by the person or entity that holds rights to the licensed work. Works may contain components (e.g., photographs, illustrations, or quotations) to which the rightsholder in the work cannot apply the license. It is ultimately your responsibility to independently evaluate the copyright status of any work or component part of a work you use.

Published in the United States of America

29 28 27 26 25 24   6 5 4 3 2 1

Library of Congress Cataloging-in-Publication Data
Names: Van Alst, Emily C., editor. | Shield Chief Gover, Carlton, editor.
Title: Indigenizing archaeology : putting theory into practice / edited by
   Emily C. Van Alst and Carlton Shield Chief Gover ; foreword by Roger
   Echo-Hawk.
Other titles: Putting theory into practice
Description: 1. | Gainesville : University Press of Florida, [2023] |
   Includes bibliographical references and index.
Identifiers: LCCN 2023017173 (print) | LCCN 2023017174 (ebook) | ISBN
   9780813069869 (hardback) | ISBN 9780813080338 (paperback) | ISBN
   9780813073002 (ebook) | ISBN 9780813070667 (pdf)
Subjects: LCSH: Indians of North America—Antiquities. |
   Archaeology—Research—United States. | Human remains
   (Archaeology)—Repatriation. | BISAC: SOCIAL SCIENCE / Archaeology |
   SOCIAL SCIENCE / Anthropology / Cultural & Social
Classification: LCC E77.9 .I53 2023 (print) | LCC E77.9 (ebook) | DDC
   930.1—dc23/eng/20230526
LC record available at https://lccn.loc.gov/2023017173
LC ebook record available at https://lccn.loc.gov/2023017174

The University Press of Florida is the scholarly publishing agency for the State University System of Florida, comprising Florida A&M University, Florida Atlantic University, Florida Gulf Coast University, Florida International University, Florida State University, New College of Florida, University of Central Florida, University of Florida, University of North Florida, University of South Florida, and University of West Florida.

University Press of Florida
2046 NE Waldo Road
Suite 2100
Gainesville, FL 32609
http://upress.ufl.edu

CONTENTS

List of Figures   vii

List of Tables   ix

Foreword   xi

Acknowledgments   xvii

Indigenizing Archaeology: Putting Theory into Practice   xix
Emily C. Van Alst and Carlton Shield Chief Gover

Part I. Recontextualizing Archives of Knowledge

1. Story of Your/My/Our Skull: The Museum as a Haunted and Haunting Space   3
Zoë Antoinette Eddy

2. Biidoban in the Museum   22
Kay Kakendasotkwe Mattena

3. Rubber Yardsticks: Emic Methods in Indigenous Archaeology   33
S. Margaret Spivey-Faulkner

4. Archives in Conversation with Indigenous Archaeology: Creating Sustainable Partnerships in Work and Practice   50
Lydia Curliss

Part II. Reclaiming Cultural Heritage

5. A Journey of Growth and Personal Observations from an Indigenous Archaeologist   65
Patrick Cruz

6. Place as Indigenized Archaeological Knowledge   82
Nicholas C. Laluk

7. Living Our Relationships in the NAGPRA Process   96
Ash Boydston-Schmidt

8. Truth and Reconciliation in Archaeology   109
   Honey Constant-Inglis

Part III. Retelling Indigenous Stories

9. Indigenizing Rock Art Research: Indigenous Archaeological Methods
   to (Re)Contextualize and (Re)Claim Rock Art Sites   125
   Emily C. Van Alst

10. Storywork as Method and Theory in Indigenous Archaeology   139
    Ashleigh BigWolf Thompson

11. Histories within Radiocarbon   155
    Carlton Shield Chief Gover

Afterword: Archaeology as a Manifestation of Sovereignty, Self-
   Determination, and Activism   173
   Joe Watkins

List of Contributors   187
Index   189

FIGURES

2.1. *Biidoban in the Museum* 23

3.1. American, English-language folk taxonomy of animals 41

3.2. Idealized generic hierarchy within a folk taxonomy 42

3.3. Primary lexical items and secondary lexical items in English 43

11.1. Sequence of archaeological cultures in the Late Prehistoric and Protohistoric Central Plains 161

11.2. OxCal produced Start and End Boundaries of Central Plains tradition 167

TABLES

3.1. Dissection of the Mvskoke word Cetto-lanuce into constituent parts   44

3.2. Thirty-eight genera in Mvskoke that have sub-genera as produced through lexical item analysis   45

11.1. Impressionistic and glottochronological dates for time depths of separation of the Caddoan language family   160

11.2. Proposed direct relationships of historic Tribes to archaeological cultures   162

11.3. Posterior density estimates for the chronology of late prehistoric archaeological cultures in the Central Plains   168

FOREWORD

The papers in this book explore the panoramic intellectual geography of Indigenous archaeology. Since the 1990s the growth of this field of scholarship in Indian Country has been somewhat incremental, but it has proven a dynamic world, a slowly sprawling realm of discourse ever more difficult to pin down with generalizations. The increase of racial Indian archaeologists and the community institutionalization of archaeology programs, as well as the more general embrace of the field in archaeology, has been significant. As this book demonstrates, Indigenous archaeology is here to stay.

Observing the gradual rise of Indigenous archaeology, certain events in Pawneeland can illustrate a central theme of the field. Through the twentieth century as archaeology took shape, there were no Pawnees in Pawnee archaeology. In the 1920s Asa T. Hill became a leading archaeologist in Nebraska, and he spent decades promoting a lively regional community of scholars. In 1925 he met some of the leading Elders of the Pawnee people, and for a few years he corresponded with one Pawnee community leader, hoping that Pawnees would visit Nebraska, and inquiring about Pawnee tradition. This modest project did not inspire ongoing mutual interest. During the decades that followed, archaeological inquiry thrived in the Central Plains. But there is no record of archaeologists meeting with Pawnees and hosting visitors at sites; and archaeology publications gave minimal attention to Pawnee oral tradition as a source of history. It also does not appear that the Pawnee Elders who dealt with Asa T. Hill felt moved to encourage young Pawnees to explore archaeology. By the 1980s the Pawnee world and the world of archaeology seemed set to proceed along entirely segregated paths. Over a century after Asa T. Hill began giving thought to Central Plains archaeology, Carlton Gover became the first Pawnee academic archaeologist, as this volume attests.

On the verge of the 1990s, I found myself delving into archaeology. Over the decade that followed, I flew to various cities, and I discovered a thriving world, very lively. Throngs of archaeo-elders and students hurried off to conferences to sit down in lecture rooms and ballrooms, and hundreds of them stood up year after year to tell thousands of interesting stories. Years passed as I sat listening. In time I learned several truths. To study ancient history, I needed to study archaeoprehistory; to ponder the doings of my ancient pre-racial ancestors, I had to ponder archaeopaleoindians. And one day in 1992, attending the Plains Conference, I found myself listening to an Indian archaeologist. I listened with great interest, watching as he stood there alone, his tone serious and momentous and aloof. He finished his storytelling and the room emptied, and he paused to shake my hand and we stood for a moment in a swirl of people, a milling flood. We spoke a few words about ourselves and why we were there. That moment felt mysterious. I didn't know why we were the only Indians there that day. Nowadays, all these years later, whatever I have learned about such matters, that history still feels mysterious.

To weave meaning into history we must often organize impressionistic abraded moments into coherent memoirs of selfhood and identity, aligning random threads of heritage into narrative trajectories. I usually begin with the notion that the more complexity we introduce into our stories, the more options we have for becoming ourselves. Exploring those options, we create personal identities that are nuanced and resilient and empowered and maybe somewhat seamless.

And by the first years of the 1990s, I learned that archaeological inquiry and the study of oral tradition could indeed be merged to create more nuanced history, expanding the horizons of the worldbuilding essential to cultural identity. I thought this kind of dialogue would energize new forms of mutual respect. We could have the necessary cultural collisions—but Indians and archaeologists would ultimately merge their worlds. This perception eventually took me down some unexpected paths. Thinking about oral tradition and ancient history, I stood in some of the rooms where they invented "repatriation"; and by the end of the 1990s, I came to the view that someday we would begin to rethink the idea of race.

Mythological texts preserve our deepest oral insights into antiquity, and to assess this historical content, we need archaeology. But skeptical disinterest long ago discouraged inquiry into oral literature. During the days of Robert Lowie, when Franz Boas and his students studied oral tradition, they deliberately set it aside from archaeology. By the end of the 1990s, observing the emergence of Indigenous archaeology, I thought it would generate a new kind of momentum, a growing literature that would explore how archaeology and oral tradition together can illuminate ancient history. A trickle of research slowly appeared. But perhaps it has not much troubled the consensus waters of scholarship. In fact, one extreme of that consensus received national attention in 2021 when a bioanthropologist demanded that scholars ignore "creation stories" as religious "creationism." And yet I feel optimism. As oral tradition–based ancient history takes shape, the old consensus will yield to new research, and a good part of that work will come from scholars who affiliate in some way with Indigenous archaeology.

Many of the papers in this collection touch on the Native American Graves Protection and Repatriation Act (NAGPRA) of 1990. NAGPRA opened various kinds of doors in archaeology. Standing at the edge of the crowd that entered those doors, I thought NAGPRA research would help to create an enduring record of new understandings about the past. Pursuing this principle, watching the gears of NAGPRA slowly shift among the various bureaucracies of repatriation, I saw how the multidimensional implementation of NAGPRA could proceed not just from community and institutional politics—I also saw that deepening the precision of history under this law would inherently deepen our various cultural legacies.

NAGPRA can be effectively implemented by variable adherence to its historical protocols. By the end of the 1990s, I also saw that governments and public heritage institutions could sometimes treat academic research principles as negotiable, and nominal application of the law could dispense with even minimal history. Practical political flexibility and negotiation have necessarily shaped the culture of NAGPRA. But ethical academic idealism prefers shared protocols of scholarship that say research should go where the evidence goes, and history should follow carefully examined historical evidence. For effective implementation of NAGPRA, mutual respect and partnership does matter. In fact, as NAGPRA transformed the political context of relations between the academic world and Indian Country, very quickly a vast literature began to appear, an enriching legacy of scholarship.

History is a chronology of self and society, a realm where we enact the many collisions and conjunctions of our social diversity. A great spectrum of cultural shadings illuminates Indian Country. The architects of NAGPRA affirmed that the structures of race can provide a primary mechanism for energizing shared multicommunity bonding, and if we just glance at

xiv · Foreword

this process, it seems to affirm a monolithic definition of racial identity. But in actuality, implementation of the law is most often community centered. Repatriation projects harness the bonding powers of our race-based social contract to shape not just the personal meanings of racial Indianhood, but also to produce the social meanings of racial Indian sovereign communities.

And then during the mid-1990s I became aware of an interesting fact. Anthropology empowered race as an idea, and I suddenly noticed that anthropologists were having professional regrets about that. Through the twentieth century a growing anthropological consensus said that the cultural belief systems of race promote a distorted understanding of humankind. The construct of race disfigures the true nature of our inherited physical diversity, and "race" is actually an idea contrived in recent history, a system born in Europe and naturalized in America as a project of colonialism. This research wafted through the halls of academic anthropology, a tangled issue of tremendous import. And in those days, to a large degree, post-NAGPRA archaeology moved toward the idealism of racial diversity and interactive dialogue, addressing the legacies of racism. This opened the door for the rise of a new kind of archaeology.

Indian archaeologists modernized into Indigenous archaeologists. As this project proceeded through the first decades of the new century, an ever-growing anthropological consensus continued to challenge race— and the new practitioners of Indigenous archaeology made an interesting ideological choice. It became standard protocol for them to bond through a unifying critique of the legacies of racial whiteness and white colonialism. This meant that race would be embraced, but it would also be interrogated. And in the end, the primary momentum of Indigenous archaeology served to direct social energy into specific local sovereign communities, building a diverse cultural infrastructure across Native America.

The scholars in this collection each have their own paths to explore, their own ways of interpreting and enacting the idea of Indigenous archaeology. Each of the authors has traveled a unique path with unique narrative trajectories. This is vastly significant. To be sure, this diverse journeying often enough explores consensus destinations, and we can see that the scholarship in this book follows some of the intellectual traditions of the founders of Indigenous archaeology, the handful of Indian archaeologists who came together between 1996 and 2001. And so, the worldbuilding in these twenty-first century Indigenous-centered projects is communal, but it is also personal. The papers that follow touch on oral tradition, archaeology, bioanthropology, museology, library studies, and many other realms of scholarship. And this diverse storytelling summons the original mythmaking of archaeology into the new mythmaking of Indigenous archaeology. Visiting the immense remnants of antiquity and history, when we enter the past that gave rise to our world, we journey onward into the mysterious places where we keep becoming ourselves.

Roger Echo-Hawk

ACKNOWLEDGMENTS

We are incredibly grateful for all the support from so many people throughout this entire process. First, thank you to Mary Puckett for taking a chance on two graduate students putting together their first edited volume; we would not have been able to do it without you. Thank you to our contributors for their amazing work and for putting up with our constant barrage of emails. Through navigating graduate school, new jobs, and COVID-19, you all put your heart and soul into these chapters. You should all be so proud of the work you do with your communities and thank you for giving us a chance to share your work with the world. We also want to thank Roger Echo-Hawk for writing us a fantastic foreword. And thank you to Dr. Joe Watkins for not only inspiring the next generation of Indigenous archaeologists but also for concluding our volume with your profound words. I, (Emily), would like to thank Carlton for being my coeditor; I would not have been able to do this alone. Thank you to Dr. Pyburn for your mentorship and advice. My family for their continued support of my career. And of course, my husband, who is always there with love and support.

Indigenizing Archaeology

Putting Theory into Practice

EMILY C. VAN ALST
AND CARLTON SHIELD CHIEF GOVER

This volume came to be after long conversations between the two of us. We met many years ago at an archaeology meeting in Bismarck, North Dakota, where we talked about being the only Native students at the conference trying to incorporate ideas from Indigenous archaeology into our thesis/dissertation research. During another archaeology meeting in 2018, after realizing there were not many sessions devoted to the topic of Indigenous archaeology and that many other Indigenous students were all in separate sessions, we decided we wanted to create a session devoted to the topic of Indigenous archaeology and its future. We wanted to bring together the current generation of Indigenous archaeologists to discuss what the next steps of this groundbreaking theory might look like. We began reaching out to folks that we either knew or heard of; we both quickly realized that many of us were experiencing similar situations in graduate school and professional settings. Soon our list of contributors began to grow, and with it, our connectedness to one another. Though COVID-19 prevented us from physically coming together to discuss our work and this topic, we began to meet digitally as we wrote these chapters. The volume you see here is the product of mentorship, relationships, and connectedness during an extremely isolating time in many of our lives.

We had conversations about the type of expectations our communities have for us when doing this work and that these expectations are very different from our non-Native colleagues. All of us continue to converse with our Tribal Elders and community members to make sure the archaeological work we are doing is in the best interest of our communities. So, in essence, this volume is a collection of the archaeology we all do for our different communities.

Past

Anthropology is a discipline fraught with colonialism that has systematically changed how Indigenous people and their culture have been represented, collected, interpreted, and even desired by non-Native people. Archaeology as a part of the larger anthropological discipline has equally helped in this process of marginalizing Native communities. Archaeology, at the end of the day, has been a method of colonialism used to study the deep past, and in North America, mostly studying Indigenous people from a western worldview. Gordon Willey defines archaeology as "the study of human cultural and social past whose goals are to narrate the sequent story of that past and to explain the events that composed it" (Willey and Sabloff 1980:1). But how can an archaeologist explain the entirety of a Nation or a society's past without including the descendants of peoples whose ancestors' cultural heritage, land, and resources were used to build that contemporary society? If archaeology attempts to reconstruct the past, Indigenous archaeology practices work to rebuild a more inclusive past where Indigenous peoples' knowledge, voices, objects, and ancestors are acknowledged, cared for, and celebrated.

In this introduction, and throughout this volume, the term *Indigenous* is utilized by Native scholars as it allows for the implication of solidarity with Indigenous people around the world (Conkey 2005). *Indigenous* encompasses the variety of first peoples around the world, including American Indians, First Nations, Aboriginal, Métis, Inuit, and more. In this instance, it makes sense that Indigenous is used in order for this theory to exist in a globalized world and we will argue later that Indigenous archaeology is a theory with an activist approach. It is important to note that the majority of the literature surrounding Indigenous archaeology comes out of Nations where settler colonialism exists. Australian anthropologist Patrick Wolfe defines settler colonialism as an ongoing process where descendants of settlers are still a part of that Nation, and it actively works to destroy Indigenous people's relationship to land and their culture with the hope that Indigenous people will assimilate and therefore be eliminated (Wolfe 1999). Because the scholars in this volume are working within settler-colonial Nations, this means that we cannot truly decolonize archaeology because we do not live in a decolonized/postcolonial world in North America. Therefore, this volume argues that *Indigenized* archaeology is the path forward in our discipline. Colonialism in North America has resulted, in the eyes of Indigenous people, in a complete apocalyptic upheaval of Indigenous ways of knowing, living, and being (Dillon 2012). In Linda Smith's (Māori) (2013) early work *Decolonizing Methodologies*, she does not argue for a decolonized approach to academic research but for the use of academia to create a world that allows Indigenous people to practice self-determination. Archaeology has been used as a tool of settler colonialism to actively destroy the cultural heritage of Indigenous people. Our work as young Indigenous scholars reclaims the cultural heritage that may have been lost or destroyed by utilizing our specific Indigenous communities' ways of knowing and being in the world.

At its inception, Indigenous archaeology was theoretical; it asked archaeologists to reconsider their relationships with local and descendant communities and it called for the incorporation of more Indigenous people as archaeologists (Watkins 2000, 2005). Others called for an archaeology that is with, by, and for Indigenous people (Nicholas and Andrew 1997). George Nicholas further argued that in order to address and combat the inequalities and power dynamics that historically exist between archaeologists and Indigenous communities, these two groups need to work together (Nicholas 2008). Though Indigenous archaeology as a theoretical framework was solidified in the early 2000s, Indigenous and Native American people were involved in the discipline of archaeology far before that. Gladys Tantaquidgeon was one of the earliest Native American women to study anthropology in 1919 at the University of Pennsylvania, she worked doing ethnographic research with East Coast tribes as well as working for the Indian Arts and Crafts Board in the early 1930s (Bruchac 2018). Other early Native Americans were also involved in anthropology, such as Ella Deloria and George Hunt, both of whom worked with Franz Boas. Their positionality as Native American anthropologists would lead them to advocate for better public and academic understandings of Native people at a time when the US government was actively pushing for Native people to be fully assimilated into American society. There were also early Native American archaeologists. Arthur C. Parker was of Seneca descent and served as the first president of the Society of American Archaeology (Bruchac 2018). His research looked at and contributed to the field of archaeology and museum anthropology. He was also an advocate for educating the public on issues related to Native Americans and helped found the Society of American Indians in the early 1900s (Berg 2000). His advocational work and research career in archaeology would influence the work of his daughter Bertha Parker, the first Native American woman archaeologist (Bruchac 2018). These early Native American anthropologists and archaeologists advocated for the inclusion of Indigenous people and viewpoints into the discipline and as such laid the groundwork for Indigenous people to continue to advocate for their communities.

As we have said, facets of Indigenous archaeology exist as an activist approach to archaeology, and the foundation of this aspect has its roots in the work of the American Indian Movement (AIM) and the Native American Rights Fund (NARF). AIM was an American Indian civil rights organization founded in 1968 by Dennis Banks, Clyde Bellecourt, Eddie Benton-Banai, and George Mitchell in Minneapolis, Minnesota (Busacca 2007; Fine-Dare 2002; Horton 2017; Johansen 2013; Watkins 2000). Although the goal of AIM was not directly concerned with Indigenous perspectives in archaeology, it was concerned with Indigenous values, beliefs, and practices being recognized by the United States government as valid expressions of culture and becoming protected under federal law (Echo-Hawk 2000; Horton 2017; Watkins 2000). The primary goals of the American Indian Movement encompassed a broad spectrum of Indigenous demands such as protection of legal rights, revitalization of traditional culture, economic independence from the United States, sovereignty over Tribal areas and lands, and the restoration of lands that the United States government illegally seized (Busacca 2007; Horton 2017; Johansen 2013). Their goal of revitalizing traditional Indigenous cultures created social and political momentum for the American Indian Religious Freedom Act (AIRFA) of 1978 (Fine-Dare 2002; Watkins 2005). Without AIRFA, we would not have had the Native American Graves Protection and Repatriation Act of 1990, and, therefore, Indigenous archaeologies would not have come into existence in the 1990s. However, we would not have had AIRFA without AIM and NARF.

The American Indian Religious Freedom Act of 1978 was a pivotal moment in Indigenous religious rights and protections (Vecsey 1991). Before this act, American Indian religions and sacred ceremonies were prohibited by federal law in the United States (Vecsey 1991). Meaning, before 1978, Indigenous peoples in the United States did not have the freedom to practice their Indigenous religions. Therefore, objects and locations critical in Indigenous religious practices were not protected and not given statuses equal to other sacred items in the United States (Echo-Hawk 2018; Fine-Dare 2002; Vecsey 1991; Watkins 2000, 2005). The passage of this act allowed Indigenous peoples in the United States to practice their religions freely and protected their sacred spaces and objects, as well as set aside rules and regulations for federal agencies, such as the US Forest Service and US Department of the Interior, to allow Indigenous ceremonies and religious practices to be conducted on federal land (Vecsey 1991). By recognizing and protecting Indigenous expressions of worship, this act set the stage for the Native American Graves Protection and Repatriation Act (NAGPRA) which had a serious impact on archaeology and museum practices in the United States, beginning at a federal level.

Post-AIM activism, coupled with Native American scholars such as Vine Deloria Jr., Roger Echo-Hawk, and Beatrice Medicine in and around the field of archaeology, resulted in writings about the tense relationship between Native Americans and archaeologists while calling for the inclusion of Indigenous knowledge within the discipline (Deloria 1995; Echo-Hawk 2000; King 2012; Medicine and Jacobs 2001). They not only called on archaeologists to work with Indigenous people but to evaluate their knowledge in the interpretation of Indigenous cultural heritage. Around this same time, archaeologists begin to work closely with descendant communities through the paradigm of community-based research and public archaeology (Atalay 2012; Nicholas and Andrews 1997; Pyburn 2003; Silliman and Ferguson 2010; Yellowhorn 2002). The practice behind community-based archaeology and public archaeology would become integral parts of Indigenous archaeology. Indigenous archaeology moves archaeology from a passive discipline that works *on* Indigenous people to working *with* Indigenous people. With the passing and implementation of NAGPRA, archaeologists were forced to not only reflect on their relationship with Native people but their own ethics within the discipline (Lynott and Wylie 1995). This created an environment that allowed for Indigenous practitioners' space to be an authority within the discipline.

Present

As community-based and public archaeology took off, so did the inclusion of Indigenous people within the discipline. Indigenous archaeologists such as Joe Watkins, Sonya Atalay, Dorothy Lippert, Desiree Martinez, Sven Haakanson Jr., Davina Two Bears, Eldon Yellowhorn, Michael Wilcox, and so many more began writing about and advocating for Indigenous archaeology within the field (Nicholas 2010). We, as young Indigenous archaeologists, recognize our forebearers, or as we like to call them our fore-Aunties and fore-Uncles—Aunties and Uncles being a Native term to describe esteemed members of our communities. They have also contributed to pushing our discipline forward and creating a more ethical, inclusive, and better archaeology. With Indigenous practitioners in the discipline, Indigenous archaeology moved from an abstract idea to a solidified theory, with the aforementioned Indigenous archaeologists beginning to conceive of an archaeology that was inclusive of Indigenous people and worldviews while pushing non-Native archaeologists to not just consult but collaborate with Indigenous people.

Collaboration became a key tenet in Indigenous archaeology and community-based archaeological practices (Silliman 2008; Zimmerman 2005). Sonya Atalay defined the importance of collaborative work as the pillar of Indigenous archaeology, she argues that "developing collaborative methods and practices for archaeology while creating the theoretical and ethical guidelines that must accompany such practices holds the promise of building a possible future for archaeology. It is an archaeology that is engaged, relevant, ethical and, as a result, sustainable" (Atalay 2012:3). By using collaborative methods, a clearer and holistic history can be created within an archaeological framework for Indigenous communities. This means that research design and research questions should be influenced by and created with the community the archaeologist wants to work with (Gonzalez 2016). The community should be involved with the actual digging and artifact collecting. The community must be informed every step of the way, and the results of the project must also be disseminated to the community, not just published for other archaeologists. At its roots, Indigenous archaeology pushes for collaboration, and that drives scholars to expand and change the discipline in order to meet the needs of all Indigenous communities (Silliman 2018). Archaeologists began to take Indigenous archaeology as a theoretical framework and put it into practice in order to push for even more collaborative approaches. Scholars in *Indigenous Archaeologies: A Reader in Decolonization* (Bruchac et al. 2010) and *Transforming Archaeology* (Atalay et al. 2014), brought together Indigenous and non-Indigenous archaeologists to write about the importance of involving Indigenous people not just as consultants but as collaborative members and stewards of their own cultural heritage.

Though Indigenous archaeology is a newer theoretical framework in archaeology, it should be noted that there is no singular approach to how to employ Indigenous archaeology. Joe Watkins explains that "American Indians do not have any singular way of dealing with archaeology and archaeologists, but rather have adopted various processes to suit their particular situations" (Watkins 2000:169). This distinction can be applied to Indigenous groups around the world who have experienced a similar erasure within the discipline of archaeology, though it is certainly not a "one size fits all" approach. The beauty of Indigenous archaeology is that as a new approach it allows for growth and adaptation. Our volume further develops this paradigm by including case studies and new culturally specific ways to work with communities. We argue that Indigenous archaeology *must* be Indigenous archaeolog(ies) to reflect the many different ways Indigenous scholars are doing this work (Colwell-Chanthaphonh et al. 2010:229). Each contributor shows how they work with their community to better showcase the varying practices of this discipline. The past decade saw Indigenous archaeology (Watkins 2000) become Indigenous archaeologies (Nicholas and Watkins 2018) with the introduction of new scholars adopting and promoting this inclusive approach. Scholars such as Watkins, Nicholas, and Atalay are still publishing on Indigenous archaeologies during this time and are even collaborating on coauthored works (Atalay et al. 2012, 2014; Nicholas and Watkins 2014, 2018; Watkins 2010). Most recently, *Archaeologies of the Heart* (Supernant et al. 2020) has been published, an edited volume by both Indigenous and non-Indigenous archaeologists who argue for an archaeology that comes from the heart, where truth and healing are outcomes of using this approach. Our volume shows how, although archaeology has been a tool of colonialism, it can now be used as a tool to reclaim our community's cultural heritage. Indigenous archaeology is a guiding principle in the archival, museum, and archaeological work done *by* our young scholars, *with* their communities. All of these case studies show how Indigenous archaeology can push the discipline of archaeology to do work *for and with* Indigenous communities. Indigenous and non-Indigenous archaeologists can use this approach (Atalay 2008). Indigenous peoples and their perspectives move Indigenous archaeology beyond just a theoretical framework, pushing archaeology to do right by Indigenous communities. By putting Indigenous archaeology into practice, Indigenous people's voices and ways of knowing are centered, which can aid in the interpretation and reclamation of material culture.

Future

Though many archaeological scholars have brought together Indigenous and non-Indigenous archaeologists to make sense of Indigenous archaeology, the volume that you are about to read is, to our knowledge, the first volume dedicated only to early-career Indigenous scholars and their research. Archaeology has not always been open and accessible for Indigenous people, but we believe that our generation of scholars will find the tools, both western and Indigenous, to make archaeology more accessible to our communities. Each one of us represents a different Tribal Nation, different cultural backgrounds, and different archaeologies. There is no set Indigenous archaeology; it is always evolving and growing (Colwell-Chanthaphonh et al. 2010). The research conducted by our scholars for this volume weaves together western scientific research and traditional Indigenous knowledge, ontologies, and epistemologies, all of which work "to reconceptualize notions of time, space, and material culture" (Preucel and Cipolla 2008:130). western science and Indigenous knowledge can be combined to provide fuller interpretations of the archaeological record. So, what are the goals of this volume? The following chapters show that the outcomes of Indigenous archaeology when implemented as a guiding principle can bring reconciliation, reclamation, decolonized histories and stories, and an understanding of Indigenous ontologies and epistemologies.

We organized our volume into three parts—*Recontextualizing, Reclaiming*, and *Retelling*. Currently, there is a movement within Native American and Indigenous studies and Native communities to reconnect and reclaim cultural heritage, knowledge, stories, language, and more. Our contributors show through their archaeological work the process of returning our ancestor's material culture and heritage through a wide variety of methods and practices while employing the guiding framework of Indigenous archaeology. In the first part—*Recontextualizing the Archives of Knowledge*—our contributors show how they have found Indigenous voices within colonial institutions such as museums, archives, and libraries that have kept and controlled various aspects of Indigenous knowledge and culture. In chapter 1, Zoë Eddy shows how museums can be sites of trauma for Native people but also spaces where Native people can begin to heal. Kay Mattena shows how Indigenous material culture can be misinterpreted and misclassified by museum collections, but Traditional Ecological Knowledge and the literal embodied knowledge of communities can be used to re-interpret our material culture. Along the same lines, in chapter 3, Margaret Spivey-Faulkner shows us how to Indigenize the classification process to better reflect and understand Indigenous language and culture. In chapter 4, Lydia Curliss advocates for the important role that archivists and librarians can play in supporting Indigenous archaeologists and centering Indigenous voices. By recontextualizing the material culture that has been hidden in these curatorial institutions through collaborative methods, we can better center Indigenous voices and ontologies.

Part 2, *Reclaiming Cultural Heritage*, focuses on community-based practices and relationship building in order to better preserve cultural heritage. Patrick Cruz illuminates for us the important advocate role archaeologists must play between multiple stakeholders to better establish working relationships between archaeologists and descendant communities. Nicholas Laluk takes us through why cultural resource practitioners must incorporate Indigenous ontologies in their work when reclaiming cultural sites. Ash Boydston-Schmidt describes NAGPRA and the multitude of stakeholders that are part of the repatriation process, ultimately arguing that Indigenous communities' needs must be at the heart of this work. Honey Constant explains the hard but important work of reclaiming the cultural site of *Wanuskewin* for her community and the educational component that is critical for her community to do so. Reclaiming the material culture of our ancestors can help rebuild important relationships between Indigenous communities and cultural heritage. With collaborative approaches and relationship building, archaeologists can begin to facilitate Indigenous preservation protocols.

In the final part, *Retelling Indigenous Stories*, our contributors explain the importance of weaving together Indigenous stories with western archaeological and anthropological methods. Ashleigh Thompson argues for the importance of storywork and the use of ethnographic data to better center Anishinaabe voices to interpret cultural landscapes. Emily Van Alst illustrates how to incorporate Indigenous knowledge to re-interpret rock art sites; the images, she argues, must be seen as more than art but an Indigenous archive of knowledge. Carlton Shield Chief Gover finishes the volume by connecting Pawnee and Arikara oral traditions with multivariate statistical analyses of radiocarbon data to provide more holistic interpretations of archaeological investigations into ethnogenesis and population dynamics. This section redefines how Indigenous knowledge can be utilized to interpret material culture and data sets that have been only interpreted from a western perspective. These scholars utilize oral traditions and Indigenous stories to create a holistic understanding of their communities' cultural heritage.

As the next generation of Indigenous archaeologists, we hope that this volume will showcase examples of new and exciting methodologies that were inspired by the foundational works of Indigenous archaeology. All of our contributors utilize the tenets of Indigenous archaeology to put this theoretical framework into practice. We see collaborative methods utilized to elevate Indigenous voices, epistemologies, and knowledge that help archaeologists and community members to better understand and interpret the material past. Joe Watkins concludes in his pivotal book *Indigenous Archaeology* that for an Indigenous archaeology to truly work, non-Indigenous archaeologists must relinquish their control over Indigenous heritage, and for Indigenous archaeologists to work with their communities to protect their cultural heritage. We hope that the following chapters show what Dr. Joe Watkins envisioned over twenty years ago. Archaeology is utilized as a tool by both Indigenous and non-Indigenous archaeologists to work toward the preservation and reclamation of Indigenous voices and material culture for future generations.

References

Atalay, Sonya
2008   Multivocality and Indigenous Archaeologies. *In* Evaluating Multiple Narratives: Beyond Nationalist, Colonialist, and Imperialist Archaeologies. Junko Habu, Claire Fawcett and John M. Matsunaga, eds. pp. 29–44. New York: Springer.
2012   Community-Based Archaeology: Research With, By, and For Indigenous and Local Communities. Berkley: University of California Press.
Atalay, Sonya, Lee R. Claus, Randall H. McGuire, and John R. Welch
2014   Transforming Archaeology. Walnut Creek: Left Coast Press.
Berg, S. C.
2000   Arthur C. Parker and the Society of the American Indian, 1911–1916. New York History 81(2):237–246.
Bruchac, Margaret
2018   Savage Kin: Indigenous Informants and American Anthropologists. Tucson: University of Arizona Press.
Bruchac, Margaret M., Siobhan M. Hart, and H. Martin Wobst, eds.
2010   Indigenous Archaeologies: A Reader on Decolonization. Walnut Creek, CA: Left Coast Press.
Busacca, Jeremy
2007   Seeking Self-Determination: Framing, the American Indian Movement, and

American Indian Media. Unpublished PhD dissertation, The Claremont Graduate University, California.

Colwell-Chanthaphonh, Chip, T. J. Ferguson, Dorothy Lippert, Randall H. McGuire, George P. Nicholas, Joe E. Watkins, and Larry J. Zimmerman

2010 The Premise and Promise of Indigenous Archaeology. American Antiquity 75(2):228–238.

Conkey, Margaret

2005 Dwelling at the Margins, Action at the Intersection? Feminist and Indigenous Archaeologies, 2005. Archaeologies 1(1): 9–59.

Deloria, Vine

1995 Red Earth, White Lies: Native Americans and the Myth of Scientific Fact. New York: Scribner.

Dillon, Grace L., ed.

2012 Walking the Clouds: An Anthology of Indigenous Science Fiction. University of Tucson: Arizona.

Echo-Hawk, Roger

2000 Ancient History in the New World: Integrating Oral Traditions and the Archaeological Record in Deep Time. American Antiquity 65(2):267–290.

2018 The Enchanted Mirror: Ancient Pawneeland. CreateSpace Independent Publishing Platform.

Fine-Dare, Kathleen S.

2002 Grave Injustice: The American Indian Repatriation Movement and NAGPRA. Fourth World Rising Series. Lincoln: University of Nebraska Press.

Gonzalez, Sara L.

2016 Indigenous Values and Methods in Archaeological Practice: Low-Impact Archaeology Through the Kashaya Pomo Interpretative Trail Project. American Antiquity 81(3):533–549.

Horton, Jessica L.

2017 Art for an Undivided Earth: The American Indian Movement Generation. DOI: 10.1215/9780822372790, accessed November 30, 2020.

Johansen, Bruce Elliot

2013 Encyclopedia of the American Indian Movement. Santa Barbara: Greenwood.

King, Thomas F.

2012 Cultural Resource Laws and Practice. California: AltaMira Press.

Lynott, Mark, and Alison Wylie

1995 Ethics in American Archaeology: Challenges for the 1990s. Society of American Archaeology. Washington, D.C.: The Society for American Archaeology.

Medicine, Beatrice, and Sue-Ellen Jacobs

2001 Learning to Be an Anthropologist and Remaining "Native": Selected Writings. Urbana: University of Illinois.

Nicholas, George P.

2008 Native Peoples and Archaeology. Encyclopedia of Archaeology 3:1660–1669.

2010 Being and Becoming Indigenous Archaeologists (Archaeology & Indigenous Peoples). New York: Routledge.

Nicholas, George P., and Joe Watkins

2014 Indigenous Archaeologies in Archaeological Theory. *In* Encyclopedia of Global Archaeology. Claire Smith, ed. pp. 3777–3786. New York: Springer.

2018 Indigenous Archaeologies in Archaeological Theory. *In* Encyclopedia of Global Archaeology. Claire Smith, ed. pp. 1–10. New York: Springer.

Nicholas, George P., and T. A. Andrews, ed.

1997 At a Crossroads: Archaeology and First Peoples in Canada. Burnaby (BC): Archaeology Press.

Preucel, Robert W., and Craig N. Cipolla

2008 Indigenous and Postcolonial Archaeologies. *In* Archaeology and the Postcolonial Critique. Matthew Liebmann and Uzma Z. Rizvi, ed. pp. 129–140. Lanham: AltaMira Press.

Pyburn, K. Anne

2011 Engaged Archaeology: Whose Community? Which Public? *In* New Perspectives in Global Public Archaeology. Katsuyuki Okamura and Akira Matsuda, eds. pp. 29–33. London: Springer.

Silliman, Stephen

2008 Collaborating at the Trowel's Edge: Teaching and Learning in Indigenous Archaeology. Tucson: University of Arizona.

2018 Engaging Archaeology: 25 Case Studies in Research Practice. Hoboken: Wiley-Blackwell.

Silliman, Stephen W., and T. J. Ferguson

2010 Consultation and Collaboration with Descendant Communities. *In* Voices in American Archaeology. W. Ashmore, D. T. Lippert, and B. J. Mills, eds. pp. 113–127. The SAA Press.

Smith, Linda T.

2013 Decolonizing Methodologies: Research and Indigenous Peoples. London: Zed Books.

Supernant, Kisha, Jane Eva Baxter, Natasha Lyons, and Sonya Atalay

2020 Archaeologies of the Heart. New York: Springer.

Vecsey, Christopher, ed.

1991 Handbook of American Indian Religious Freedom. New York: Crossroad.

Watkins, Joe E.

2000 Indigenous Archaeology: American Indian Values and Scientific Practice. Walnut Creek: Alta Mira Press.

2005 Through Wary Eyes: Indigenous Perspectives on Archaeology. Annual Review of Anthropology 34(1):429–449.

Willey, Gordon R., and Jeremy A. Sabloff

1980 A History of American Archaeology. 2nd edition. San Francisco: W.H. Freeman.

Wolfe, Patrick

1999 Settler Colonialism and the Transformation of Anthropology: The Politics and Poetics of an Ethnographic Event. London: Cassell.

Yellowhorn, Eldon

2002 Awakening Internalist Archaeology in the Aboriginal World. Thesis, Department of Anthropology, McGill University.

Zimmerman, Larry

2005 First, Be Humble: Working with Indigenous Peoples and Other Descendant Communities. *In* Indigenous Archaeologies: Decolonizing Theory and Practice. Claire Smith & Hans Martin Wobst eds. pp. 301–314. New York: Routledge.

I

RECONTEXTUALIZING ARCHIVES OF KNOWLEDGE

Biidoban, by Kay Kakendasotkwe Mattena. Mixed media on canvas. 2023.

1

Story of Your/My/Our Skull

The Museum as a Haunted and Haunting Space

ZOË ANTOINETTE EDDY

Welcoming Specters

I like to think that I have encountered both theoretical and actual ghosts during my academic career. While the former is more comfortable to explain than the latter, they are, to me, one and the same: our literal and figurative specters haunt one another recursively. As anthropologists, we are stuck in the middle of this haunting. We exist in spaces—particularly those of us working in privileged, wealthy institutions—that reap the rewards of violent histories; at the same time, we often see ourselves as researchers positioned to engage with the past in a way that exposes those histories. The work of anthropology often hovers in a space of cognitive dissonance: as anthropologists follow various decolonial theories to their logical conclusion, so too do we simultaneously benefit from colonial structures of violence. Our intangible ideas and values buck up against the material reality of empire, power, and knowledge gained through exploitation.

Various writers have framed these material realities within cultural theories of spectrality (Blanco and Peeren 2013). Spectrality asks us to accept that specters of empire, both material and immaterial in the institutional record, haunt our work. These specters are, as I understand them, the permanent vestiges that speak to a history *done* but not *over*. And our anthropological texts are nothing if not haunted by colonial violence: I have many times found myself reading through a canonical work and staggering as I stumble over a word or a sentence or a paragraph that indicates the violence of history and the ethnographer's complicity in such violence. I feel myself react in the same way a ghost story protagonist might: incredulous, wary, nauseous, and, finally, frightened to the point where I close the book and find something else to do. To borrow from Derrida's original theory of hauntology (Derrida 1994), these are the specters that feed into our theorizing: in our discipline, intimate with violence, we often find ourselves gazing into secret corners haunted by confusing pasts and devastating presents. These theoretical specters, to me, are more or less the same as actual ghosts. They are reminders that past violence is not truly dead but instead endless and returning.

And what of this return? In many cultural ghost stories, there is often an implication that specters can be laid to rest: that is, once apologies are made or some sort of appeasement completed, the haunting stops. Haunted as we are by our spectral worlds, I see this impulse among my colleagues and in my own work: how can "we" (as a privileged class of researchers with access to institutional power) rectify damage and make things *right?* How can we better *collaborate?* How can we best *represent?* How can we make meaningful reparations for the centuries of violence our academic institutions have maintained? How can we cede our own authority to communities historically subjugated by the academic project?

These are undoubtedly ethical directions in anthropology and research more broadly. However, I still question the impulse "to make things right." The motivation to make return or reparation to a community should not be out of a sense of quieting ghosts, but instead out of ethical obligation to acknowledge damage. I argue that, as anthropologists, we must learn to live with ghosts: rather than seeing them as upsetting reminders of the past that can be excised, it is better to look at specters and haunting as disruptions to settler-colonial notions of temporality (Hickey 2019; Rifkin 2017). Such ghosts remind us, whomever "we" may be, that the past and the present feed on one another. They are cyclical, returning, and growing in relation to themselves.

A conversation with a friend, Arnold (he/him/his), reveals the subtlety of these disruptions, as well as their importance.[1] Arnold, an Anishinaabe man, was traveling with two of his friends, Joshua and Mary. Joshua (he/him/his) was a second-generation Jewish American who identified as white, while Mary (she/her/hers) identified as a white woman of a prestigious family in USA settler-colonial history. Mary's family, through their connection to this history, owned a residential New England summer camp. Mary would invite her friends to the camp for weeklong excursions; Joshua and Arnold were two of these friends. The camp, while only seasonal in use, was private and, to quote Arnold, "rich." In addition to private lakeside houses and fully outfitted sporting facilities, the gated camp, opened in the nineteenth century, also housed historical landmarks and a private restaurant. The restaurant was fully staffed by locals and specialty chefs when the family visited. The camp was private and only open to the public on special occasions.

During their stay, Arnold and Joshua were impressed by the obvious vestiges of wealth and political empire. Arnold, who had grown up just outside his reservation service area and had been unhoused throughout his childhood, found the hundreds of acres of grounds staggering in their expanse. He noted that Mary was apologetic about the wealth, and she frequently explained that she was not proud of her family's history. One day, Mary, Joshua, and Arnold explored one of the older historical buildings, a hunting lodge for nineteenth-century politicians and their gentlemen guests. The lodge had been converted into a private museum that now housed family heirlooms, art, and, by Mary's estimation, "artefacts." When he entered the room, Arnold noticed not only the portraits of long-dead family patriarchs, but also romantic landscapes of plains and "the American Indian"—or so this was engraved on silver-plated labels. Additionally, Arnold noticed a small collection of lithic tools. He looked to Mary and asked of their provenance. Mary admitted she did not know, but that one of her great-great uncles had been a "collector." She then said that the family had surrendered marine mammal bones to the local fish and game authorities and, in the same spirit, were attempting to repatriate the tools to local tribes.[2]

It was an awkward moment that Joshua eventually broke: playfully elbowing Arnold in the ribs, Joshua joked, "You know, there was a time not too long ago when people like you and me wouldn't be allowed in here." Mary and Arnold quickly laughed, though the comment suggested the strange haunting of the space. The past—physically manifest in testaments to collection and representation of Indigenous people by settlers— reminded Mary and Arnold equally of their own histories. For Mary, this space indicated her family's complicity in centuries of violence from which she still benefited.[3] Arnold indicated that she expressed guilt and bewilderment when it came to her own subjectivity within violence: although she had never participated in the active subjugation of Indigenous people, the specters of subjugation loomed large on her family's estates—estates inaccessible to those outside her family's immediate circles. For Arnold, the moment was both a figurative and literal haunting: the museum reminded of his own family's decades-long displacement from unceded territories;

the lithic materials, he said, might still be living, but were removed from their proper context. Even if Mary's family repatriated the objects, the tools would be wrapped within the context of trauma and theft. Though saddened, Arnold explained the juncture as a moment of power: it was an indelible colonial encounter where a settler family could not hide its legacy and, through the specters left by their empire, had to confront that the past was very much still wound up in the present.

Such is the nature of haunting. It interrupts us and reminds us that, while the world may spin ever forward, our lives remain circular and entangled with our pasts. Our histories do not leave us though we try to abandon them. As suggested by the example of Arnold, Joshua, and Mary, museums are places that haunt our presents.

(Re?)Conceptualizing the Museum

Anthropology is inextricably connected to museums; museums are the places where the objects we collect[4] are stored, studied, and exhibited. Indeed, first-time visitors to museums are often enthralled by the "amount of stuff" that museums hold. For those interested in the material past, the museum is a behemothic resource: in both its popular and professional image, the museum is a "treasure trove" wherein things extraordinary and/or mundane are guarded from the passages of time and decay. The Euro-American celebration of the museum as a space of wealth, knowledge, and meaning belies the documented histories of these places. The museum is a manifestation of not only the colonial empire, but also of the violence done to communities and individuals, among them Indigenous people. Conceptualizing the museum as a space haunted by violence is the focus of the rest of this chapter.

In the context of Indigenous anthropology, the relationship between empire, colonization, genocide, and the museum should be obvious. Archival research into collections' records indicate the lives and passions of the late nineteenth- and early twentieth-century ethnographers, archaeologists, collectors, and donors: researchers and casual visitors alike can see the objects, people, and places that these individuals attempted to possess through collection and curation in museum archives. Within related accession records are implied less obviously the genocidal complicity of these actors. The earnest cataloguing of dates reveals in exactly what historical context a picture, an object, or a piece of cultural knowledge was taken, stolen, appropriated, and/or exploited.

Even a quick perusal through an archive demonstrates that museums and anthropologists have profited from the colonial wars on Indigenous peoples.

A conversation with an Indigenous researcher exemplifies the violence of the archive. This unstructured interview, part of a larger conversation about Indigeneity in the archive, was conducted in the summer of 2018. The researcher had been working in a collection well known for late nineteenth-century travelogues. Her research was mostly benign: she was attempting to catalogue the travelogues and identify the authors and interlocutors. It had proved difficult, as the collections were a ramshackle mass of decades-old donations. One day, the researcher opened an anonymous scrapbook: various diary entries and unrelated photographs were pasted to the book's pages. While the researcher could identify the late nineteenth-century authorship, nothing else was clear—only that the author, barely visible in fuzzy photographs, was a man given to frequent travel across the United States. As she paged through the moldering photojournal, she stopped at a blurry, water-stained picture labeled only with a location: on what seemed to be a barren cliffside, the author stood in front of a cairn, hands on hips; a bulky shape lay at the author's feet. The researcher could not make out the details of the photograph until they squinted: they immediately realized that the staged picture was not of a cairn, but of an exhumed grave—the shape in the picture was clearly the body of a dead person, removed from their grave. The researcher immediately identified the body as a member of a tribe associated with the region in which the picture was taken. The researcher stopped her work; she felt a complex pang of anger and shock that melted into nauseous guilt—she described the situation as uniquely "haunting."

It is worth mentioning that, in this case, the researcher and museum handled this material quickly. They immediately contacted the affiliated Tribal group for guidance and, in the meantime, pulled the object from the publicly available collection. The researcher finished her fellowship before the situation reconciled and was not sure how it was resolved. In a recent correspondence, I followed up on this, explaining this essay and this larger volume—she laughed and admitted she was not sure. She assumed it had been "taken care of" given the general ethos of the museum staff, but stated "who knows?" She added: "I think about it from time to time, you know? It was so weird. It will just pop up in my mind, and I remember, specifically, how the photograph was pasted in, and you could see the dried glue." Such is the purview of a ghost.

In the United States context, NAGPRA and repatriation movements demonstrate the contours of the museum as violent actor against Indigenous populations. Very simply, museums hold the bodies, beings, and materials of Indigenous people and their landscapes; descendant communities want these returned to their appropriate cultural context. For a museum to possess any of these things[5]—whether through intentional collection or unknowing accident—is for a museum to have a physical manifestation of empire: the human remains and objects of cultural patrimony taken from their origin demonstrate the structures of colonial power that have enabled such taking (Bruchac 2018; Colwell 2021; Jones 2009; Rassool 2015; Turnbull 2020). Indeed, many museums are aware of this and working to repatriate collections as quickly as possible. Many, however, are not. The debates that have resulted in opposition to repatriation movements demonstrate the colonial structures of anthropology that continue to govern Indigenous life.

So what do we, as anthropologists, do with this? Is the answer to advance community practices and better repatriation policies? Is it to establish radical and diverse anthropology programs that destabilize and challenge violence? Is it, as many have questioned, to burn anthropology down and start over (Jobson 2020)?

There are pragmatic answers to the issues presented. In the United States, the suite of ethical and radical repatriation, curation, accession, and stewardship of objects are new directions that museums are taking (Ariese 2018; Atalay 2019b; Ronan 2014; Sleeper-Smith 2009; Viau-Courville 2016). Equally important, Tribal museums grounded in Indigenous knowing and reclamation have come to the forefront of museum best practices (Goff et al. 2019; Lonetree 2012; McChesney 2019; Spears 2020). Within institutions, collaboration and representation are both developing values, even though Indigenous communities are justified in their skepticism and/or unwillingness to engage with museum practice.[6] As various scholars and activists have indicated, museums might be able to exist within Indigenous life, however precarious that existence may manifest.

This essay, however, does not address material pragmatics. Quite frankly, people more qualified than I have proposed frameworks with which to reconsider the Indigenous presence in and outside of museums (Atalay 2018, 2019a, 2019b; Bramlett 2018; Colwell and Nash 2020). To conclude this essay, I instead offer a way of theorizing museums; this theory positions them within methods of Indigenous knowing and spectrality. Since anthropology, and certainly archaeology, are social sciences grounded in both empire and empiricism, I suggest this framework as a radical reappraisal of how anthropologists and other museum professionals approach their work. I view this only as a single step as the Indigenous community moves through our relationship and futures with museums.

Within this conversation, I situate as haunted spaces within spectrality and hauntology.[7] I offer this not as an answer to how any researcher, Indigenous or non-Indigenous, should do their work, but instead as a provocation. I hope to encourage a reconsideration of the museum project and our individual and communal ethical obligations to people living, deceased, and existing as spirits outside of settler-colonial frameworks of the (implied imaginary) ghost.

Before I continue, there is an important note on such imaginary ghosts. Spectrality scholars often muse on the presence of ghosts both "real" and "imagined." Within the spectral turn, theorists, particularly Euro-American theorists, have spilled a good amount of ink wondering on this "imagined ghost." In such pieces, the specter is theoretical: it is a cultural impression left by histories and the lasting ramifications of social networks. It is crucial, as I attempt to bring a largely settler framework in line with Indigenous experience, that I destabilize the notion of spirits, ghosts, and specters as fictional or unreal. Importantly, understandings of the supernatural are individually conceived, and there is no singular belief in spirits among Indigenous people. All the same, it is important for researchers—particularly non-Indigenous ones—to note that the reality of haunting is not only physical and present but ingrained in many Indigenous cultural and personal values.

To return to the museum, those interacting with Indigenous people should respect the existence of specters that know and feel. While there is a general understanding of the sentience of some cultural objects, very few non-Indigenous museum professionals have written on the living ancestors we see in human remains, photographs, and accounts of/by Indigenous people. Museum professionals must pay more than lip service to our context as Indigenous people: some of us encounter humans who remain as more than lifeless objects left behind and, by definition of the museum's endeavor, existing as objects of study rather than subjects deserving of consent, respect, and return.

To add to the argument of real/unreal ghosts: museums must further be thought of as spaces of potential trauma for Indigenous participants.

In their introduction to *The Spectralities Reader*, María del Pilar Blanco and Esther Peeren provide a landscape of the "contact zone between trauma studies and theories of spectrality" (Blanco and Peeren, 2013). They offer a trajectory of this contact, positing theorists' connections between haunting and memory, as well as the traumatized individual existing as a historical figure girded by a reoccurring past. While the authors caution against a disciplinary bandwagon, the application of trauma studies to Indigenous experience is well studied, and the intersection of ghosts/hauntings and trauma is powerful. Within the context of Indigenous participation in museums, the collection of Indigenous materials, people, and other living beings is not only a physical vestige of the colonial project, but also a manifestation of communal and individual trauma. In short, the museum encounter is one that, for many people, is traumatic and/or retraumatizing.

If ghosts serve as reiterations of trauma, and museums can function as haunted spaces, then spectrality allows us to reframe Indigenous trauma within the museum space. In her introductory chapter to the edited volume *Haunted by Empire*, Anne Stoler writes on the position of haunting within the larger United States colonial project. Stoler explains haunting within the bounds of ambiguous encounters:

> To haunt is "to frequent, resort to, be familiar with," to bear a threatening presence, to invisibly occupy, to take on changing form. To be haunted is to reckon with such tactile powers and their intangibilities. To be haunted is to know that such forces are no less effective because of disagreement about their appropriate names. *Haunted by Empire* is a book stepped in such predicaments. It works through—and rests uncomfortable in—the fierce clarity of intimacies and in those ambiguous zones of empire that refused or refuted colonial appellations. To be haunted is to be frequented by and possessed by a force that not always bares a proper name. (Stoler 2006)

Stoler's final line—the inability to express effectively that which scares us—points to the importance of understanding haunting.

In order to unpack this haunting, I will reflect on my own experiences[8] within collections. This is part autoethnographic evocation and part personal storytelling: haunting is difficult and awkward, particularly when the sensation of being in contact with a past is dismissed as pseudoscience in formal academic circles.

Semah, Pebbles, Visitations

Early in my graduate career, I worked as a research fellow in a museum: the museum in question was not associated with my university and, as a new researcher, I was unfamiliar with the collections themselves. In particular, I was not aware that the museum housed a large collection of human remains; these remains were stored in the same building in which the graduate research office was located. During one of my first weeks, a conservator gave me a tour of the entire collection. I was both flattered and surprised: it felt like a privilege to be invited into the labyrinth of objects that, prior to my fellowship, were inaccessible. I was all the more excited as the museum had a good reputation of working with descendant communities—local and National news had lauded the institution multiple times for their ethical curation of sensitive collections. In skimming such press releases, I had failed to consider that the topic of "return" was seldom mentioned.

The conservator took me through the spaces and breathlessly indicated their favorite objects. A taxidermy mount of a brown bear recently returned to her luster after a moth infestation. A collection of gourd dippers incised with swirling loops. A marimba, steel and bone, which still sounded deep, resonant notes. Appreciative of the knowledge, I nevertheless grew uneasy. Something had started to feel wrong. I could not pinpoint the moment when my wariness started, but I knew I felt less like an Indigenous woman scholar and more like a gentrified adventurer plundering a very nebulous grave. Shivers ran up my back and a nauseous pang of guilt settled in my stomach. It was the same sort of anxious fear described in horror novels of haunted houses.

As we bustled through the collection in the conservator's whirlwind of enthusiasm, I grew increasingly nervous. Why was I here? Why were we rehearsing the trials of Mr. So-and-So as he systematically catalogued the language and ceramics of Such-and-Such two hundred years ago? I felt the guilt seep deeper. Jewish and Anishinaabe in its manifestation, I wondered if I should be placing pebbles and *semah* on the dutifully shuttered storage units.

My guilt shifted, in a moment, to confusion, anger, and, eventually, sadness. This shift was obvious and catalyzed by the moment we passed by the photography station: between light stands and two battered cameras, a human skull was propped on a staging table. The lights were carefully filtered so that the bones cast no shadow upon the muted background. In

12 · Zoë Antoinette Eddy

the immediate moment, I was struck by a grim admiration: it is difficult to negate the shadows artifacts cast—I could not imagine the challenges a human skull might present.

This admiration, of course, quickly melted into a tangle of emotions. A quick glance at the accession label confirmed what I assumed: *Skull, Human, Unknown Provenance (American Indian? Canada?)*. My prior questions returned furious and ugly: What was this doing here? What was I doing here? Why were any of us here? Why was this place?

The conservator caught my expression. They checked their watch, "Oh, the photographer is out to lunch, I think." I said nothing, though a part of me empathized with them. How do you explain the intrusion of unexpected human life into a house of the (presumed) dead? To borrow from Mbembe and Mitsch, the skull and its livingness—the presence of a ghost that I felt—announced itself as both there and not there, something that indicates the irreversibility of time. As Mbembe and Mitsch write, "If stories and events have a beginning, they do not necessarily have an end, properly speaking. Indeed, they may be interrupted. But a story or an event may continue in another story or in another event, without there necessarily being a causal relationship between one and the other" (Mbembe and Mitsch 2003). My presence in the museum interrupted the existence of this skull—the skull of a human being with a life story—and the skull interrupted my space through the museum; I became a witness to the continuation of this person's life story. We were not causal to each other, two humans caught in an accidental moment, but so too were our existences rooted in colonial violence. The difference being that my own skull was not abandoned on a table nor was I the person who had taken the skull in the first place (though the branches of my lineage could have facilitated either outcome). Nevertheless, we existed in each other's presence, resonances of one another's trauma and my complicity in that violence.

Bizarrely, this moment reminded me foremost of the city sparrow who flies into the rafters of a local grocery store. Screeching and fluttering their wings, they call out for both release and witnessing. Though no shadow bounced from their planes, the skull did the same thing, I felt, in these halls.

The curator, in earnest good faith, explained that they had a sizable collection of skulls from, "a collector." They were "a sensitive collection" and "being photographed for reappraisal—potentially deaccessioning." I nodded but continued staring at the skull. The thinning bone and worn-down teeth—the missing incisor, clearly jangled loose postmortem. I ran my tongue against my own teeth, the clinical phrases *eagle talon cusp* and *shoveled incisors* ringing in my brain.

How did the tooth go missing? I wondered silently.

Did a well-intentioned intern drop it during storage transport?

Did a researcher carefully remove it and place it among other specimens?

Was it merely poorly packed, clattered around, and then bumped, some 150 years ago, as its collector sped hundreds of miles to his own home?

I remembered a line from a textbook about postmortem dental damage: the incisors come loose during excavation, transport, and analysis. "Take care during handling."

I thought of my grandmother's skull rattling around in a hastily packed trunk.

I thought of my uncle's skull, carefully removed from shelving and placed on a lab table. I knew his bones must have been ravaged by disease, and I imagined *advanced periodontitis* scribed into some database somewhere.

I thought of many of my Elders' skulls, dug up from gravesites, dropped by an intern in a drafty collections' hall. I know some of them had gold teeth, and I saw these teeth skittering across the linoleum tile. A 115-year-old tooth reflecting fluorescent light across a fifteen-year-old floor.

I thought of my skull. How it must have hairline fractures and funny teeth once riddled with *caries*. How it was, for now, mine and mine alone. I had never considered that it might eventually be someone else's.

I looked at the conservator and smiled. They beamed back at me, nervous but still energetic, and wondered if I had any questions. Many, I thought. "No, I'm good!" I said too joyfully.

As the conservator hurried away from the photography station, I followed them, noticing their practical sneakers and well-tended fingernails. I saw my history reflected both in their effortless professionalism and genuine enthusiasm. I wondered if I saw myself in the skull still resting on the table.

I left no *semah* nor pebble. In a petty act of defiance and reverence, I nudged the overhead lamp. The light swayed, and the skull cast a sharp and deep shadow across the wall. It was a moment wherein I felt I could demonstrate that this still life was very much still alive. It was a moment, moreover, where I clung to reconciling my own betrayal.

This experience is not unique to me. Furthermore, as a scholar who has received her anthropology PhD from an institution implicated for the same things, I am as complicit as any other institution's faculty, staff, and affiliated professionals. This is all to say, the experiences of other Indigenous people are more traumatic than mine and, as are all professionals working in/with museums, I am in part responsible for their trauma.

That does not make the realness of my own haunting any less powerful. It is painful. It is raw and real. It is embarrassing, as an Indigenous scholar, to acknowledge that I sometimes cry when I enter museum spaces. To acknowledge this pain, a pain that comes from mourning people's lives manifest and captured in a museum, is to acknowledge my own difficulty navigating a space that holds/jails/curates the bones, memories, and spirits of my cultural ancestors. Recognition of this pain—born of both cultural practice and my understanding of historical trauma—seems to me an important step in allowing Indigenous people to reclaim the violence of museums. Our pain is not figurative grief brought on by conceptual ghosts. Very simply, recognizing and embracing the Indigenous experience of spectrality makes both conceptual and tangible the existence of descendant community pain. Acknowledging ghosts—letting ourselves feel anger, violence, and the perpetual presence of life lost yet persistent and maybe alive—allows us to better tackle the museum as an institutional space.

Genocidal Complicity and the Future of Hauntings

So where do we go from here? I have presented theory, personal account, and a call for settler scholars to, once more, acknowledge the visceral pain that history causes for Indigenous communities. To conclude this essay, I turn to a new rupture into the museum space: the work of Che Applewhaite[9] and his 2021 short film, *A New England Document*.

Applewhaite's 2021 short film, *A New England Document*, offers what I consider a profound rupture into museum practice and research. The film considers Applewhaite's ethnographic research on the Lorna J. and Laurence K. Marshall Archive currently housed in the Peabody Museum of Archaeology and Ethnology at Harvard University. Applewhaite's archival research, the basis for the film, focuses on material, specifically photographs (numbering over 40,000 in the collection) taken of Ju/'hoansi, 'Gwi, and Khoisan people from 1952 to 1961. In particular, Applewhaite details his interactions with the image "/Gaishay focusing the camera." Through exploration of this collection, and focus on this particular image and person, Applewhaite highlights how anthropologists and collectors contribute/d to the genocide of Indigenous populations—genocidal complicity, he argues, justified by Euro-American ideals of scientific inquiry.

While the scope of Applewhaite's work is striking in and of itself, his autoethnographic process is particularly relevant to a rupture of the imperial museum space. Applewhaite positions himself—as both a Harvard College researcher and Black man—as someone caught in the haunting of colonial violence. Applewhaite writes:

> The photograph's caption told of "/Gaishay focusing the camera," just like I did some mornings in Peabody's underground reading room [during research into the Marshall collection]. It wasn't possible to differentiate my position as a student, an academic knower, from what I saw in /Gaishay, a boy dressed in a park ranger outfit typical of fifties American male attire. We were both given our recording instruments with the support of Harvard University; his came directly from the Marshall family, mine from the Art, Film and Visual Studies Department. We both grapple with our emergences as knowers in a world made from imperialism, his South African and American, mine British. The effortful tension he holds in stillness reminded me of the tripod I turned ever so slightly to get the dappled streetlight upon an undulating Charles River. Our desire for cinema narrowed the distance between our positions as credible knowers and curtailed my ability to put him in a Savage Slot. (Applewhaite 2021)

Applewhaite's empathy for not only the individual collected through photography, but the larger process of knowing and knowledge making speaks to the importance of rupture. Throughout Applewhaite's film and writing, the past and present blur together as if to remind the viewer that the specters of the colonial past are not mere ghosts, but living, often silen/t/ced presences within the institutional world. Applewhaite's work points to the multitude of constituencies erased in the museum: collections, his work suggest, are more than pieces of information. They are spaces of frustrating ambiguity, to return to Stoler's work—the past seems knowable, yet the lived experiences of those people represented in archives remain quiet. A quiet achieved through the routine silencing that has accompanied the larger anthropological project. Applewhaite's work demands that we allow absence to inform us as strongly as presence. He necessitates a reality that the past is not memory, but instead a spectral social web that stretches beyond notions of settler time (Rifkin 2017).

Haunting then is not an absence but a rupture and fission: specters, regardless of whether you think they are real or imagined, interrupt us. They interrupt us from moving through our work unbothered by the things that, though not quite living, remain. As anthropologists in this current moment, I argue that we need to embrace and come to understand our ghosts, whether or not we believe in them. We have made ourselves, whoever we are and however we try to fight it, storytellers responsible for communicating this confusing tangle of past and present: recognizing our disciplinary specters can help us do that work.

And, indeed, they perhaps move us out of trauma/tizing frameworks. In a recent article, Joseph P. Gone challenges dominant IHT (Indigenous historical trauma) narratives that position Indigenous people as at-risk victims of a prolonged colonial history. Writing from a public health perspective, Gone asks: ". . . we might ask what it means when entire generations of Indigenous people are said to suffer from IHT and therefore to be 'at risk' for mental health problems? What does it mean when Indigenous community-based 'healing' projects promote these ideas among their Indigenous clients, many of whom arrive to these programs by professional or legal mandate, only to be considered successful cases if they learn to disclose their vulnerability, open up to their counselors, and inaugurate a 'healing journey'?" (Gone 2021:9). Gone's critique challenges not only settler models of therapeutic healing, which often decenter communities in favor of the individual (Burrage et al. 2022), but also questions the centrality of trauma and victimhood when considering Indigenous legacies. Gone continues, "[i]n sum, is this what Indigenous liberation and emancipation from the legacy of colonization should look like? Whereas proponents of IHT find hope and possibility in the therapeutic ethos, I instead explore what Indigenous self-determination today might resemble if we were to celebrate mastery more so than fragility and to cultivate 'survivance' rather than 'victimry' (Vizenor 1999)" (Gone 2021:10). While Gone writes as a medical anthropologist, his critiques benefit my own consideration of the larger field. Can ghosts and the haunting of our field bring us to a point of survivance?

I return to Arnold's story that I presented earlier in this essay. Arnold spoke to me not only of his upset at seeing Indigenous materials in a private, exclusive family museum. He spoke to the power that came from the indelible ghosts of a haunted space: "Any museum is a haunted house, and from those hauntings come our proof that history happened." When settlers are forced to confront the materialized specters of their histories—

Notes

1 This conversation was part of an informal ethnographic interview, for this volume, which occurred in December 2020; I conducted this interview with Arthur. I have changed names, used pseudonyms, and excluded some identifying information to preserve anonymity. Arnold is a Tribally enrolled Anishinaabe man.

2 In the state where Mary's family camp was located, the collection of protected species parts is prohibited without special permit. Government offices control the collection and stewardship of protected species including the remains of animals collected on beaches. Mary stated to Arnold that, while her family was able to contact wildlife offices easily, the return of materials connected to descendant communities proved more difficult. A state archaeologist worked with the family to identify the materials and determined the objects were potentially associated with Alaskan Native descendant communities. Mary explained it had been simple to report the marine mammal bones, but the lithic materials remained in the liminal bureaucracy surrounding objects connected to cultural patrimony. Especially since Mary's family had no expertise in NAGPRA and no real connection to local tribes, let alone non-local ones, Mary and her family found themselves confused about the repatriation process. I locate this as an insidious example about the complexities of NAGPRA and repatriation of materials within settler-colonial frameworks.

3 As I am presenting the history of another person, I think it is important to also present the privilege my own affords me. I am of mixed heritage, but I am also white and benefit from not only white privilege, but the continuing legacy of white supremacy in North America that is reified by not only my family history, but also my existence as a mixed white person living in the United States.

4 I present "collection" and "collect" as two words that indicate not only the physical violence of museum practices but also the mindset that goes into "collection." "Collection" is the process wherein materials and living/non-living beings are chosen and assembled. The logic of collection, as it pertains to museums and nineteenth-century foundational collecting practices, is one wherein a presumed expert constituency—whether formally recognized as professional or romanticized as the interested donor amateur—deigns certain objects worthy of possession, decontextualization through seizure (sometimes consensual, sometimes non-consensual), curation, maintenance, and analysis. Within the context of Indigenous human remains, this is particularly upsetting as it advances a collecting logic wherein the bodies of Indigenous people are deemed objects rather than subjects. Even in cases where descendant communities consent to museum stewardship of human remains, there is a larger conversation that non-living people are not able to consent to their

18 · Zoë Antoinette Eddy

own collection and storage. While there are movements among living people to donate their bodies to museums and other research institutions, these efforts should emphasize that non-living people who offered no consent cannot consent. The issue of consent is outside the scope of this current discussion but warrants meaningful attention and serious appraisal.

5 Throughout this essay, I have found it difficult to refer to the materials held in museum collections. "Thing" in the English language generally implies a lack of sentience and, furthermore, a generalized lack of importance. This is troubling when talking about Indigenous materials wherein Indigenous languages often used grammars of sentience to communicate the living-ness of "things" deemed lifeless in the English language. I will use an example from my own cultural practice. When I started seriously beading, I was taught that beading is medicine and a practice wherein you connect with not a lifeless material object, but the life of beads. I was taught the word for beads in Anishinaabemowin, *manidoomin*. Manidoomin translates as "spirit berry" and, in the cultural practice I was taught, speaks to the sentience and living-ness of beads. I was taught that manidoomin think and speak and, through the process of making materials, I could learn how to understand their living agency. This is but one example of how "living-ness" is lost in settler colonial frameworks of objects. Furthermore, it suggests that, particularly in settler-colonial collecting logics, the bodily remains of humans and non-humans are conceived, through language, as, if not "things," non-sentient objects devoid of agency and lived experience. When I use the word "things" I invite readers to consider how a material imagined lifeless might in fact have sentience and presence and to further consider how the English language, which has been imposed globally on Indigenous people, erases this sentience.

6 As an anthropologist and researcher who has worked in museums, I, like many of my colleagues, hold to a narrative that museums can be "good." This is my own bias as a researcher who has benefited from and found joy in museums. As this essay is a provocation within a volume that seeks to Indigenize archaeology, I respect the perspective that extant settler-colonial museums cannot be ethical and can only serve as continuations of violence. This essay makes a pitch that museums, if reconceptualized by experts, can be understood in a way that makes space for the experience of Indigenous people. The counterargument that their histories of violence render this impossible is just, ethical, and crucial.

7 My framework for spectral studies and hauntology is informed first by Derrida's work and, more holistically, by the various cultural theorists who contributed to Blanco and Peeren's 2013 volume *The Spectralities Reader: Ghosts and Haunting in Contemporary Cultural Theory*. While nominally a reader, this collection of essays invites a diversity of responses in conversation with one another. I consider it foundational to discussions of museums and spectrality; additionally, I posit museums as one of the places where spectrality theory is best made tangible.

8 These reflections draw on my experiences when I was a graduate student (2011–2019) working in various United States and international museums and archives.

9 With thanks to Che Applewhaite for his consultation on his film and thesis.

References

Applewhaite, Che
2021   A New England Document. Undergraduate Honors Thesis, Harvard University, 2021.

Ariese, Csilla Esther
2018   The Social Museum in the Caribbean: Grassroots Heritage Initiatives and Community Engagement. Leiden: Leiden University.

Atalay, Sonya
2019a   Braiding Strands of Wellness: How Repatriation Contributes to Healing through Embodied Practice and Storywork. The Public Historian 41(1):78–89.
2019b   Can Archaeology Help Decolonize the Way Institutions Think? How Community-Based Research is Transforming the Archaeology Training Toolbox and Helping to Transform Institutions. Archaeologies 15(3):514–535.

Atalay, Sonya
2018   Repatriation and Bearing Witness. American Anthropologist 120(3):544–545.

Blanco, María del Pilar and Esther Peeren, eds.
2013   The Spectralities Reader: Ghosts and Haunting in Contemporary Cultural Theory. London: Bloomsbury Publishing.

Bramlett, Katie
2018   Legible Sovereignties: Rhetoric, Representations, and Native American Museums. Composition Studies 46(2):219–235.

Bruchac, Margaret
2018   Broken Chains of Custody: Possessing, Dispossessing, and Repossessing Lost Wampum Belts. Proceedings of the American Philosophical Society 162(1):56.

Burrage, Rachel L., Sandra L. Momper, and Joseph P. Gone
2022   Beyond trauma: Decolonizing Understandings of Loss and Healing in the Indian Residential School System of Canada. Journal of Social Issues 78(1):27–52.

Colwell, Chip
2021   Plundered Skulls and Stolen Spirits. Chicago: University of Chicago Press.

Colwell, Chip, and Stephen E. Nash
2020   Why We Repatriate: On the Long Arc Toward Justice at the Denver Museum of Nature & Science. *In* Working with and for Ancestors. Chelsea H. Meloche, Laure Spake, and Katherine L. Nichols (eds.). pp. 79–90. London: Routledge.

Derrida, Jacques
1994   Specters of Marx: The State of the Debt, the Work of Mourning, and the New International. New York: Routledge.

Goff, Sheila, Betsy Chapoose, Elizabeth Cook, and Shannon Voirol
2019   Collaborating Beyond Collections: Engaging Tribes in Museum Exhibits. Advances in Archaeological Practice 7(3):224–233.

Gone, Joseph P.
2021   Recounting Coup as the Recirculation of Indigenous Vitality: A Narrative Alternative to Historical Trauma. Transcultural Psychiatry. Online publication. https://doi.org/10.1177/13634615211054998, accessed January 15, 2022.

Hickey, Amber
2019   Rupturing Settler Time: Visual Culture and Geographies of Indigenous Futurity."
        World Art 9(2):163–180.
Jobson, Ryan Cecil
2020   The Case for Letting Anthropology Burn: Sociocultural Anthropology in 2019.
        American Anthropologist 122(2):259–271.
Jones, Lucy T.
2009   The "Sleazy" Underbelly of Museum Collecting: Archiving Theft in Museums.
        Library & Archival Security 22(1):19–32.
Lonetree, Amy
2012   Decolonizing Museums: Representing Native America in National and Tribal
        Museums. Chapel Hill: University of North Carolina Press.
Mbembe, Achille, and R.H. Mitsch
2003   Life, Sovereignty, and Terror in the Fiction of Amos Tutuola. Research in African
        Literatures 34(4):1–26.
McChesney, Meagan Donnelly
2019   Exhibiting Sovereignty: Tribal Museums in the Great Lakes Region, 1969–2010.
        PhD dissertation, Department of Anthropology, University Chicago.
Rassool, Ciraj
2015   Re-storing the Skeletons of Empire: Return, Reburial and Rehumanisation in
        Southern Africa. Southern African Studies 41(3):653–670.
Rifkin, Mark
2017   Beyond Settler Time: Temporal Sovereignty and Indigenous Self-Determination.
        Durham: Duke University Press.
Ronan, Kristine
2014   Native Empowerment, the New Museology, and the National Museum of the
        American Indian. Museum and Society 12(2):132–147.
Sleeper-Smith, Susan, ed.
2009   Contesting Knowledge: Museums and Indigenous Perspectives. Lincoln: University of Nebraska Press.
Spears, Lorén M.
2020   Indigenous Collections: Care, Research, and Representation. DigitalCommons@
        URI, The University of Rhode Island, 20 Apr. 2020, digitalcommons.uri.edu/
        lib_events/6/, accessed September 1, 2020.
Stoler, Ann Laura
2006   Haunted by Empire: Geographies of Intimacy in North American History. Durham: Duke University Press.
Turnbull, Paul
2020   Collecting and Colonial Violence. *In* The Routledge Companion to Indigenous
        Repatriation, pp. 452–468. New York: Routledge.

Viau-Courville, Mathieu

2016 "Museums Without (Scholar-) Curators: Exhibition—Making in Times of Managerial Curatorship." Museum International 68(3–4):11–32.

Vizenor, Gerald R.

1999 Manifest Manners: Narratives on Postindian Survivance. Lincoln: University of Nebraska Press.

2

Biidoban in the Museum

KAY KAKENDASOTKWE MATTENA

Long before the fourth fire was lit by the Nishnaabe, I came to rest and began my journey with aki, mother earth. I was laid next to my keeper Keshnekwe on a hill overlooking Lake Michigan alongside her traveling supplies, and the braids of her kin. Tobacco leaves between her fingers on one hand, and me in her other. We laid together for a great long while feeling the cool rain trickling down the roots that now caressed our bodies, the summer sun warm and dry, the soil around us, and the last fall moisture in the soil frozen in the winter hugging our decaying skin. Around us sprouts sweetgrass and wild geraniums from the nutritious gift we both get to return.

Now my leather skin is fragmented, the bone needles and medicines within me are now decaying as they should. Keshnekwe carries us into the ancestral village. Ready to give the last manitou, spirit, a tobacco leaf we are all at once thrust into the light of father sky . . . but there is no comfort here. Pale faces stare down at us speaking a language we cannot understand, as red burnt backs and necks scramble for small paper tags, and clear bags. I hear among the language the word Potawatomi and turn to ask my companion, "do they mean Bodwewadmi?" She does not reply; where her body once laid next to mine there only remains some of her teeth and the nutrient rich earth that filled in around her. I thank her for her gift, and I'm grateful for her journey, but now I wonder what is mine? These "hunters" seem interested in us and our resting place, and yet they do not understand what harm they have caused all of us.

Kenyan artist Ng'endo Mukii compares the work of the ethnographer to the work of taxidermy stating that, "Both of these practices involve an act of deletion, of drying out, of editing an Indigenous species for the sake of representing it as an icon in a foreign context" (Mukii 2020). Archaeology, conceived alongside anthropology, has been a science of studying the material past of primarily "prehistoric" and "other" cultures, resulting in "othering" the individuals and communities from their own culture, from

Figure 2.1. *Biidoban in the Museum,* by Kay Kakendasotkwe Mattena.

their materials, and the present communities from their ancestors (Trouillot 2003). This taxidermy of the past as separate from the present and future limits the speculations archaeology can engage with, and also draws a theoretical line in the sand between the subjective times themselves. It erases other ways of understanding time and the materials encapsulated within. If archaeologists seek to avoid researching simply for the sake of research, and instead search for ways to make archaeology meaningful, they must redefine these temporal categories into more of a continuum, undulating waves, or the twisting roots of a tree (Atalay 2012). The unilinear sense of time and space (temporality) is often forced onto Indigenous people and their ancestors, whose own temporalities are assimilated and appropriated into the settler-colonial mold, and in many ways it colonizes Indigenous ways of viewing time itself (Rifkin 2017). A more engaged archaeology requires recognition of multiple ways of viewing time, and the people who draw connections to that temporality allowing for forms of *temporal sovereignty* (Rifkin 2017).

This "entrapment" within progressive constructs of time is oversimplified and limiting in many ways (Olivier 2011; Dawdy 2010). Ideologies of "progress" (Imperial, Colonial, Industrial) are often tangential to destruction. Progress is a storm that carries us away from the past, leaving rubble and ruins behind us, blindly hurdling into the future (Benjamin 1968:ix–259). Landscape in these progressive ideas center the land as commodity and property, rather than life-giver and place as many Indigenous groups view the land (Atalay 2020). Land *her*self represents and encapsulates, much like time, heritage, history, and Traditional Ecological Knowledge (TEK) for Indigenous communities and non-Indigenous communities alike. TEK is difficult to define generally, but it is mostly synonymous with or includes Indigenous science, and knowledge that is specific to each cultural group

(Whyte 2013). Land, and her knowledge, is where intersections of hegemony and archaeology, time and earth, walk hand-in-hand, and archaeology has hope to expose the oppressive destruction of people and communities for the sake of "progress." These flaws of progress showcase the destructive nature of western views of progression that have been hidden, alongside the erasure of Indigenous Knowledge and Indigenous heritage.

I laid resting when the "hunters" found me. They placed my body on the cold table, removed what remained of aki, my mother, from my skin. Cutting loose my flesh, piece by piece, much like the deer who gifted me their skin, and released my spirit into the bright unnatural light. Panic sets in as I look around for Father Sky, Mother Earth, and Grandmother Moon. I catch a glimpse out of the singular small window in this basement room. My family is so far away now.

As I lay on the table staring out at my only hope to see the great manitou, the Aliens spill my guts on the table before me, picking me apart. I call out to my creator asking, "why are they doing this to me?" All at once I hear shouts in many languages around me . . . I am not the only one. I hear one distant voice call back to me in Haudenosaunee which I recognize, "they want to learn from us . . . but they think our creators are dead." "They are not!" I shout back, "They can't be!" The small child's voice responds, "we know, but their knowledge keepers say that the Bodwewadmi no longer exist and refuse to learn from our makers and their descendants." "But why?" I ask. She responds, "Because like the Windigo they cannot see their own cannibalism." As I glance around the room to see the source of the voice, she is a small corn husk doll made by our neighbors. "They cannot see us or learn from us because our spirits don't speak English."

I cry for the little girl, she cries for me, and together we cry for our people. One of the Aliens looks around as if they heard our cries, and I hope one day they will hear our joy. I worry what my creator will do as these poor creatures dissect, organize in their way, and label my most sacred parts no one else was meant to see. They put me in a box made of paper without any of my medicines and tools, they stole my name, and renamed me "tattoo kit."

Museums are a primary example of the proliferation of the ideology of linear progression that regularly omits and silences Indigenous ways of knowing. This can take form in something as small as a lower case *g* for non-Christian Gods in a display description, and as large as encapsulating an "entire" culture within glass boxes with historical-fiction settler fantasies about the Indigenous other (Ames 2010; Benjamin 1969). Museums with settler-colonial origins and practices often promote progressive time, fabricate exotic narratives, and silence Indigenous heritage and knowledge, justifying (or hiding) colonial legacies. Museums construct miniature narratives similar to those fantasies seen in the Paris arcades described by Benjamin (1969)—dioramas of worlds outside their own, with whom the upper classes both fantasize, and reflect their power over the landscape and the people living in the landscape. Museums similarly often display Indigenous heritage as if frozen in time, frozen in the past and the dead. Much like how the taxidermist tries to create life where there is none, the ethnographer, curator, archaeologist creates death where there is life (Mukii 2020).

This destruction by fantasy and hidden histories has material traces: the heritage itself, the colonial traumas, and the acts of hiding them (Hawkins 2009). These materials require an archaeological sensibility and rigor to unearth them. The origins of archaeology as a discipline, and the origins of museum institutions, are two branches on the same tree. Both originated as colonial power displays and controls, not only dictating the narrative of colonization, but also justifying the objectification and hegemony over Indigenous people and their heritage. Indigenous voices, however, were not regularly viewed as significant enough a resource to be commodified alongside them. Objects and traditions that represented Indigeneity were hidden and destroyed through a lack of curatorial care if they did not fit the constructed colonial narrative (Turner 2017). An archaeology of these material traces of destruction through fantasy within museums has potential to show these hidden truths in tangible ways.

The museum catalogue itself is a "feature" of excavation and critical analysis (Turner 2020). Reducing heritage to numbers, data points, and classifications erases, or "dries out," the history and ancestry carried with them. When the people, and their ancestors, are removed from material heritage their voices are erased. However, when the work of museums is done collaboratively it can also be a work for healing by including multiple forms of Knowledge (Atalay 2020:110). An archaeology of these institutions interrogating these hidden heritages can illuminate colonial injustices at the hand of museum institutions, and has the potential to reawaken stolen Indigenous traditions. This reawakening requires care and attention to the potential for healing colonial traumas. It can be a medicine of the heart to heal the wounds of the ancestral past. Remembering and healing traumas requires careful critical analysis of what has been remembered, what has been forgotten, and what has been erased (Wilson 2011; Lucas 2002).

Father Sky must be laying his head to rest as his light fades from the view of the small hole I have to see out of my box high up on a shelf. The voices of the Aliens, and the whirls and whorls of their machines quiet. The bright artificial light goes out and a heavy door in the distance clicks shut. The grinding of a key in the lock shuts us in for the sake of keeping others out. Laughter echoes and the voices joke as they drift further away from the door, "maybe they aren't so different from my creator" I mumble to myself, "but what is their purpose with me?"

Around me I hear the moans, cries, and songs of my neighbors. Some have been here much longer than me. Their voices dry and tired. As I was being put inside my new prison I caught a glimpse of a red catlinite pipe, broken and missing his stem. His song is one of sorrow because he has not been gifted sema, tobacco, or been used to communicate with manitous, spirits, for some time. Next to him, a bag of animal bones labeled "fauna." I immediately recognized my friend, the Northern Alligator Gar. Their mandible I once protected in my now torn skin. They used to make such beautiful designs on the skin of our people that would heal mind, body, and spirit. Their designs marked our people for the spirits to see, and now they cannot breathe, suffocating in clear bags. As I lay in my box listening to the songs of my kin, I join in the singing. Suddenly, the voices fall silent as a shadow approaches the door.

click As the lock slides open, and the door swings in allowing a small breeze to permeate the dusty air. A young figure enters the room. I hear the shuffling of tired feet drag across the linoleum floor. A chair slides out from a lab table as the figure plops down a heavy bag. Another chair slides out, they take their seat and rest their heavy head in their palms. Heavy breathing is pierced by quiet sobs. "Exhaustion," I think to myself, "I know it well," as I lay here in my tattered scraps gutted of my mind and spirit. I too begin to quietly sob like the figure before me; then, grief stricken by the loss of my creator and my home, I'm overcome by emotion. Wails erupt from my box . . .

"Hello?" shouts the figure, "is someone there?"

I lay silent deciding what I should do next, my despair tying my heart into knots . . .

An excavation of the material record, and reinvigoration of traditional heritage braided together requires a new attention to the materiality of this record. Experimental archaeology, woven closely with Indigenous Knowledge, can bring light to these silenced stories by producing and critically engaging with material culture. Producing items and using them guided by TEK weaves the once objectified numeric item with cultural histories, heritage, tradition, and Knowledge. Doing so may reveal the colonial fantasies of "progress," and dust off the hidden histories within the vast collections of artifacts (González-Ruibal 2008). Experimentation seeks to reach out to these memories as they "flash . . . up in a moment of danger" (Benjamin 1968:vi–256, 257). In this continuing "state of emergency" archaeologists should seek to "brush history against the grain" and expose "alternative" narratives of the oppressed (Benjamin 1968:vii–viii, 258–259). When in the hands of Indigenous people, experimental archaeology can flush memories out of the artifacts themselves as they emerge within the descendants working with them. Gaining ancestral knowledge from once hidden artifacts, Elders, youth, and archaeologists can generate a decolonial future together.

"Traditional" archaeology has always consisted of excavation, or removing artifacts and samples from the geology they sit in for study. However, the process of doing this is destructive and irreversible. As soon as an archaeologist cuts into the soil it cannot be undone. The other issue of traditional archaeology is the lack of care for artifacts once they are removed. Artifacts are excavated, if they were something of interest or offered potential prestige for the archaeologist, they may have been photographed and described. The majority of the artifacts, however—the debitage, the refuse, the smaller things—are lost to storage to collect dust, or returned with the backfill. Historically, and occasionally perpetuated in the present, archaeology was far more focused on excavation itself. Cataloguing, labeling, and analyzing after the excavation built far less prestige than a tantalizing photograph of a white man in khakis looming over an excavation site. This means that numerous collections held in curation facilities and museums are poorly documented, let alone cared for. Facilities left to care for these collections are often poorly funded and understaffed, leaving thousands of artifacts abandoned to collect dust. Archaeologists cannot only look outside archaeology to see the destruction and ruination of the contemporary; we must be reflexive and see our role in the destruction (Buchli and Lucas 2001). The acts of "construction, fortification, destruction, and reconstruction" leaves material traces "as the dust settles" (Weizman 2014:16). To see the ruination and abandonments, archaeologists must seek to excavate these curation facilities and legacy collections. Researchers must brush off the dust as carefully and systematically as we would in the field to re-unearth the hidden and forgotten truths, stories never heard, and voices of the voiceless left behind for another time.

Another way artifacts of cultural heritage have been hidden in plain sight is through miscategorization. As mentioned previously, the museum catalogue itself served to erase the Indigeneity out of the artifacts themselves via the reduction of heritage to numbers and data (Turner 2020). Without TEK with, by, and for Indigenous people, archaeologists were, and still are, unable to discern a tattoo needle from their curatorial "haystack." Teasing out these miscategorizations requires experience and community involvement to parse out the images and items set aside for a time when a new generation of Indigenous scientists will find the voices of their ancestors among the rubble of a careless archaeology. Involving Indigenous people thoughtfully and collaboratively can shed light on these items and push for decolonizing museums (Bruchac et al. 2016).

The figure rolls their chair back from under them and quietly steps to where I sit on the shelf. The young face, streaked with tears and heavy bags under their eyes, approaches my box. "Now is my chance!" I think to myself.

"Child, you are too young to have such a tired face."

The figure jumps, not expecting to hear a voice coming from the curation lab shelves, but shakes their head saying, "I really must be losing it! I'll get some rest once I catalogue this." They carefully open the lid to the box labeled "tattoo kit." Inside they see the bag of faunal remains, the pipe, and then they find me . . . my sad flesh suffocating too inside a clear bag. They pick me up and carry me to the table where they've been working. On the table sits a notebook labeled "Thesis: Tattooing in the Great Lakes Region." They open a spreadsheet on the computer in front of them, glancing back at the paper label here keeping me company in my lonely bag.

"What troubles you child?" I ask, hoping they hear me this time, or maybe just to have someone to talk to whether they hear me or not.

Their eyes widen and look down at me lying on the table, "Did you . . ."

"Yes! Please hear me. I have so many questions. Don't be startled, all of us here have our own stories to tell but no one will hear us." The figure seems to calm themselves and gingerly picks me up and carries me to a tray lined with paper. They open the bag and gently pour me onto the tray.

inhale *exhale* "Migwetth—thank you," I say with relief to finally breathe. My concept of time must have escaped me, because from all the time sitting and listening to the Aliens I have learned their language; "now," I say to myself, "It is time they learned mine."

> *"You're welcome," says the wide-eyed young scholar staring down at my tattered body, "what questions do you have?"* . . .
>
> *Together we talked for hours until Biidoban dusted away the yesterdays from the surface of the earth. The student answered my questions about the Aliens, why I was here, and where my people were today, and I answered hers. However, I stated that, "I am not my own creator, so I only know those stories and medicines that I carry. To know my purpose, to know my stories and how they are braided with so many others, you must know my creators."*

Ojibwe artist, Lisa Jackson, in her virtual reality world *Biidoban: First Light*, brings to life the liminal space between past and future, and Indigenous and settler (Astle 2018). Shedding the "first light" or *biidoban* on museum collections means engaging with the temporalities they exist in, all the people who have impacted and been impacted by them, establishing good relationships with all. The act of weaving the critical attention to materiality through experimental archaeology, with Indigenous Knowledge makes visible traditions, stories, histories, and heritage hidden among the artifacts themselves. When producing things such as beadwork and jewelry, or when doing things such as drumming or tattooing, it is a time where youth and Elders can spend time together. This is important because Elders, and knowledge keepers, can gift their wealth of knowledge to future generations ensuring TEK continues to be passed on. Following traditional protocols for storytelling, gift giving, and ceremony woven with these hidden heritages, stories can be shared within the cultural group and to the archaeologist digging for a decolonial future. The objects, medicines, and symbols themselves become tightly woven with these healing stories. In this vein of research, the archaeologists' hands are clasped around the medicines of the ancestors, and the generations with us today (Supernant et al. 2020).

This relationship between archaeologists and Indigenous peoples is a necessary cultivation. The destruction and trauma of progress at the hands of historically colonial institutions and disciplines is not an easy trauma to heal. Archaeology alone has erased and left out the voices of the people still here today by erasing the traces of their ancestors or devaluing their lineage. The very act of relationship building is a decolonial project (Atalay 2012; Bruchac et al. 2016). Relinquishing the researchers' power over the research, although difficult for many, is necessary to address the destruction and wounds caused by research itself (Atalay 2012). The potential loss of nishnabek tattooing is a result of colonization and Anglicization.

In *Archaeologies of the Heart*, Atalay concludes with sowing the seeds for healing (Supernant et al. 2020:261–264). These seeds are "patience," "emotions," "empathy and compassion," "focus and care," "stories," and "relationality." Through Indigenous experimental archaeology, I hope to investigate what an "Archaeology led by Strawberries," an archaeology that is led by the heart with empathy and care, might look like when it aims to reawaken sleeping material traditions. Strawberries are a medicine that heals the physical and spiritual heart. "Patience" shows commitment and allows time for ourselves as well as our relationships with others. Archaeology can cultivate and entice out "emotions" as a time for celebrations, remembrance, mourning, and togetherness. All struggles for justice require empathy and care for the people and communities with whom archaeologists work to engage thoughtfully, and critically while remembering our humanity (Supernant et al. 2020). For all the previous seeds to be sown, "relationality," or relationships, must be cultivated in a heart-centered way. Atalay reminds us why the analogy of the heart berry is so necessary and that an archaeology for healing colonial traumas and generating a hopeful future for generations of Indigenous people is an *Archaeolog*[y] *of the Heart* (Supernant et al. 2020).

A heart-centered, Indigenized Experimental Archaeology thoughtfully engages with materiality and all the real and tangible emotions braided within the materials we work with as archaeologists, students, curators, librarians, and people. As one might dust off a picture of their ancestors tucked away in their attic, there is hope in dusting off the pictures of ancestors and their material belongings in museums. With this Indigenous people can reflect on stories, healing, emotion, empathy, care, patience, and relationships for a braided future built in collaboration with all who have touched and been touched by these materials. With the right medicines archaeologists and Indigenous people alike can seek to debride the wound caused by colonialism and heal as we start this long journey together rooted in heart-centered practices.

"Today is the day!" I shout to my cousins and neighbors who too will be returning home soon. Since the first time I met this student they have grown much. Together, with, by, and for myself and my people the Bodwewadmi, we shared knowledge and teachings. Our research together will now be turned into a book so this knowledge of our relationship together might be known by all others. Now they carry me to a table surrounded by my people, my creators. They brought with them medi-

cines I have longed to see since the day my journey was interrupted by the Aliens I now call friends. Tobacco ties clasped in their Hands. A Nokomis, grandmother, who looks much like my old friend Keshnekwe thanks the student with a firm, loving hand.

"Migwetth," they say.

"Migwetth," I say.

"It's been an honor to learn and grow with you," says the Archaeologist.

Together, they leave the artificial underground of the lab and bring me into the light. For the first time in decades, I can feel the warmth on my skin. I finally get to complete my journey, and I get to do so while knowing that my medicines, my story, and my people will never be forgotten. We are still here, and always will be. In mind, body, and spirit.

Bama mine jaganeganon—Later on to all my relations.

References

Ames, Michael M.

2010   Cannibal Tours and Glass Boxes: The Anthropology of Museums. Vancouver: University of British Columbia Press.

Astle, Randy

2018   "'Our Culture is in Our Language': Lisa Jackson on Her VR Film Biidaaban: First Light and Indigenous Futurism." Brooklyn: Filmmaker Magazine.

Atalay, Sonya

2012   Community-Based Archaeology: Research With, By and For Indigenous and Local Communities. Berkeley: University of California Press.

2020   An Archaeology Led by Strawberries. *In* Archaeologies of the Heart. Kisha Supernant, Jane Baxter, Natasha Lyons, and Sonya Atalay, eds. pp. 258-269. New York: Springer.

Benjamin, Walter

1968   Illuminations. Hannah Arendt, ed. Harry Zohn, trans. Illinois: University of Chicago Library.

1969   Paris: Capital of the Nineteenth Century. Perspecta 12:163–172. Cambridge: MIT Press.

Bruchac, Margaret, Siobhan Hart, and H. Martin Wobst

2016   Indigenous Archaeologies: A Reader on Decolonization. London: Routledge.

Buchli, Victor, and Gavin Lucas

2001   Archaeologies of the Contemporary Past (1st ed.). London: Routledge.

Dawdy, Shannon Lee

2010   The Taphonomy of Disaster and the (Re)Formation of New Orleans. American Anthropologist 108(4):719–730.

González-Ruibal, Alfredo

2008 Time to Destroy: An Archaeology of Supermodernity. Current Anthropology 49(2):247–279.

Hawkins, Gay

2009 History in Things: Sebald and Benjamin on Transience and Detritus. *In* W. G. Sebald: Schreiben Ex Patria / Expatriate Writing. Gerhard Fischer, ed. pp. 161–176. Netherlands: Brill Publishing.

Lucas, Gavin

2002 Disposability and Dispossession in the Twentieth Century. Journal of Material Culture 7(1):5–22. London: Sage Publications.

Mukii, Ng'endo

2020 "Re-Animating Ancestors and Those to Come." CSPA Quarterly Spring/Summer 2020:8–27. Center for Sustainable Practice in the Arts.

Olivier, Laurent

2011 The Dark Abyss of Time: Archaeology and Memory. Lanham: AltaMira Press.

Rifkin, Mark

2017 Beyond Settler Time: Temporal Sovereignty and Indigenous Self-Determination. Durham: Duke University Press.

Supernant, Kisha, Jane Eva Baxter, Natasha Lyons, and Sonya Atalay

2020 Archaeologies of the Heart. Switzerland: Springer International Publishing.

Trouillot, Michel-Rolph

2003 Anthropology and the Savage Slot: The Poetics and Politics of Otherness. *In* Global Transformations: Anthropology and the Modern World. Michel-Rolph Trouillot, ed. pp. 7–28. New York: Palgrave Macmillan US.

Turner, Hannah

2017 Organizing Knowledge in Museums: A Review of Concepts and Concerns. Knowledge Organization 44, 472–484.

2020 Cataloging Culture: Legacies of Colonialism in Museum Documentation. UBC Press. Weizmann, Eyal, Susan Schuppli, Shela Sheikh, Anselm Franke, Thomas Keenan, and Paulo Tavares

2014 Introduction: Forensis. *In* Forensis: The Architecture of Public Truth. Berlin: Sternberg Press.

Whyte, Kyle Powys

2013 On the Role of Traditional Ecological Knowledge as a Collaborative Concept: A Philosophical Study. Ecological Process 2(7). https://doi.org/10.1186/2192-1709 -2-7.

Wilson, Ross

2011 Remembering and Forgetting Sites of Terrorism in New York, 1900–2001. Journal of Conflict Archaeology 6(3):200–221.

3

Rubber Yardsticks

Emic Methods in Indigenous Archaeology

S. MARGARET SPIVEY-FAULKNER

The sciences, as we are accustomed to the use of the term, are western "folk theories" of the phenomenological world . . .
(Dunnell 1971:13)

In this new wave of Indigenous archaeology, when the necessity of Indigenous guidance and participation in the archaeological research process has already been firmly established by those Indigenous archaeologists who came before us, we have the luxury of teasing out more radical ways of embedding Indigeneity into the discipline. To that end, I seek to resurrect an old argument of analytical perspective in archaeology: can we take an emic perspective in our analyses? More specifically, can we use aspects of Indigenous cultures to study the material remnants of their ancestors? When Ford and Steward (1954) and Spaulding (1953) duked it out on this topic during the rise of processualism, new disciplinary mores that preferred positivistic frameworks prevailed. Though ironic, I posit here that new advances in the biological sciences have shown that the "Science" of anthropological yore was, in fact, more akin to cultural product. Our archaeological hard sciences were, and often still are, European folk sciences that are by definition no more objective than Indigenous folk sciences. This chapter will demonstrate what the use of Indigenous folk sciences could yield if systematically applied in the analyses of Indigenous ancestral material cultures.

As a rule, scientific analyses are conducted from an objective, etic perspective. This is in an effort to ensure replicability of methods and interpretations across individual researchers and through time. Consistency and clarity about what constitutes the objective for a particular type of analysis is an immovable necessity. Often missed, however, are the many and pervasive cultural lenses that have been inserted into scientific objectivism by researchers who are not encouraged to reflect on, much less inspect, if these lenses have crept into their own work.

Efforts to tease out these lenses would not have been fruitful only a few decades ago. New advances in fields like phylogeny allow for producing a data set that is disassociated with cultural biases embedded in western science. So, let us use these new tools to better our anthropological methods of analysis in the deeply anthropological vein of examining culture alongside the culture of scientists and science itself. For Indigenous archaeology, this exchange of cultural lenses from western to one purpose-built for use in analyses of a particular Nation or culture can result in drastically more refined interpretations of material culture. Beyond that, the development of these hyperlocal analytical lenses would necessitate deep engagement between scholars and contemporary Indigenous communities, providing a boon for community relations and the increased entrance of Indigenous individuals into the field of anthropology. I would argue that the playing out of this process would enrich the discipline massively by reifying the primacy of traditional knowledge keepers from Indigenous cultures, bringing anthropology back to its four-field roots, and producing better science than our current methods allow. There are only winners here.

Below you will find a case study of this process focusing on animal taxonomies, wrapped in a discussion of the history of anthropological theory surrounding the uses of emic or etic categories within these typologies and taxonomies. Focusing on this case study is critical, as my proposal to shift our disciplinary standards toward emic analyses is not worth much through mere telling; showing is far more effective. Some of the theoretical detail is dense, but it is included here as a necessary proof of concept.

What Are *Emic* and *Etic*?

Anthropological discussions of emic and etic are borne out of the discussion of phonemic and phonetic in linguistics, first coined by Pike in 1967 (Markee 2012:1). In colloquial terms, emic is a view from inside a culture and etic is a view from outside a culture. In his original work, Pike emphasizes that etic and emic are not a true dichotomy (1967:41), but instead are likened to two images with very slight differences aligned within a stereoscope. When the two lenses are brought together, each in front of a separate eye, they enable the onlooker to see a scene in three dimensions

(Pike 1967:41). The emic lens displays vital information to those who use a language, and the etic lens clarifies that which is important to a researcher analyzing said language (Markee 2012:1; Pike 1967).

Fundamentally, etic analyses rise from the western intellectual tradition, and for our purposes, can be firmly understood as an outgrowth of western objectivism and science. None of these traditions are sterilized from cultural considerations inherent within western ontologies and epistemologies; in fact, they are the fruition of those very structures. This is the rub. As the production of an etic investigatory framework is inexorably tied to its western cultural birth, it inevitably distorts analyses through that cultural framework. As anthropologists, our research goals are to understand culture better. The more we can reduce error and noise through incidental injections of culture outside the group we are studying with, the more accurate our results and interpretations will be.

A Case Study in Emic Categorization as Analytic Method

The universality of categorization of things as a facet of human cognition can be cited as the unstated reason why typologies persist in archaeological inquiry (Keil 1989; Santos et al. 2002). More than this, the universality of categorization by humans is the underlying reason why we, as archaeologists, posit that our typologies could in some way connect to the cultural lifeways of people who exist within a wholly different temporal, cultural, and linguistic context than we do.

When an archaeologist pulls an artifact from the screen, when they clean and sort bags of artifacts fresh in from the field, and when they record artifact frequencies and make data tables, that archaeologist is applying an analytical method as old as the discipline of archaeology itself: the creation and reification of the artifact typology. Though the typology fundamentally underlies nearly all archaeological research, little consideration has been given to the implicit assumptions about human nature embedded in the use of typologies in archaeological research and the applicability of our own typologies to the past since the debates between Spaulding and Ford in the 1950s (Spaulding 1953; Ford and Steward 1954) and Binford's New Systematics (1965). Most pertinent of the more recent works on typologies to my research here are Hayden (1984), Fradkin (1990), and Berlin, Breedlove, and Raven (1973).

Rote interest in antiquities has existed through human history, with older heirlooms being found in much more recent contexts archaeologically. The earliest reference to a "typological method" can purportedly be found in an 1816 scientific publication by de Blainville to create a zoology built from his advisor Cuvier's work (de Blainville 1816; Gorodzov 1933:95; Gräslund 1987:110; von Hofsten 1922:395, 402). By 1933, the use of typologies to order excavated archaeological materials had already begun to be used widely in archaeology (Gorodzov 1933). Early analytical archaeological typologies were most proficiently used when analyzing ceramics but had been descriptive when first developed (Ford and Steward 1954:42). The use of typologies for seriation and the development of relative chronologies is most prominently seen early in the American Southwest (Ford and Steward 1954:43; Kidder 1915).

Not all categorization schemes are made alike, with scholars such as Hayden (1984), in following Krieger (1944), defining a classification system as fundamentally different than typologies and taxonomies because it does not "pretend to relate artifact categories to concepts of their makers, users, or any other problem of evolutionary or anthropological importance," (Hayden 1984:80). I will extend that definition to this work by pushing you, the reader, to produce not just classification systems but also endeavor to imbue those classification systems with some shadow of the meaning their creators saw within the artifacts.

In modern archaeology, typologies are consistently employed, and their constituent types or categories are the basis for long-running and frequent debate in regional or specialized journals. However, the method itself is frequently running in the background as a kind of archaeological operating system. While many other methods or models developed contemporaneously to the typology have been thoroughly interrogated, dismantled, or discarded as rudimentary or based on anti-scientific or racist ideas, the typology has persisted as a nearly invisible filament allowing the whole web of archaeological inquiry to remain intact.

The mid-1950s saw a spirited debate on the constitution of archaeological types and the appropriate deployment of them as a methodological tool. Two early articles best summarize the two opposing interpretations by Spaulding (1953) and Ford and Steward (1954). This discussion was vital to later conceptualizations of archaeological typologies and the care with which we should apply ethnographic analogies to data drawn from the archaeological record.

Spaulding's (1953) work was an early exploration in analyzing archaeological materials statistically to determine typologies. In this work, a type is defined as "a group of artifacts exhibiting a consistent assemblage of attributes whose combined properties give a characteristic pattern" (Spaulding 1953:305). Though he notes that artifact attributes are a result of cultural processes and "not an arbitrary procedure of the classifier," he asserts that the analysis of attributes and sorting into types "must be carried out . . . independently" (Spaulding 1953:305). This point of view is asserted in direct opposition to Krieger's conceptualization of the type as "the result of sound inferences concerning the customary behavior of the makers of the artifacts" (Spaulding 1953:305).

Ford and Steward assert the normative theory that any quantification of archaeological data presupposes the "use of cultural types" (1954:42) and differentiates between "types" used for "descriptive systematization" and those used for seriation, lamenting that the same term has been carried over from past usage (1954:42). Most significantly, they connect Krieger and Rouse's earlier works with their own to build an argument that archaeological types, and therefore archaeological typologies, must necessarily have "historical meaning" and should apply to the "living culture" of those who created the materials being typologized (Ford and Steward 1954:43; Krieger 1944; Rouse 1939). In this work, they directly refute Spaulding's 1953, work stating that

> This discussion takes for granted the assumption that types do exist in culture and may be discovered by competent methodologies. This I doubt. (Ford and Steward 1954:42)

In all, Ford and Steward's fundamental point is that human cultures and human history do not behave in ways that can be neatly described by mathematical formulas or models (1954:44). The oversimplification inherent to the collection of data influenced by depositional and taphonomic forces, as well as obfuscating cross-cultural misunderstandings, renders all archaeological data immune to the ahistorical statistical determination of types championed by Spaulding.

I specifically reference this debate because it gets to the heart of the tension inherent in our reliance as archaeologists on typologies, particularly because our own lived realities are fundamentally different from those of the peoples we are studying through those typologies. An archaeologist requires several stages of inference, many of which are derived from ethnographic analogies, to traverse the intellectual space from examining wholly unknown artifacts to interpreting their human origin.

The natural discursive outgrowth of the Spaulding-Ford debate on typologies and types that began with the works described above was Binford's development of the New Systematics (Binford 1965). Following Dunnell (1971), here, the term *phenomenon* is used in these discussions to mean actual, material events or artifacts, and the term *ideational* refers to how people conceptualize and make ideas about their reality.

Binford discusses Ford's normative stance as taken by "one who sees as his field of study the ideational basis for varying ways of human life—culture" (Binford 1965:203). Binford criticizes this normative view by positing that for the normative theoretical understanding of cultural types to be observable, they must transmit between people in a rational, model-able manner, an assertion he then deconstructs as unreasonable (Binford 1965:204). I assert that many of the analogies Binford deduces from the normative typological paradigm are straw man fallacies. While one could conclude that these are necessary conditions of the paradigm, they do not, in fact, necessarily apply to all situations where normative ideas of typologies could be applied. In other words, these analogies are not universal, and thus they cannot be used to dispense with Ford's point of view universally. Specifically, Binford's reduction of the normative stance to one of a diffusion model from a central point is so divorced from the nuance present in Ford's discussions to make it moot (Binford 1965: 204).

Systematics is interested primarily in "what is done by scientists, and not the way or ways in which non-scientists care to rationalize the procedures" (Dunnell 1971:13).

> To use folk units as the units of study is not terribly unlike a taxonomist asking a frog to what species he belongs. (Dunnell 1971:134)

While adherence to objectivity is a central pillar of western science, it is impossible to disarticulate a person from their cultural context. Implicitly, the categories and "units" western scientists use to analyze and understand the world around them (or in the past) will be tied to their own intellectual heritage, a heritage that may not wholly align with that of those studied (Dunnell 1971:13). In studying past cultures, it would be ideal to develop a system that simultaneously and accurately reflects the cultural processes that led to the deposition of material into the earth and worked within "our own system of ideas and things" (Dunnell 1971:14).

While this era of archaeological systematics appeared particularly intent on categorizing material and phenomena into "ahistorical units," which could be analyzed through archaeological methods (Dunnell 1971:20), it is useful for this study in its understanding of the delineation between how we, as western intellectual scientists, categorize phenomena and how the people who created the materials we study categorized phenomena. Vital to creating analytical units and designations in the study of archaeological materials is the awareness that these created units are themselves artificial and in no way securely connected to the lives of those who produced these materials (Dunnell 1971:26). This "ideational realm . . . include[s] those things which have no objective existence" and thus should not be treated as the analytical product themselves (Dunnell 1971:26). While Dunnell's initial breakdown of these ideas is particularly valuable, I disagree with his organization of "kinds of arrangement" (Dunnell 1971:Figure 3) and many conclusions about the arrangement of phenomena he draws from his original posits.

The use of emic categories in archaeological analysis has been critiqued by several eminent archaeologists who argued for New Systematics (Binford 1965, 1967; Heider 1967; Hayden 1984), with most coming to a conclusion that doubts the utility of emic typologies for the purposes of archaeological research and others claiming that the effort will obfuscate any analysis, in essence forcing a researcher to use "rubber yardsticks" (Dunnell 1971:133–135). For all of his infinite classifications and thin parsing of the appropriate ways of conceptualizing categories and the most ideal tack to take in analysis, Dunnell fundamentally wholly undermines his enterprise with the following:

> The absence of an identifiable phenomenological unit above the scale of discrete object may be the most serious conceptual void in prehistory's formal theory, but by far the most serious operational difficulty is the chronic lack of problem and consequent lack of rational means of evaluating classifications. (Dunnell 1971:161)

Beyond simply an admission of flaws in applying deductive or inductive reasoning to a field that can nearly only reasonably lean on abductive reasoning for evaluating material culture, Dunnell here deconstructs his reliance on the classification of phenomena through the observation that ideational hierarchies must meld with phenomenological hierarchies, as in reality hierarchies of things cannot exist exclusively within the ideational world. Moreover, Dunnell posits here that cultural classifications cannot be evaluated in a scientific, systematic manner, a concern central to the archaeological paradigm in place at the time of the publication of his book. With that, he rips away the utility of classification within the narrowly deductive analytical window he has left for himself.

Indigenizing Typologies and Taxonomies

Archaeologists from non-western intellectual traditions recognize the divergent analytical applications of typologies in archaeology (Hein 2016). While some archaeologists adhere to a strictly etic perspective, others assert that an emic perspective in creating typologies can "tell us about the underlying conceptual system of the artisans" (Hein 2016:7; Rouse 1960). Though, unsurprisingly, such a fundamental method can serve many purposes in archaeology, recognition of the typology's flexibility is necessary to exploit its potential fully.

Starting from the understanding that the categorization of phenomena is an inherent function of human cognition, we can safely assume that Indigenous people(s) categorized the objects and animals around them in some manner. Getting at how these categorizations were structured requires a look outside of archaeological datasets and a folk taxonomy concept.

Popularized in the 1960s and still used consistently in ethnobiological studies, folk taxonomies are a record of the colloquial categorization of things by groups of people who share a common culture. These folk taxonomies use an emic set of attributes to create classifications of flora and fauna. Following that process results in taxonomies and typologies that are fundamentally dissimilar to those developed in western science. The primary data type used in the recreation of folk taxonomies by anthropologists is either ethnographic interviews or linguistic information. Most pertinent is Fradkin's dissertation titled *Cherokee Folk Zoology* (1990). Fradkin uses a mixture of linguistic information, oral traditions, and ethnographic data to delve into its titular subject in great detail, considering the cosmology and ceremonial lives of Cherokee peoples (Fradkin 1990). By adopting folk taxonomic methods à la Fradkin, as opposed to categorizing artifacts or animals using western scientific methods, entities in the world can be categorized into typologies more accurately reflecting the reality of those who produced any material culture question.

A folk taxonomy is how a culture classifies its "biological universe" (Berlin et al. 1973:214). The collection and description of folk taxonomies of animals and plants began to be a focus of research in the mid-1950s (Berlin et al. 1973:214).

The American, English-language folk taxonomy in Figure 3.1 is a fair demonstration of the differences between an American, English-language folk taxonomy and a scientific, Linnaean taxonomy or phylogeny. This folk

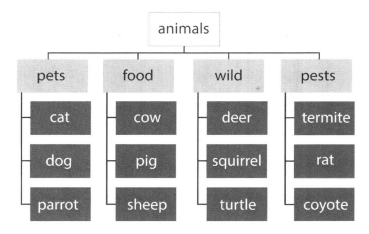

Figure 3.1. An example of an American, English-language folk taxonomy of animals.

taxonomy demonstrates one way Americans categorize animals, but it also conveys a great deal of information about how they culturally consider the world around them. For example, American ideas about ownership, animal welfare, and even legal statute concerning these animals are embedded in this folk taxonomy, simply due to the categorization method used colloquially. Understanding the categorizations made by peoples who have a language and culture different than our own could provide enormous, unique insight into human-animal interactions in that group that would be otherwise inaccessible.

Berlin, Breedlove, and Raven enumerated nine principles consistent cross-culturally in folk taxonomies (1973:214–216). These deal primarily with "universal ethnobiological categories" that form any folk taxonomic structure (Figure 3.2) (Berlin et al. 1973:215). For this research, their sixth principle provides the basis to form a method. There, they state that

> Life form taxa are labelled by linguistic expressions which are lexically analyzed as primary lexemes and may be illustrated by the classes named by such words as *tree, vine, bird, grass, mammal*, etc. (Berlin et al. 1973:215)

Furthermore, in their eighth principle, they indicate that

> Both specific and varietal taxa are linguistically recognized in that they are most commonly labelled by secondary (versus primary . . .) lexemes . . . (Berlin et al. 1973:216)

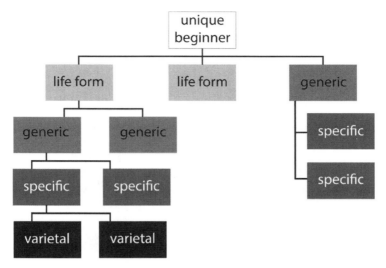

Figure 3.2. Idealized generic hierarchy within a folk taxonomy. Adapted from Berlin et al. 1973:Figure 1.

With these principles, we can identify primary and secondary lexical items within a language to approximate the folk taxonomies that people who spoke those languages would have developed (Dougherty 1978:68). It follows that one can examine traces of folk taxonomies in Indigenous languages, if crudely, by examining contemporary Indigenous languages for the presence of primary and secondary lexical items in words identified as relating to animals, for example.

An at-hand example of primary and secondary lexical items in action within a general American folk taxonomy would be that of trees known as oaks. The word "oak" in this context would be a primary lexical item. The words "black oak," "live oak," and "red oak" are secondary lexical items, given the fact that they use the primary lexical item "oak" and a further identifier (Figure 3.3).

I employed this lexical item analysis in my work to produce a folk taxonomy from Indigenous languages of the Southeast that could be used in an emic analysis of an assemblage of iconographic artifacts depicting animals (Spivey-Faulkner 2018). As the assemblage I was working with predated 1000 CE, there was no way to verify which Indigenous language the artists who created these images spoke. To overcome that hurdle, I attempted to bring together all extant Indigenous languages of the region to hunt for similar lexical structures seen across multiple languages. In turn,

Figure 3.3. An example of primary lexical items and secondary lexical items in English. Dougherty 1978:68.

I inferred that lexical structures seen across many linguistically dissimilar languages were likely to have been germane across the region. As many of these languages were collected when the overall speaking population was in remarkable decline, I treated each language dataset as incomplete.

The method I developed to locate primary and secondary lexical items within the Native American languages of the Southeast goes as follows:

1. Collect all known words referring to animals in a single list for each language.
2. Group word lists by like root word or affix to aid in the search for primary and secondary lexical items.
3. Create hierarchical charts to illustrate lexical item structures from these groupings, with the caveat that these have been produced from incomplete language datasets if the researcher is not fluent in the language or of the community where the language is spoken. If there was a similarity between some primary and secondary lexical items, I combined taxa with notation under the assumption that language loss had occurred between European Invasion and language collection.
4. Examine the resulting folk taxonomies to find similar taxonomic structures across languages.

As a demonstration of this method, let us cast our eyes to Mvskoke, a Muskogean language of the Southeast spoken in different dialects today by citizens of the Muscogee (Creek) Nation, the Seminole Nation of Oklahoma, the Seminole Tribe of Florida, and the Poarch Band of Creek Indians. Using Martin and Mauldin's Mvskoke language dictionary (2000), I made a master list of each word concerning animals, animal actions, or animal parts. This list was composed of 573 different Mvskoke words.

An understanding of the grammatical structure of the language with which you are working is key to executing any analysis of this type of word

44 · S. Margaret Spivey-Faulkner

Table 3.1. An example of the dissection of the Mvskoke word Cetto-lanuce into constituent parts

Cetto (snake)	For example
Cetto-kvcēkv (joint snake)	
Cetto-lane (green snake)	
Cetto-lanuce (small green snake)	Cetto /lan /uce
Cetto-lvste (black snake)	
Cetto-mēkko (rattlesnake)	Snake / "natural" color / diminutive suffix
Cetto-tokohe (bullsnake)	
Cetto-tvstvnkuce (ground rattlesnake)	
Ue-cetto (water snake)	
Ue-akcetto (green water snake)	
Hvyakpo-cetto (prairie kingsnake)	

list. Mvskoke is an agglutinative language that makes liberal use of affixes to indicate part of speech, tense, subject, object, and person. Armed with this knowledge, I evaluated the Mvskoke word list by dissecting apart the roots and affixes from each word.

The example in Table 3.1 illustrates this process. *Cetto*, the word meaning snake in Mvskoke, is the root and primary lexical item in these genera. When secondary lexical items in the form of affixes are added to *cetto*, a more specific type of snake is indicated by the new word. So, the word *cetto-lanuce* can be broken down into parts that include *cetto*, meaning snake, the diminutive suffix -*uce*, and *lanē*, the Mvskoke word for a color that includes colors of nature (green, yellow, and brown). Together, *cetto-lanuce* is translated as "little green snake" a folk taxon that includes species like *Opheodrys aestivus* and *Opheodrys vernalis*. As you can see from the words *ue-cetto* and *hvyakpo-cetto*, the exact organization of affixes is not perfectly consistent, so when working with Mvskoke, one cannot rely solely on simple grouping mechanisms like alphabetization.

Repeating this deconstructive process across the entire word list provided me the ability to group the words by root, here serving as both the primary lexical item and genera in our new folk taxonomy. This process of grouping produced thirty-eight distinct genera that are populated with sub-genera animals (Table 3.2). Description through the use of a secondary lexical item denotes containment within a taxon. Many animal names, however, are primary lexical items that can only be truly integrated into

Table 3.2. The thirty-eight genera in Mvskoke that have sub-genera as produced through lexical item analysis

Mvskoke primary lexical items/genera

Wenhokv (insect)	Efv/etv (dog)
—Fo (bee)	Ero (squirrel)
—Rono or canv (fly)	Hvlpvtv (alligator)
—Tvopvss- (insect)	Kaccv (puma)
—Vcoklepv (spider)	Kono (skunk)
—Akwenhokv (insect that is small and wiggles in water)	Kote (small frog)
Fuswv (bird)	Kvnsvkatkv (lizard)
Opv / pov (owl)	Vcoklopv (lizard)
Ayo (hawk)	Lucv (turtles, terrapins, and tortoises)
Tolose (chicken)	Lvmhe (eagle)
Pvce (dove, parrot, pigeon)	Nerē (night)
Sule (buzzard)	Nokose (bear)
Fuco (duck)	Rakko (horse)
Pen- (turkey, peafowl)	Rvro (fish)
Tuske (woodpecker)	Sakkelv (blackbird)
Cetto (snake)	Sokhv (pig)
Cufe (rabbit)	Pofkv (trumpeting horn)
Cowatv (goat)	Wakv (bovine)
Eco (deer)	Wotko (raccoon)

this folk taxonomy through close consultation with fluent Mvskoke informants.

This basic folk taxonomy allows for a window into categorization methods that differ from what we, in our own modern western-influenced context, would impose upon our taxonomic data. It is not, and could not, be truly complete without deep collaboration with fluent speakers, but this method does re-create a kernel of the folk animal taxonomic structure for peoples who speak Mvskoke. In an analysis of a zooarchaeological assemblage, knowing how Mvskoke-speaking peoples categorized birds, for example, provides great interpretive insight into human-animal interactions with particular species that would be absent from a standard zooarchaeological analysis.

Such a folk taxonomy is inherently flawed, but it also comes with several great benefits when applied to archaeological analyses. First, the dataset is entirely independent from any previous archaeological interpretations and divorced from most intrusions of the western culture within which our discipline lies. Independent datasets are often beyond our grasp as archaeologists, so I felt this was deeply valuable to my research. Second, this dataset is firmly rooted in contemporary Indigenous lives. One cannot work on Indigenous linguistics or ethnography without longitudinal and affirmative engagement with living Native people(s). Vitally, it placed me in the correct pedagogical positioning on Indigenous lives: I am a student, and traditional knowledge keepers are the instructors. Third, the deployment of this taxonomy in analyses produces a result that I can be sure is much closer to the lived realities of the artists who created the assemblage I was studying than the ones provided by western science.

To expand on that third point, the entrance of phylogenetic trees produced solely based on genetic sequencing into science should revolutionize what archaeologists feel are scientifically valid taxonomies for reporting purposes. I say this because the introduction of this data has upended Linnaean taxonomies by showing many of the extant phylogenetic structures archaeologists traditionally rely upon are not based on scientific reality. Species previously thought to be related have been found to simply be morphologically similar through processes of convergent evolution. A great example of western folk taxonomic structures bleeding into scientific standards can be seen in the Anglo folk taxonomic unit of "raptor" or "bird of prey." This is a categorization unsupported by phylogenetic data or Linnaean taxonomy; however, it is pervasive as a good analytical category in an archaeological discussion of birds and their images in North America. Using folk taxonomies in our analyses, we can simultaneously remove an erroneous western lens and substitute it with an Indigenous lens, bringing us twice as close to what we strive for: a peek into a culture we do not know.

Closing Takeaways

The time is nigh to revolutionize the way we perceive objectivity and subjectivity in scientific methods used in anthropology. Just like each ethnographic study is highly tailored to the cultural realities it is situated within, and advances in genomics are beginning to provide genetically tailored medical applications in the health sciences, we now can tailor our analytical and interpretive scientific methods as well.

My hope is that the case study above has adequately convinced you that returning to the question of emic methods in archaeology is not just possibly fruitful but also an ethical and enriching process that will only bolster our work's scientific validity. The new wave of Indigenous archaeology represented by this volume is just that: the operationalization of the decades of work our forebearer Indigenous anthropologists have conducted to convince people Indigenous perspectives are vital to understanding Indigenous peoples. Not only is this work good for our communities and our discipline, but it is also good for our results and our interpretations. To that end, I would like to provide a list of action items that could help archaeology develop our emic methods in Indigenous archaeology.

1. When reporting results of zooarchaeological and paleoethnobotanical analyses, add an additional table, clearly labeled, that does the same tabulations under a culturally and linguistically appropriate folk taxonomy, with this dual reporting forming a new disciplinary standard.
2. We must build capacity in junior archaeology colleagues to longitudinally engage with Indigenous languages through collaboration with living communities.
3. Reform archaeological professional guidelines to encourage more participant observation with traditional practitioners, with payment to those traditional knowledge keepers commensurate with what we pay faculty who teach students. We must not simply be extractive cultural consumers that build our careers off of others. Instead, be true partners participating appropriately within traditional knowledge systems that are not of our own design. If we can require undergraduates to attend sometimes expensive and onerous field schools to learn archaeological field methods, we certainly can do this as well.

References

Berlin, Brent, Dennis E. Breedlove, and Peter H. Raven
1973   General Principles of Classification and Nomenclature in Folk Biology. American Anthropologist 75(1):214–242.
Binford, Lewis R.
1965   Archaeological Systematics and the Study of Culture Process. American Antiquity 31(2):203–210.
1967   *Review of* K. C. Chang's "Rethinking Archaeology." Ethnohistory 15:422–426.
de Blainville, Henri Marie Ducrotay
1816   Prodrome d'une Nouvelle Distribution Sytematique du Regne Animal. Bulletin des Sciences, par la Société Philomatique de Paris 8:105–124.

Dougherty, J.W.D.

1978   Salience and Relativity in Classification. American Ethnologist 5(1):66–80.

Dunnell, Robert C.

1971   Systematics in Prehistory. New York: The Free Press.

Ford, James A., and Julian H. Steward

1954   On the Concept of Types. American Anthropologist 56(1):42–57.

Fradkin, Arlene

1990   Cherokee Folk Zoology: The Animal World of a Native American People, 1700–1838. New York and London: Garland Publishing Inc.

Gorodzov, V.A.

1933   The Typological Method in Archaeology. American Anthropologist 35(1):95–102.

Gräslund, Bo

1987   The Birth of Prehistoric Chronology: Dating Methods and Dating Systems in Nineteenth-Century Scandinavian Archaeology. Cambridge, NY: Cambridge University Press.

Hayden, Brian

1984   Are Emic Types Relevant to Archaeology? Ethnohistory 31(2):79–92.

Heider, Karl

1967   Archaeological Assumptions and Ethnographical Facts. Southwestern Journal of Anthropology 23:52–64.

Hein, Anke

2016   The Problem of Typology in Chinese Archaeology. Early China 39:21–52.

Keil, Frank C.

1989   Concepts, Kinds, and Cognitive Development. Cambridge: MIT Press.

Kidder, Alfred V.

1915   Pottery of the Pejarito Plateau and of Some Adjacent Regions in New Mexico. Memoirs of the American Anthropological Association, vol. 2. Lancaster, Pennsylvania: The New Era Printing Company.

Krieger, Alex D.

1944   The Typological Concept. American Antiquity 9(3):271–288.

Markee, Numa

2012   Emic and Etic in Qualitative Research. *In* Encyclopedia of Applied Linguistics. Carol A. Chapelle, ed. pp. 1–4. Hoboken: Wiley-Blackwell.

Martin, Jack B., and Margaret McKane Mauldin

2000   A Dictionary of Creek/Muskogee. Lincoln, London: University of Nebraska Press.

Pike, Kenneth, L.

2015   Language in Relation to a Unified Theory of the Structure of Human Behavior. Janua Linguarum. Series Maior. Book. Berlin: De Gruyter Mouton.

Rouse, Irving

1939   Prehistory in Haiti; A Study in Method. Yale University Publications in Anthropology Vol. 21. New Haven: Yale University Press.

1960   The Classification of Artifacts in Archaeology. American Antiquity 25(3):313–323.

Santos, Laurie R., Gregory M. Sulkowski, Geertrui M. Spaepen, and Marc D. Hauser
2002 Object Individuation Using Property/Kind Information in Rhesus Macaques (Macaca mulatta). Cognition 83:241–264.

Spaulding, Albert C.
1953 Statistical Techniques for the Discovery of Artifact Types. American Antiquity 18(4):305–313.

Spivey-Faulkner, S. Margaret
2018 Fort Center's Iconographic Bestiary: A Reanalysis of the Site's Carved Wood Assemblage. Unpublished PhD dissertation, Department of Anthropology, Washington University in St. Louis.

von Hofsten, N.
1922 Från Cuvier till Darwin. Ett blad ur den jämförande anatomiens historia. Nordisk tidskrift 1922:389–411.

4

Archives in Conversation with Indigenous Archaeology

Creating Sustainable Partnerships in Work and Practice

LYDIA CURLISS

Throughout my own work as a library practitioner, student of the archives, and as a Tribal researcher, I have observed how archives are essential to the work and efforts of Indigenous communities in their efforts to Indigenize, decolonize, and recontextualize their relationships to knowledge and often, these collections and materials are not easily accessible to these communities. Even in cases where communities can access these materials, challenges arise due to the nature of how this information is organized and described within these spaces. For many archival collections in archaeology and anthropology, Indigenous related records are held in collections named after the white anthropologists who "discovered" these communities, and therefore seen through a white, male, western lens which have valued these knowledge systems as less than or other (Smith 1999; Atalay 2006). As an Indigenous researcher and student focused on archival studies, I aim to contextualize the relationship of archives to archaeological work and demonstrate how archives and archivists are uniquely positioned to be important partners to Indigenous archaeologists and the communities they work with. While this will not propose perfect solutions, I intend to demonstrate how critical and reciprocal practices and partnerships can benefit both archival institutions and Indigenous archaeologies.

This chapter will identify the ways in which archives, and other similar cultural heritage institutions, have been connected to and can be positioned to help support the efforts, goals, and work of Indigenous archaeology. This chapter will outline (1) the roles of archives and archival institutions, (2) how their current institutional structures and scopes of work have affected how archaeological work is done, and (3) suggestions for how archives must pivot to provide opportunities for supporting Indigenous Archaeology. It will also address areas of current alignment in archival work to Indigenous Archaeology and some of the barriers that make this work and these partnerships challenging. Last, this chapter will examine models of creating sustainable partnerships with Indigenous communities and developing infrastructure among libraries and archives to support this work. While the other chapters of this book focus on Indigenous archaeological methods, this chapter looks at the methodologies employed by archivists and archival studies especially in the places where the work intersects. It will examine the roles of these institutions, and how they can better align with Indigenous archaeological practices and considerations. This includes ensuring the discoverability of collections and materials to address issues surrounding the curation crises in Archaeology, reparative description and the ethical care of Indigenous archaeological materials held in these institutions.

What Are Archives? What Do They Do?

Archives, as defined by the Society of American Archivists (SAA), can be used in three different ways—to refer to the records of people, organizations, businesses, or governments; to refer to the group or organization tasked with preserving the documentary heritage of a particular group; or to refer to the literal building or physical space where materials are held (Society of American Archivists 2016). Generally, the role of archivists and those working in archival institutions is to assess or decide what is collected, collect, preserve, and create access to the materials (Society of American Archivists 2016). Within archival studies, this field has been primarily considered through a western epistemological lens and theoretical framework. This means that the creation and structuring of these institutions and the ways in which we understand the knowledges held within the archive, is largely seen in a Western context. In Terry Cook's (2013) article, "Evidence, memory, identity, and community: four shifting archival paradigms," he outlines how the role of archives has shifted over time. In the first paradigm, "evidence," Cook explains how archives as they first formed were designed to collect records of the colonies or states to document or create a record for the government and other related information. In the next paradigm, the shift focuses to memory. In shifting from only collecting government records to creating memory, the focus becomes about creating a historical record, and in doing so, the archivist begins to play a role in determining what materials are collected and which are not. In the third paradigm, the archivist is envisioned as a mediator, collecting items and materials—leading to a shift in the archives in the ways in which collections are used to create a collective memory. In his last paradigm, Cook describes the shift away from previous models, focusing more on community-based archives and community as archivists. However, the role of archives in history have been explicitly through a western context and has meant that archives are often co-conspirators in violence and oppression which have led to power imbalances and a need for reconciliation with how we incorporate suppressed voices in these spaces (Hughes-Watkins 2018).

Shifting Views in Archival Studies and Practice

Within the field of archival studies, there is a shift taking place as more scholars are now engaging with more critical views of archives and ideas around archival neutrality. In the past, archival studies have focused on areas of archives as related to problems of space, access, accessibility, and many others. For example, in learning about archives there are often conversations around problems of funding, staffing shortages, and the pursuant problems that occur because of these shortages. While these have historically been observed through western understandings, new approaches such as considering social justice (Duff et al. 2013) or critical race theory (Dunbar 2006; Punzalan and Caswell 2016) and Indigenous Knowledge (Christen 2011; Christen and Anderson 2019; O'Neal 2019; Littletree et al. 2020) have begun to take hold across the field. In looking toward more critical engagements with archives, scholars and practitioners have begun examining impacts and relationships of these collections to power structures including how to make archives more accessible (Marsh 2019), reparative description (Wood et al. 2014; Lougheed et al. 2015), community-based archival practice (Caswell et al. 2017; Caswell et al. 2018) and crowdsourcing (Van Hyning et al. 2017; Blickhan et al. 2019)

Problems in Archives and Archaeological Collections

Within archives, the inability to process collections as they come in has long been a problem, leading to large institutional backlogs and persistently uncatalogued records. To address this problem, the archival field came up with the concept of "More Product, Less Process" (MPLP) in 2005 (Greene and Meissner 2005). Through this proposed process, Greene and Meissner laid out a bare minimum amount of description and collections information to allow for archival materials to be findable, especially amid huge backlogs of archival collections that had been secured by an institution, but to the public or researcher were virtually unfindable. These concerns can also be seen within archaeological collections and archives, where space and the preservation of materials often prove challenging. Since 1977, archaeological discourse has focused on the curation crisis, which is used to describe the lack of resources, space, time, and ability to manage archaeological collections as they continue to grow.

Archives of archaeological materials pose different challenges than standard archives as they not only house paper records and materials but often act as repositories for archaeological artifacts. Amid concerns of a "curatorial crisis," there is a general lack of documentation and understanding of what happens to archaeological collections once in archives (Friberg and Huvila 2019). This, in tandem with the continued excavations and collecting of artifacts, provides questions on what should or should not be kept in these spaces and how to preserve records that may be important, while creating room for new objects and records.

Organizational Hierarchies of Archival Knowledge

Throughout history, archival and museum methods of "collecting" objects and knowledge were and continue to be harmful for Indigenous and Tribal communities globally. It is well documented that during the conquest of the "new world" through imperialism and colonialism, many objects' materials and knowledge were taken from Indigenous communities worldwide (Smith 1999). These objects and information were transformed and hidden away in museums and other centers of cultural heritage. In the stealing and claiming of these knowledges they were re-interpreted through these white supremacist lenses that also debased and othered these communities (Smith 1999) as well as creating new social categories that upheld these beliefs (Stoler 2010). As these knowledges and items were shifted in the cultural view, this affected how they were described, and the organizational systems and structures these institutions used to categorize and organize their collections (Turner 2020).

The systems and organizational structures of archives have been created to maintain the status quo of dominant society. This has meant that there is an emphasis on collecting materials that fit into this lens while categorically ignoring narratives that counter these points or creating new narratives that "other." For Indigenous communities, this has meant that often the archival documentation and materials collected were acquired by or interpreted by white scholars, ethnographers, and archaeologist and recontextualized in ways that deny Indigenous communities their own identities and sovereignty (Smith 1999).

Working within Archives

For Indigenous archaeologists who find themselves working with archives, the materials they are likely to find within the archives usually counters Indigenous archaeology perspectives. One way that this is prevalent is with the passage of NAGPRA (Native American Graves and Repatriation Act 1990). While NAGPRA was created to protect objects related to burial and cultural patrimony, archival spaces are not necessarily held to NAGPRA in the same ways as other institutions and are, therefore, allowed to do with these materials as they wish. Additionally, due to the limited scope of NAGPRA, it fails to protect other types of knowledges and sacred objects that are important to Indigenous communities' rights to their own knowledges. For archives to be partners with Indigenous archaeology efforts, archives will need to consider their own practices, protocols, and engagement with communities to align with Indigenous archaeologies' principles.

Both in archaeology and archival studies, research shifts are taking place to refocus and recenter the disciplines around issues of social justice. In Indigenous archaeologies, according to Atalay (2006), practices must focus on communities, using methodologies that align with their own worldviews and knowledge while also critiquing and deconstructing traditional and western archaeological canon. George Nicholas and Thomas Andrews (1997) conceptualize Indigenous archaeology as practices that are "with, for, and by" Indigenous communities. For archival research and practices to support *with* this work, the archival field needs to consider how it critiques and deconstructs practices to center Indigenous worldviews. Archives need to engage with projects that align with community goals through ethical and sustainable partnerships.

Engaging with Indigenous Archaeologies in the Archives

While archives are beginning to engage in more critical work within their institutions, there is still progress that must be made to fully become engaged in community-oriented work. The following section looks at projects and approaches to archival work that can serve as models for institutions on how to successfully engage in this work.

Protocols for Native American Archival Materials

The "Protocols for Native American Archival Materials" were created by a group of Indigenous and non-Indigenous librarians and archivists as a culturally responsive framework for working with Tribal materials (First Circle Archivist 2008). These protocols function on the basis that Indigenous tribes are their own sovereign Nations, and they recognize that archival and museum collecting methods are not always ethical and/or do not account for Indigenous knowledge or Indigenous beliefs and practices. The protocols serve as guidelines and a framework to rework each individual institution's policies, such as how they approach community partners, or display information about collections. Like other government protocols (for example, NAGPRA), the protocols set forth a bare minimum standard for how to approach Indigenous communities and engage in repatriation work.

The protocols include ten areas or practices for those engaged with archival materials to consider and work into practice. Among these include guidelines on "Building Relationships of Mutual Respect," "Culturally Sensitive Materials," "Native American Intellectual Property Issues," and "Reciprocal Education and Training." For each protocol, there is a description explaining what a given protocol means and why it is important. Additionally, each protocol includes a set of guidelines for archives/libraries and a separate set of guidelines for Native communities. In creating both sets of guidelines, the protocols support both sides of the partnership, providing ways relationships can be cultivated. While the protocols include guidelines, it is important to understand that they are designed to get archives and libraries to think about these issues and to encourage shifts toward community-based practice. For example, under "Building Relationships of Mutual Respect," the protocols state

Native American communities have had extensive first-hand experience with the ways that information resources held in distant institutions can impact their quality of life, their practice of religion, and their future as a people—sometimes with disastrous consequences, sometimes to their benefit. Libraries and archives must recognize that Native American communities have primary rights for all culturally sensitive materials that are culturally affiliated with them.

Within this protocol, we begin to see how archives must adapt practices in work with Indigenous collections to allow for the expert knowledge of communities and centering their concerns, needs, and priorities throughout the work. Additionally, in creating dialogue and building mutually beneficial and respectful relationships with communities, we begin to see how this can lead to more ethical stewardship and care of collections.

Other examples of recommendations for institutions include, "[s]eek opportunities for Native American community consultation by contacting the chair's office of each tribe that is or may be culturally affiliated with collections held by the archives or library," and "[e]nsure equitable treatment in negotiations, whether a collection is culturally affiliated with one or more than one community. Offer comparable arrangements and agreements regarding access and use to all communities." For Indigenous or Tribal communities, the protocols offer recommendations such as "[p]ublicize who may speak for them, by informing archives and libraries of the individuals who will act as community representatives for these matters, i.e., a Tribal archivist, historic preservation officer, cultural liaison, records manager, etc." and "[o]ffer expertise to institutions interested in developing culturally responsive archival management policies as well as exhibits, lectures, storytelling, teaching, workshops, and other forms of public education" (First Circle Archivists 2008).

The protocols have the potential to align with Indigenous Archaeologies. Indigenous Archaeology forefronts and centers Indigenous ways of knowing, community engagement, and collaboration, while also countering colonial views on how Archaeology is done (Atalay 2012; Silliman 2008). Along these same lines, the protocols guide libraries to take on similar practices, including collaborating and building relationships with Indigenous communities, engaging in repatriation, and demonstrating culturally informed care for objects within collections, and working with Indigenous communities to understand their priorities for collections, which have historically been inaccessible through library and archival gatekeeping. Like the tenets of Indigenous Archaeology, the protocols allow for a reframing of the type of work that is done in libraries and archives to better align with Indigenous knowledge and traditions, creating a more inclusive archival space.

Digital Technologies and Digital Scholarship

With the rise of new technologies, new projects—especially digital archival projects—are increasing public access to collections to tell counternarratives and to reframe our understanding of archival histories. Digital technologies have also been harnessed to support archaeological research, particularly within digital humanities and scholarship. Examples of archaeological digital projects include the Digital Archaeological Record (tDAR) a project that aims to digitally represent archaeological collections and materials globally and the Center for Collaborative Synthesis in Archaeology at the University of Colorado. Digital Methodologies applied to many different disciplines are widely becoming adopted by researchers, and the archives that support them (Burdick et al. 2012; Mackenzie and Martin 2016). In many ways the expansion in digital technologies allows for integration of some of the most trivial and challenging parts to both Indigenous archaeological work and archival work.

As projects use digital methodologies to create access to collections, issues are raised related to the protection and ethical care of Indigenous materials. Within archives, the Social Networks and Archival Context (SNAC) Platform is one example. This platform was born out of a project at the University of Virginia and operates as a conglomerate of archival repositories globally. Within the platform, SNAC enables partnering institutions to deposit their archival metadata, and then throughout the platform link records together based upon authority control. This database allows for disparate records linked to a person, family, or corporate body to be connected. Additionally, editors within SNAC can use authority control and create record documentation to represent these entities more accurately. Within archaeology, the Digital Archaeology Record (tDAR) project through the Center for Digital Antiquity at Arizona State University aims to fill a similar role. tDAR is a digital archive that holds archaeological data sets, documentation, images, and other digital sources for the preservation of the archaeological record into the future.

While both systems are examples of the potentials for digital projects to align with the goals of Indigenous archaeology and Indigenized archival practice, there are still shifts to be made in both platforms. As both integrate different archival collections, there is no way to control or mitigate risk with materials that should be protected. While tDAR does require NAGPRA compliance for institutions that are required to, NAGPRA only provides bare minimum protections, and, in many cases, does not protect archival documentation. While SNAC does allow for editors to create ethical description and control, the overall platform is not integrated with Indigenous knowledge practices that allow for the complex information ecologies of Indigenous knowledges.

Pivoting Archives to Become Sustainable Partners

By refocusing the archival landscape, and Archaeologies, we allow for new ways of existing that respect and accept Indigenous knowledge and viewpoints as equal to those that have historically been considered superior. To successfully support efforts of Indigenous Archaeology, archives need to partner in sustainable ways to ensure long-term success and longevity. One of the most important things archives can do to support Indigenous Archaeology is to educate themselves on Indigenous knowledge practices and decolonizing frameworks, and actively implement these practices into daily work and policies. To support Indigenous Archaeology at its core, there must be an understanding of Indigenous knowledge and the way it frames the worldview of Indigenous scholarship. Texts such as *Decolonizing Methodologies* propose a framework for decolonizing academic and research contexts and spaces by integrating Indigenous knowledge as core and center to the practice. This text is the foundation for many contemporary efforts to integrate and create space for Indigenous knowledge in the academy. While Smith's work only begins to provide the necessary knowledge on these issues, it demonstrates the importance of supporting other worldviews and frameworks of knowing that exist outside current practice.

While education is important, creating and acting on plans are equally as important within archives. For archives to support Indigenous Archaeology, ongoing support and understanding of the issues and barriers to collaborating with communities as well as the complex issues of archaeological archives needs to be present. Building relationships with communities that support the work of Indigenous archaeological efforts requires building trust between communities and the institution. In practice, this will require rethinking archival policy, developing more ethical practices, and an understanding that there will be times when the institution is not the priority. This requires re-examining archaeological collection management practices, looking to other models of stewardship or repatriation, and developing policies for the ethical collecting of materials to support the research and scholarship of Indigenous Archaeology. Additionally, more thought needs to be given to how library and archival staff can work on projects and utilize technologies, services, and spaces that support these efforts.

Archives must become diligent and respect the rights of communities to say no to requests made by them. Engaging in community-oriented work with respect and openness is important not only for these relationships specifically but for setting precedents for interactions in the future. An understanding that each community is its own entity with its own perspectives and practices on materials and knowledge is essential for being able to support this work (First Circle Archivists 2008). Especially as archaeologists have long extracted knowledge, objects, and human remains from these communities, understanding how these complex histories affect contemporary relationships is essential in ethical partnership.

For archaeologists, scholars, and practitioners, the greatest way to integrate and to consider archives as a partner is to understand how archives and archival practices work. In partnership, understanding how each other operate, and their respective understandings and cultural norms is crucial to understanding how to collaborate. In addition, for Indigenous archaeologists, pushing on institutions to make change and consider more ethical practices may be crucial for widespread change across the discipline. In both archives and archaeology, practitioners are making change, but with greater support and communication between fields, some of these critical gaps and policy changes may occur at faster rates.

Along these same lines, archival expertise could alleviate the curation crisis, which has plagued archaeology for decades. As discussed above, the curation crisis describes the poor management of archaeological items, materials, and records, due to poor organization, lack of funds or resources, or improper handling of these materials (Friberg and Huvila 2019; Kersel 2015; Thomson 2014). While these issues remain large problems in all archives, especially around materials or resources that have not been prioritized, there are projects that could be employed to help in the work. Archives, as advised in the Protocols, could use funds and resources to help connect Tribal communities to archaeological materials and collections, which in turn could lead to more ethical stewardship and processes, and research that could prevent the desecration of sacred sites.

For Indigenous Archaeology to take place, involvement with community is central. Community members or Tribal Historic Preservation Officers (THPOs) should approach libraries and archives especially if they know that materials relating to their Nations and communities are being kept at these institutions. Additionally, building mutual relationships with staff members and engaging with them on projects can encourage community building. Inversely, Tribal communities should make sure their needs are heard and met and feel able to remove themselves from relationships or partnerships that are not beneficial to them, or do not respect their autonomies.

Conclusion

Archives contain a host of resources, services, and spaces that when utilized could provide important partners for Indigenous Archaeology. While challenges remain, efforts to build more inclusive spaces and work to correct past wrongs against Indigenous communities provide important frameworks. Integrating library and archival resources with Indigenous archaeological philosophy and practice provides a more robust discipline that has the potential to expand the ways in which Tribal communities, librarians, archivists, and archaeologists engage in community-oriented work.

References

Atalay, Sonya
2006   Indigenous Archaeology as Decolonizing Practice. American Indian Quarterly 30(3/4):280–310.
2012   Community-Based Archaeology: Research With, By, and For Indigenous and Local Communities. Berkley: University of California Press.
Blickhan, Samantha, Coleman Krawczyk, Daniel Hanson, Amy Boyer, and Andrea Simenstad
2019   Individual vs. Collaborative Methods of Crowdsourced Transcription. Special Issue, "Collecting, Preserving, and Disseminating Endangered Cultural Heritage for New Understandings through Multilingual Approaches," Data Mining and Digital Humanities.
Burdick, Anne, Johanna Drucker, Peter Lunenfeld, Todd Presner, and Jeffrey Schnapp
2012   Digital_Humanities. Cambridge: MIT Press.
Caswell, Michelle, Alda Allina Migoni, Noah Geraci, and Marika Cifor
2017   "To Be Able to Imagine Otherwise": Community Archives and the Importance

of Representation. Archives and Records 38(1):5–26. DOI: 10.1080/23257962.2016.1260445.

Caswell, Michelle, Joyce Gabiola, Jimmy Zavala, Grace Brilmyer, and Marika Cifor

2018 Imagining Transformative Spaces: the Personal—Political Sites of Community Archives. Archival Science 18:73–93. https://doi.org/10.1007/s10502-018-9286-7.

Christen, Kimberly

2011 Opening Archives: Respectful Repatriation. The American Archivist 74(1):185–210. https://doi.org/10.17723/aarc.74.1.4233nv6nv6428521.

Christen, Kimberly, and Jane Anderson

2019 Toward Slow Archives. Archival Science 19:87–116.

Cook, Terry

2013 Evidence, Memory, Identity, and Community: Four Shifting Archival Paradigms. Archival Science 13:95–120. https://doi.org/10.1007/s10502-012-9180-7.

Duff, Wendy M., Andrew Flinn, Karen Emily Suurtamm, and David A. Wallace

2013 Social Justice Impact of Archives: A Preliminary Investigation. Archival Science 13:317–348. https://doi.org/10.1007/s10502-012-9198-x.

Dunbar, Anthony W.

2006 Introducing Critical Race Theory to Archival Discourse: Getting the Conversation Started. Archival Science 6:109–129. https://doi.org/10.1007/s10502-006-9022-6

First Circle Archivists

2008 Protocols for Native American Archival Materials. https://www2.nau.edu/libnap-p/, accessed January 12, 2023.

Friberg, Zanna, and Isto Huvila

2019 Using Object Biographies to Understand the Curation Crisis: Lessons Learned From the Museum Life of an Archaeological Collection. Museum Management 34(9):362–382. DOI:10.1080/09647775.2019.1612270.

Greene, Mark, and Dennis Meissner

2005 More Product, Less Process: Revamping Traditional Archival Processing. The American Archivist 68(2):208–263. https://doi.org/10.17723/aarc.68.2.c741823776k65863.

Hughes-Watkins, Lae'l

2018 Moving Toward a Reparative Archive: A Roadmap for a Holistic Approach to Disrupting Homogenous Histories in Academic Repositories and Creating Inclusive Spaces for Marginalized Voices." Contemporary Archival Studies 5(6):26–37. https://elischolar.library.yale.edu/jcas/vol5/iss1/6.

Kersel, Morag M.

2015 Storage Wars: Solving the Archaeological Curation Crisis? Eastern Mediterranean Archaeology and Heritage Studies 3(1):42–54.

Littletree, Sandra, Miranda Belarde-Lewis, and Marisa Duarte

2020 Centering Relationality: A Conceptual Model to Advance Indigenous Knowledge Organization Practices. Knowledge Organization 47(5):410–424. http://hdl.handle.net/1773/46601.

Lougheed, Brett, Ry Moran, and Camille Callison

2015   Reconciliation Through Description: Using Metadata to Realize the Vision of the National Research Centre for Truth and Reconciliation. Cataloging & Classification Quarterly 56(5–6):596–614. DOI: 10.1080/01639374.2015.1008718.

Mackenzie, Alison, and Lindsey Martin, eds.

2016   Developing Digital Scholarship: Emerging Practices in Academic Libraries. Chicago: ALA Neal Schuman.

Marsh, Diana E.

2019   Research-Driven Approaches To Improving Archival Discovery. IASSIST Quarterly 43(2):1–9. https://doi.org/10.29173/iq955.

Nicholas, George P., and Thomas D. Andrews

1997   At a Crossroads: Archaeology and First Peoples in Canada. Burnaby, BC: Archaeology Press.

O'Neal, Jennifer

2019   From Time Immemorial: Centering Indigenous Traditional Knowledge in the Archival Paradigm. Afterlives of Indigenous Archives. Ivy Scweitzer and Gordon Henry, eds. Chicago: University of Chicago Press.

Punzalan, Ricardo L., and Michelle Caswell

2016   Critical Directions for Archival Approaches to Social Justice. The Library Quarterly 86(1):25–42

Silliman, Stephen W.

2008   Collaborating at the Trowel's Edge: Teaching and Learning in Indigenous Archaeology. Tucson: University of Arizona Press.

Smith, Linda Tuhiwai

1999   Decolonizing methodologies: Research and Indigenous peoples. 1st ed. Dunedin, New Zealand: Otago University Press.

Society of American Archivists

2016   What are Archives. Society of American Archivists. https://www2.archivists.org/about-archives, accessed June 2, 2021.

Stoler, Ann Laura

2010   Along the Archival Grain: Epistemic Anxieties and Colonial Common Sense. Princeton: Princeton University Press.

Thomson, Karen

2014   Handling the "Curation Crisis": Database Management for Archaeological Collections. New Jersey: Seton Hall University.

Turner, Hannah

2020   Cataloguing Culture: Legacies of Colonialism in Museum Documentation. Vancouver: University of British Columbia Press.

Van Hyning, Victoria, Samantha Blickhan, Laura Trouille, and Chris Lintott

2017   Transforming Libraries and Archives Through Crowdsourcing. D-Lib Magazine 23(5/6). https://doi.org/10.1045/may2017-vanhyning.

Wood, Stacy, Kathy Carbone, Marika Cifor, Anne Gilliand, and Ricardo Punzalan

2014   Mobilizing Records: Re-framing Archival Description to Support Human Rights. Archival Science 14:397–419. https://doi.org/10.1007/s10502-014-9233-1.

II

RECLAIMING CULTURAL HERITAGE

Nokomis and Mishomis at the Precipice, by Kay Kakenda-sotkwe Mattena. Mixed media on canvas. 2023.

5

A Journey of Growth and Personal Observations from an Indigenous Archaeologist

Patrick Cruz

Working with tribes has sometimes been a difficult process for many scholars. Differing goals, differing perspectives, differing cultural histories make coming together on collaborative efforts sometimes fraught with difficulty. Sometimes, this is even the case despite scholars and archaeologists having already established a history of working with Tribal communities. Caught in the middle are Indigenous archaeologists who find themselves at the crucial interphase between Indigenous communities and outside organizations or institutions. For the Indigenous archaeologist, this is not only a critically vital role they must play and responsibility which they must bear, but also gives them a unique perspective. As both participant and witness to collaborative projects, I will discuss some basic observations and offer some insight for scholars wishing to do work with Tribal communities.

Early Observations

Every perspective on Indigenous archaeology should begin with setting some context. This is important as no two people, no two organizations, no two tribes, no two regions within the US have the same histories, nor have they had the same historical trajectories of relationships between Indigenous peoples, archaeology, and the public. Each particular region, tribe, institution, and stakeholder has relationships built upon localized experiences and histories. To succeed in this effort, archaeologists and scholars need to familiarize themselves with the histories of localized interactions, the key individuals and participants, and the primary arguments and motivations of stakeholders. Otherwise, we risk fumbling the process. At the same time, we must recognize that our individual experiences color the lens through which we experience these topics and help to drive specific discussion points and interactions between differing stakeholders. For instance, the relationship between tribes and government or museum entities in the American Southwest are different from those of other regions. The same can be said on intra-regional scales as well. Each region will have its own history of relationships between individual Indigenous communities and governmental organizations and these histories will have great impact on the continued engagement of those relationships into the future. This is not to say there are no commonalities in the issues faced by Indigenous communities such as the desire for cultural preservation, similar colonial experiences of subjection of Indigenous peoples, and attempted cultural erasure as part of the history of the Americanization process. It must be recognized that localized regional histories and experiences have differed which in turn have fostered differing concerns and critiques based on those specific histories.

First some context.

My name is Patrick Cruz. I am an Ohkay Owingeh Tribal member, a museum professional, and an archaeologist. My childhood was spent growing up near my community where I would spend summers, weekends, and afternoons after school with my grandparents, aunts, uncles, and cousins. We had agricultural fields where we grew hay, alfalfa, and traditional crops, raised cattle and I participated in feast day activities, dances, and other community activities at the Pueblo. My drive to know about our past drove me to learn all that I could about the history of my own people. Most of that history was about the times before the colonization experience which started in AD 1598 with the establishment of San Gabriel, the first Spanish/European capital/settlement in New Mexico, located across the river from Ohkay Owingeh. Most of our history and stories seemed to be about the precontact period. Absent was much of the history that followed the contact period and colonization that took place afterward. The exception being the personal lived experiences of individuals recounting their experiences of growing up in the community.

My first professional experience was working at Bandelier National Monument as part of a National Park Service (NPS) work crew recruited from local Pueblo youth to work on cultural preservation projects at Pueblo sites. This was my first experience working for a governmental entity that had regular interaction with local Indigenous communities. Here I saw an NPS monument that drew much of its workforce and staff from local Indigenous communities. Here I witnessed the interaction of Indigenous youth working alongside anthropologists, historic and architectural preservationists, and their graduate students. As a youth group, we participated as observers in the consultation process between the park and leaders of local Pueblo communities with regards to the disposition of a detached park unit called *Tsankawi*, the site of a fourteenth-century mesa top Tewa community, as well as documentation and preservation efforts of other park sites. This involved recording, documenting, and attempting to mitigate the impact of visitation by the public to these important sites.

My experiences during these formative years were one in which the federal government (in the form of NPS) interacted in positive ways with local Pueblos and other Indigenous groups. Working with government supervisors' anthropology graduate students also introduced me to new ways of researching and understanding the Pueblo past, often in manners that promoted continued interaction with local communities. Conspicuously absent in this discourse were the fraught relationships faced by other Indigenous groups in other areas of the country. My experience at that young age and on the periphery of the field of anthropology was with proactive non-Indigenous proponents who supported local Indigenous communities, their perspectives, and interactions. How could it have not? It formed the very basis by which I found myself working on a park service work crew made up entirely of Pueblo youth. Furthermore, community leaders encouraged and supported the work we performed. The majority of anthropologists whom I met during this formative time were young burgeoning professionals who all seemed to support and reinforce this positive relationship between archaeology and Indigenous peoples and simultaneously formulating lifelong friendships. These burgeoning archaeologists were part of an era coming out of the late 1990s, when NAGPRA (Native American Graves Protection and Repatriation Act) was still new, and its impact was still felt by many as the turning of a new page of matured responsible anthropology. With the arrival of NAGPRA, we saw for the first time a need for archaeologists to actually interact and communicate with Indigenous peoples in a respectful and equitable way at the same table. As Steve Lekson described it: "[b]efore NAGPRA, Indians were optional; archaeology could engage or ignore at its pleasure. After NAGPRA, Indians had a seat at the head table" (2018:39). We witnessed NAGPRA related interactions between NPS and local tribes that seemed a successful answer to many of the injustices of the past as I understood them to be at that time.

The first museum professional I had ever met was an NPS museum curator/collections manager, who happened to be the only museum professional attached to the park, and who was also a member of a local Pueblo community. He was very active in promoting the relationship between the park and surrounding Native communities as well as taking a leading role in promoting repatriation efforts and consultation on local matters between the NPS and the tribes. Today, I still wonder how much of my early impressions were formulated by my observations of his dedication and hard work as *both* a federal employee and a senior member of his community. He actively fostered these favorable interactions, and their results speak more to his leadership and participation. He remains a respected mentor who to this day I continue to try to emulate.

As we know, the relationship between government and tribes was not necessarily as idyllic as my youthful, isolated, singular observations had convinced me was the case. Certainly, this was not the experience of tribes in other regions of the country as I would soon learn. It was not like I was unaware of the fraught relationships and histories between government and tribes, but with few exceptions, these fraught issues rarely manifested themselves in the world I experienced, and when they did it was no more than a temporary blip. It seems I grew up in a unique time and place where the troubles that Indigenous archaeology was meant to address were not apparent, at least not to me. Perhaps it was youthful naivety. Perhaps it was due to my being isolated at the periphery of professional archaeology, affiliated by association but not yet fully immersed in the politics from within. Could I be blamed? (Please no one answer that . . .). Many of these young non-Indigenous graduate students in archaeology who I worked with and formed lasting friendships with went on to become strong proponents for tribes, even going so far as to work on legal cases on their behalf.

Most of the difficult issues that seemed to be raised, in my observation, revolved around NAGPRA's mandate to make linkages of affiliation between descendant communities and the remains of ancestors and their materials. At the same time, communities fought to gain or preserve access to sacred spaces and landscapes that were not located areas controlled by the tribes. Certainly, there remained the conflicting mission for the NPS as both public servants to preserve and provide for the general American public while simultaneously attempting to respect and preserve the sanctity of Tribal sacred spaces (Tsosie 2003).

Lesson Learned

It was an eye-opening experience to attend a 2008 NAGPRA and Repatriation Symposium hosted at the Institute of American Indian Arts (IAIA) campus in Santa Fe, NM, attended by Indigenous peoples, officials, government employees, and others from across the country. The sessions were emotionally raw and the experiences of Indigenous peoples from outside the Southwest were expressed in full. This is where I learned that my prior experiences and observations were unique and perhaps not the norm. It was dizzyingly disorienting to see, on the one hand, federally employed Indigenous staff from differing government departments and agencies promoting the work and accomplishments they had done from within their institutions which seemed completely at odds with the perspectives of leaders and activists from beyond the Southwest. In these other regions, the relationship between tribes and government entities (including agencies such as the NPS) remained antagonistic. Grievances and wrongdoings by the government remained unaddressed and unassuaged. Those relationships between tribes and government which I had so taken for granted as the norm were in these other places stalled or nonexistent. Here, it was hammered home to me how much localized context really matters. It's incredibly crucial. To make assumptions based on the observations of one local area and assume that it was representative of the broader state of experience of other communities elsewhere was a critical error.

Museum Career

During the time of the Santa Fe repatriation symposium, I worked as a museum professional learning about the ins and outs of the museum field witnessing multiple levels of interactions between museums and Indigenous communities and individuals. Some of the programs I was associated with worked explicitly to promote and train burgeoning Indigenous museum professionals. Many of these museums worked in conjunction and partnership with local Tribal museums planning exhibitions as well as working with and learning from Indigenous artists and cultural specialists. I walked away with a feeling that museums should aspire to be conscientious stewards of histories for the public, and those museums with Indigenous collections should view their roles as stewards for their local tribes. Again, this should be viewed as a slice of my specific and particular experiences of the world that might stand in stark contrast to the museum experiences that other Indigenous people have had in other places. Not all museums play such a proactive role with Tribal communities.

I noticed that a key difference in the interests of stakeholders is that for archaeologists, the interests are in artifacts, the data they can produce, and in what can be inferred about human behavior of the past. For museums, the interests are in preserving objects in their collections and for exhibiting them in a public education format. For Indigenous people, the interests seemed to not necessarily be about the objects/artifacts themselves, but rather about the social lives of objects and their relationship to people. Objects were not connections to a broad faceless past in the history of humanity, but rather were things created and used by grandparents, great grandparents, and great-great grandparents; actual individuals in the past with whom those in Native communities shared a familial connection with.

Anthropology

In Fall of 2014, I returned to the world of anthropology/archaeology by attending graduate school. I got to witness an archaeology that attempted to promote relationships and inclusivity with Indigenous peoples. Yet, at odds with this perspective was the realization that there was a lack of Indigenous graduate students in anthropology programs. There was a deep focus on western social philosophical thought and theoretical perspectives, all based on past and current Euro-American epistemologies. Anthropological programs seem to be structured on learning, comprehending, and functioning within the strict confines of western logical theorems and being able to recite the history of their evolutionary development over time. In this light, Indigenous archaeology seemed to be nothing more than one of the many post-processual divergent branches of schools of thought, one among a myriad of many. The consideration of Indigenous archaeology could simply be seen as a subsection of a subsection of a subsection of anthropology, one where the adherents find themselves potentially isolated in self-fulfilling echo chambers isolated away from the broader field.

To many in anthropology, Indigenous perspectives, ontologies, and epistemologies, were merely supportive datapoints to an otherwise western thought-based thesis or argument they were making. Straying too far into a truly Indigenous ontology could be interpreted by science-heavy archaeology as becoming too subjective and biased, and delving into the wishy-washy world of unprovable untestable opinions. Indigenous per-

A Journey of Growth and Personal Observations from an Indigenous Archaeologist · 71

spectives that suggest that the past was knowable, comprehensible, even livable and open to experience by the people of today fell in stark contrast to the theoretical western dictates that the past was an abstract, far too removed and unrelatable world which could only be understood through the material traces of generalized, faceless, broad human behaviors. The understood relatedness of individuals to the past has tended to be construed as naive or otherwise inappropriate for conducting the science of archaeology. In this way, at its heart, archaeology might always be forever and inextricably embedded within western thought processes. Indigenous students might in such academic programs forever be forced to learn in full the theoretical perspectives of long ago dead western theorists and their theories which have come and gone as the field's paradigm perspectives have changed over time. These were theorists whose ponderings were alien and indifferent toward Indigenous perspectives, histories, and ways of knowing. "If archaeological theory and method is to become liberated from the vestiges of colonialism, it has to open itself to ways of reading the land that admit Indigenous values. Less ethnocentrically, places of low and high materiality need to be theorized and alternatives to western value scales need to be applied in analysis and interpretation" (Wobst 2004:18). Room must be made within the field of archaeology for alternative modes of knowledge.

Something that I have found most dissatisfying in writings, though I remain unsure as how to mitigate it, is how writers of archaeological publications provide clear discrete compartmentalization of research papers that often include at the very end of those publications separate chapters on "Indigenous interpretation." "Nowadays, when Native knowledge is recognized in research, it often gets compartmentalized as the 'cultural perspective,' as distinct from scientific explanation and thus—like some epistemological orphan—permitted a presence at the table, but not one to be taken too seriously. The effect is that Native and scientific perspectives appear to exist in parallel universes, and while pronounced as equally valid, with no attempt to reconcile or address any of their epistemological differences, this is a false sense of equality" (Whiteley 2018:233). Whiteley's concerns remain mine on how to better integrate Indigenous perspectives on subject matter rather than merely reflexively tacking on a "Native perspective" chapter at the end of a paper as if it were nothing more than an afterthought to the publication. Here, Native voice would seem to be an addition to an otherwise complete study, an extra chapter, and only used for the sake of protocol. Rather than this, I wrestle with how we can include or integrate a socially wholistic Indigenous perspective within what is otherwise discretely non-social scientific professional publications.

That said, one alternative way to approach this problematic issue is by understanding that by learning anthropology from within that western framework, some benefit for Native students might be that it results, even if somewhat unsatisfactorily, in empowering Indigenous scholars with skillsets necessary to engage with their non-Indigenous colleagues. Further, Indigenous anthropologists are able to provide Indigenous perspectives to a western research team and maintain a level of awareness of the impact that research might have on Tribal communities. A danger that I foresee for a lack of Indigenous archaeologists in the field is that their absence can potentially breed absence of consideration and inclusion. And it is here where the participation of Indigenous anthropologists, trained in western anthropological practices and frameworks, becomes vital. The mere presence of Indigenous archaeologists on a project can have an equalizing effect: reinforcing inclusivity as a constant reminder to consider the impact that projects can have on Indigenous communities.

Indigenous Archaeology

So, what then is Indigenous archaeology? For me, Indigenous archaeology is archaeology that is generally conducted by Indigenous people, for Indigenous communities, using Indigenous knowledge or ways of knowing in order to assist with archaeological interpretations, facilitating the inclusion of participation and consideration for Indigenous communities, and which can then give us a better more wholistic understanding of the past. I envision it as having two components: (1) Indigenous individuals practicing within the field of archaeology, as the representative middleperson between outsider archaeologists and Indigenous communities, who are beholden to those same communities and acting as both a facilitator and as a leveling mechanism that encourages respect and dignity for all parties involved, and (2) as a form of community-based archaeology that empowers those Indigenous communities with an active participating role in research projects and which can exert both community-generated agency as well as self-directed self-learning and discovery in line with the community's goals and wishes, ultimately promoting cultural preservation. Community "archaeology is largely about communities, usually anthropological and indigenous, listening to and respecting one another as they craft interpretations of the past together, producing results for both communities. The constraints that the respective communities place on one another and on the interpretation of the past often lead to more solid interpretations that meet both academic and indigenous criteria" (Preucel and Cipolla 2008:135).

According to Nicholas "Indigenous archaeology is an expression of archaeological theory and practice in which the discipline intersects with Indigenous values, knowledge, practices, ethics, and sensibilities, and through collaborative and community-originated or -directed projects, and related critical perspectives. Indigenous archaeology seeks to (1) make archaeology more representative of, responsible to, and relevant for Indigenous communities; (2) redress real and perceived inequalities in the practice of archaeology; and (3) inform and broaden the understanding and interpretation of the archaeological record through the incorporation of Aboriginal world views, histories, and science" (Nicholas 2010:234). According to Atalay, "Indigenous archaeology includes research that critiques and deconstructs western archaeological practice as well as research that works toward recovering and investigating Indigenous experiences, practices, and traditional knowledge systems" (Atalay 2010:80).

Sharon Milholland of Crow Canyon Archaeological Center further describes Indigenous archaeology as "a form of archaeology where Indigenous knowledge, values, and goals are the underpinnings of research. Processes and products define [I]ndigenous archaeology—not necessarily who is conducting the work. In fact, it's commonly mistaken as a subdiscipline of archaeology practiced only by Indigenous peoples around the globe" (Milholland 2019).

In contrast to Milholland's definition, in which she favors "processes and products" over the identity of the individual archaeologist performing the tasks, I do believe that one of the keys to the definition of "Indigenous archaeology" is in fact this last point. I have struggled to come to grips on this question of "who" actually does Indigenous archaeology, and I cannot escape the point that, for me, the identity of the archaeologist doing the work is as important an aspect as anything else concerning the term *Indigenous archaeology*. Can non-Indigenous archaeologists do Indigenous archaeology? Perhaps, but a missing tenet for me is that it is precisely by having Indigenous people from the communities working within the field of archaeology facilitating on both ends as archaeologist and community member, that Indigenous communities are able to push for better inclusivity and assert their agency through the efforts of Tribal members.

This is not to say that other non-Indigenous archaeologists who work closely with Indigenous communities are not doing similar work with a similar spirit and purpose as Indigenous archaeologists. For them I would actually use the term *Indigenous-Oriented Archaeology* to describe archaeology conducted more broadly by both Indigenous and non-Indigenous archaeologists and pertaining more to those shared aspects, purposes, and intents and using shared processes and methodologies to accomplish a similar end. The term *Indigenous-Oriented Archaeology* doesn't imply that these archaeologists are from these communities themselves, but does recognize that they play a crucial and vital role in contributing toward promoting Indigenous agency, equality, and interests. I believe that Indigenous archaeologists can bring with them the addition of an emic ontological perspective or interpretation gained through different lived and learned experiences not generally open, available, or recognizable to western archaeologists. Here Indigenous archaeologists are not only armed with the epistemologies of their communities, but they are also armed with the knowledge of how archaeology functions, thus bridging the gap between the archaeology profession and Tribal communities.

If Indigenous archaeology is about the individual conducting the research, I suggest that Indigenous-oriented archaeology is the process and methodology by which it is conducted, that is the "process and product," which Milholland speaks of. Preucel and Cipolla refer to this as Tribal Archaeology in which "[t]ribal communities often hire nonindigenous individuals as their employees to carry out the research they are interested in" (2008:133). Indigenous-oriented archaeology is only a different name for what can be more broadly understood as community-based archaeology, or as a variant there of. In fact, there is little to distinguish the two. Community archaeology assumes the presence of an academic scholar (regardless of who they are) as specialist working with and toward the benefit of a community. What they hold in common is the attempt to correct a power differential between the scholarly field and the community, with the ultimate goal being community empowerment. Whether Indigenous or not, communities subjected to scholarly research across the globe often face this same power differential with outside researchers coming into a community at a higher level of societal prestige, rank and power and the subject community being at a lower vulnerable level.

There is a question of presumed imbued or entitled ascribed authority with which a researcher brings with them to the table. "The privilege that cloaks academia affords non-Native researchers the ability to conduct research in minority populations with many assumptions and unspoken authority" (Bird 2018:15). These are many of the same shared concerns that researched communities around the world would raise. This is an often-vocalized point I have repeatedly heard during meetings when tribes are asked to participate with outside entities concerning their ancestral past. Outside academics with their education, training and degrees that confer both a societal standing and assumed expertise, coming in to tell Indigenous leaders and specialists about who their own people were, where they came from, where they would go, and how they used to live. There is resentment toward such interloping and many a Tribal leader has cautioned those at the outset of such meetings with phrases like "you may have the degrees, but remember, we are the specialists here" and "we may not have a piece of paper (degree) and fancy title in front of our names, but we are the ones in this room who know our people and our past better than anyone."

With NAGPRA and the criticism of how archaeology had been conducted in the past came calls for collaboration where Indigenous peoples were now listened to as equals. This acted as a leveling mechanism to force PhD scholars and researchers to consider what these Indigenous "laymen" had to offer, for it was these community "laymen" who were in fact the specialists on the many topics being discussed. Surely this would have been unsettling for some scholars in the field who viewed credentials as certificates of entitlement and confirmation of the prestige of this structural power differential. NAGPRA, and the work by Indigenous activists who pushed it, I believe should be viewed with exaltation not for being so comprehensive of legislation, but rather for its role as initially opening the door for change and forcing inclusion of Indigenous peoples at the policy table. Though NAGPRA is far from perfect, the pressure for today is to continue to improve upon laws and relationships between tribes and governments which were first initiated with NAGPRA.

NAGPRA also brought with it the call by Indigenous communities for community members to actively expand into fields of study that could assist their home communities, to become the researcher rather than the researched. Pueblo youth are often told by their Elders to go out and get educated, but that it is their responsibility thereafter to return to their communities in order to help them. For me, NAGPRA on the one hand, and on the other the push by elders for youth to return to their home communities armed with the skill sets necessary to assist their own people is how Indigenous archaeology was born.

I would describe community archaeology as a subfield that pushes for archaeology-community partnership, and where communities play a leading role in interpretation of the archaeology that is found. Both community archaeology and Indigenous-oriented archaeology are about communities playing a role in providing advice, direction, and interpretation. In many ways, this is better than the singular Indigenous archaeologist as it emphasizes the broader community's interpretation of the past rather than the individual's.

With community archaeology, the archaeologist, Indigenous or not, uses their trained expertise to collect data, and present that data to the community for discussion, interpretation, and final disposition. The archaeologist proposes projects to communities; in turn, the community determines if these projects are in the interest of the community or not. This overlap between Indigenous-oriented archaeology and community archaeology shouldn't be surprising. Atalay suggested that community-based archaeology was formulated in conjunction with the Indigenous archaeology movement (2012a:38).

By its very nature, community archaeology is multivocal combining the statements of a wide range of speakers which is far more representative of the society. It crosscuts class, rank, religion, gender, and age groups which allows for a wholistic and complete representation of interpretations. Further, the inclusion of the community at all levels of the research allows for a true partnership. For community-based Indigenous-oriented archaeology, "(s)haring authority is central here. And, as Strand et al. (2003:10) point out, both partners experience benefits: 'Everyone in the group is regarded as both a researcher and a learner. In this way, the research process itself become a means of change and growth for everyone involved'" (Atalay 2012b:63). The shared understanding is that each partner brings something valuable to the collaborative table. It has an added benefit of providing a centralized space for disparate parts of community knowledge to be shared for all present, providing the archaeologist more information, while also facilitating the transfer of that knowledge among the broader community, particularly among the youth. That is, by providing a space and time to be used to transmit and disperse community knowledge to the collective whole, which would otherwise remain compartmentalized into bits and pieces among different community members and factions. While not an explicit goal in and of itself, I have personally found that putting elders together with youth assists in facilitating cultural knowledge transfer and the reaffirmation of community traditions and narratives within the context of archaeological sites or materials. It is the archaeology that oftentimes initi-

A Journey of Growth and Personal Observations from an Indigenous Archaeologist · 77

ates the discourse. And isn't this a large part of the purpose of community archaeology? It would certainly be for Indigenous communities since community archaeology is meant to be beneficial to the whole community, and the cultural preservation of knowledge is one aspect.

Here it is not the job of the archaeologist to necessarily interpret a site or material, but rather to present the collected data, provide suggestions based on their trained expertise, and let community members provide interpretation and meaning to that data. And since the information learned from this process is about the community and their history, surely, they should have the final say in its eventual disposition. Also, the process of including elders and youth in archaeological activities can help to demystify the profession of archaeology and perhaps even to encourage youth to pursue some form of anthropology or related field in the future.

The efforts of archaeology can and should be viewed as a partnership that gives back as much as it takes. In the summer of 2021, I participated in a collaborative effort that brought a delegation of Arizona Tewa community members to New Mexico to participate in scholarly research regarding Tewa migrations from the Rio Grande to the Hopi Mesas which took place around the seventeenth century. Their contributions aided in my own academic studies and those of other researchers, but in turn we were able to provide assistance by creating for them an opportunity to visit culturally significant places in the Tewa region that were important to them and which they had never visited before. It also gave them the opportunity to connect with or renew connections with local anthropologists, cultural preservationists, government representatives, other interested parties in the area, and local Rio Grande Pueblo groups, something they seemed to have had a keen interest in.

As part of the effort of the Indigenous archaeologist, they have an obligation to the community they serve. They collected the data using their expertise, but they also find themselves in a critical role of providing a safe space for community leaders and Elders to discuss potentially confidential or sensitive topics or to air concerns about the project freely that might not be as open for discussion in the presence of non-community members. In this way, they can act as advisors or experts on the site and material subject matter and even provide their own concerns of potential issues such as with open public literature and public knowledge on the topics discussed. Some knowledge, by its very nature, is confidential and the retention of that level of confidentiality might be vital to the community.

In stark contrast to western perspectives where all knowledge is seen as democratically open for all and at any time, many Indigenous communities have traditions of disseminating knowledge gradually, at proscribed points in the life cycle of an individual. In some cases, certain knowledge is the sole prerogative of individuals, families, or clans within the community and not widely shared. Such knowledge would certainly be confidential and excluded from publication and dissemination to the broader general American public. Elders and leaders may feel that some knowledge is not appropriate for circulation in the public sphere. While the ultimate decision on whether or not to make public certain information rests solely on the discretion of the community, I believe that it is incumbent on the Indigenous archaeologist to make their expertise available as a resource for the community when making such decisions. Further, the Indigenous archaeologist, as a fellow community member, would be more invested in upholding the final community-based decisions on disposition of knowledge and archaeology, being more keenly aware of the potential implications if this knowledge were to get out. These are ethical considerations about what information is publishable, and what is not, and to err on the side of caution in order to protect the community and its members.

Closing Thoughts

The Indigenous archaeologist is more keenly beholden to the community and less likely to attempt to "sell" a new project to that community, providing a deciding council with more specific "pros and cons" of the project in question. They may also have a more genuine feel for the level of interests for a potential project since they often might be familiar with those community members in positions to make decision on such projects. I have witnessed, during my time as a burgeoning Indigenous archaeologist, that oftentimes meetings between archaeologists and Indigenous community leaders looks like a briefing in which the non-Indigenous archaeologist provides information of their findings to a Tribal council, and thereafter are asked to leave so that the council can openly discuss among themselves the topics presented, whereas the Indigenous archaeologist might be allowed to remain to further answer any additional questions that might come up. In this role, they can provide for a frank and truthful opinion of the project being presented.

I have also seen times when this position as an Indigenous archaeologist offers no benefit and perhaps even some level of concern. Whereas an inquisitive outsider archaeologist might be viewed as forgivably naive about the significance and community repercussions of a proposed project, the Indigenous archaeologist as a member of that community might be subject to some suspicion. Surely the Indigenous archaeologist participating in such a project understands more clearly the significance of what is being proposed. Whereas the non-community archaeologist might be forgiven for not comprehending the full impact of a project, the archaeologist from the community should and might be held to a higher standard. Direct questions that might be asked of an archaeologist include "how will you personally benefit from this project?" This question of "who" will benefit and in "what way" is a constant consideration that must be navigated. The fear remains among many communities that archaeologists (Indigenous or not) are somehow "in it for the money" or "for the fame" so it behooves the archaeologist, both Indigenous and non, to think long and hard about both the benefits and potential consequences of proposed projects in order to be able to answer such questions. "It is not an exaggeration to say that we should conduct our research 'as if someone's life is on the line,' for that is exactly the case when heritage research affects a person's or group's identity, well-being and sense of history . . . ultimately we are dealing with the essence of who people are—and that is something that deserves great care and respect" (Nicholas 2019:170–172). The hopeful and sincere self-reflective answer to this question is that it would ultimately help the community; that it is *THEY*, the community, who will benefit. That said, the archaeologist should be as open as possible about how they themselves might benefit from the proposed project if asked directly by a council. My own experience informs me that truth in the matter, sincerity, and openness are vital for building relationships.

Another point to make is on when projects might be initially planned and when to propose them to a community. Some outside researchers might already have a mature, developed project with which they want to present to the community. Be forewarned, this often has the optics of "I have the project, now I just need the Indians willing to let me do it." It ventures dangerously close to the historical anthropological dynamics of the past: that of researcher and subject. Perhaps better is to have a project proposal, partially developed just enough so that you have something to present, but still in its infancy such that one can make an inquiry on the level of interest by the community and also requesting for an active partnership. This active partnership would include community members as colleagues in the project playing an active role in the decision-making and even in the data collecting if possible. Also, pursue projects that the community finds relevant to their interests. This greatly increases the chance that they will be supportive of the project. The best supported projects are ones that address the interests and needs of both the scholarly world *and* the community. Projects that seem frivolous, superficial, or irrelevant to the community will gain little support, even if the questions being asked are of keen interest to the researcher.

In sum, I would suggest that all Indigenous-oriented archaeology essentially be community archaeology by its very nature, and that Indigenous archaeology is conducted by Indigenous scholars. Indigenous archaeologists act as agents and facilitators for their own communities. Indigenous archaeologists are in fact individuals from those communities, trained in archaeology and armed with a lived ontology created and molded from the collective epistemologies of their community and their upbringing, and who provide for that community a service as community member and a trained specialist in the field upon which they can be called upon. There is an inherent responsibility to their home community as well as a shared investment and shared stakes that non-community archaeologists don't share. Ultimately, it is a democratic and mutual respect–driven archaeology "of and for the people." It is an archaeology that serves not to merely learn about the past for the sake of learning but serves to assist and address the needs of those communities. It is a tool, one among many, which Tribal communities can call upon to promote their own cultural preservation efforts and the transmission of that knowledge of the past to future generations.

References

Atalay, Sonya
2010   Indigenous Archaeology as Decolonizing Practice. *In* Indigenous Archaeologies: A Reader on Decolonization. Margaret Bruchac, Siobhan Hart, H. Martin Wobst, eds. pp. 79–85. Milton Park, Abingdon-on-Thames, and Oxfordshire: Routledge.
2012a   Origins of Community-Based Research in Archaeology. Community-Based Archaeology: Research With, By, and For Indigenous and Local Communities. Berkeley: University of California Press.
2012b   Guiding Principles of Community-Based Participatory Research. Community Based Archaeology: Research With, By, and For Indigenous and Local Communities. Berkeley: University of California Press.
Bird, Doreen M.
2018   Towards a Pueblo Methodology: Pueblo Leaders Define and Discuss Research in Pueblo Communities. PhD dissertation, Department of Justice Studies, Arizona State University, Tempe. ProQuest (2046938440).

Lekson, Stephen H.

2018   Chaco in the Twentieth Century. *In* A Study of Southwestern Archaeology, pp. 1–49. University of Utah Press. Kindle Edition.

Milholland, Sharon

2019   What is Indigenous Archaeology—and What Does It Mean for Crow Canyon? Retrieved from https://www.crowcanyon.org/about-us/american-indian -knowledge/. Accessed June 19, 2021.

Nicholas, George P.

2010   Seeking the End of Indigenous Archaeology. *In* Bridging the Divide: Indigenous Communities and Archaeology into the 21st Century. Caroline Phillips and Harry Allen, eds. pp. 233–253. Walnut Creek: Left Coast Press.

2019   Listening to Whom and for Whose Benefit?: Promoting and Protecting Local Heritage Values. *In* Archaeologies of Listening. Peter R. Schmidt and Alice B. Kehoe, eds. pp. 155–176. Gainesville: University Press of Florida.

Preucel, Robert W., and Craig N. Cipolla

2008   Indigenous and Postcolonial Archaeologies. *In* Archaeology and the Postcolonial Critique. Matthew Liebmann and Uzma Z. Rizvi, eds. pp. 129–140. Lanham: AltaMira Press.

Strand, Kerry J., Sam Marullo, Nick Cutforth, Randy Stoecker, and Patrick Donohue

2003   Origins and Principles of Community Based Research. *In* Community-Based Research and Higher Education: Principles and Practices, pp. 1–15. San Francisco: Jossey-Bass.

Tsosie, Rebecca T.

2003   Conflict Between the Public Trust and the Indian Trust Doctrines: Federal Public Land Policy and Native Indians. Tulsa Law Review 39(4):271–312.

Whiteley, Peter M.

2018   The Native Shaping of Anthropological Inquiry. *In* Footprints of Hopi History: Hopihiniwtiput Kukveni'at. Leigh J. Kuwanwisiwma, T. J. Ferguson, and Chip Colwell, eds. pp. 230–246. Tucson: The University of Arizona Press. DOI:10.2307/j.ctt1zxsmmc.

Wobst, H. Martin

2004   Power to the (Indigenous) Past and Present! Or: The Theory and Method Behind Archaeological Theory and Method. *In* Indigenous Archaeologies: Decolonizing Theory and Practice. Claire Smith and H. Martin Wobst, eds. pp. 15–29. Milton Park, Abingdon-on-Thames, and Oxfordshire: Routledge.

6

Place as Indigenized Archaeological Knowledge

NICHOLAS C. LALUK

What does it mean to "Indigenize"? What does it mean to "decolonize"? Do Tribal communities have words for such terms that drive much of contemporary archaeological discourse? What types of Indigenous knowledge are being used to *Indigenize* archaeology? These questions are crucial if we are to continue to further decolonize a discipline that has and continues to marginalize Indigenous people around the world. As an Indigenous archaeologist involved in academic archaeology, I experience ongoing frustration at having to teach archaeology in ways that perpetuate colonialism rather than effectively "Indigenizing" archaeology through a consideration of how Indigenous knowledge can reorient our ideas of standard method, theory, and practice. I typically cover the historical underpinnings of archaeological theory (Johnson 2019; Trigger 2006), but I constantly feel that a true, full-scale Indigenization of archaeological method and theory is thwarted by structural and systemic barriers that impede an inclusive approach to the profession of archaeology. I try to integrate works by Indigenous scholars, but if I stray too far from processual, objective, and materialistic approaches I run the risk subjecting myself to criticism and questioning about my own identity and background. The bigger question for me, as an Indigenous scholar, is why do I have to use and teach such knowledge if it only distances me from my own Indigenous culture and identity?

Deloria states that "Indians are at best a marginal group within American society, but we are submarginal in terms of academia and the reading public" (2004:25). How do we then address this marginality and submarginality within academic and public contexts? Indigenous archaeologists are foregrounding powerful forms of knowledge and practice (Aguilar 2019; Atalay 2006, 2012, 2019; Campbell 2021; Gonzalez 2016; Watkins

2000; Schneider and Hayes 2020; Schneider 2021; Thompson and Marek-Martinez 2021; Supernant et al. 2020; Wilcox 2010) but continuing to center Indigenous epistemology as method and practice is ongoing. This chapter attempts to further Indigenize the discipline of archaeology by looking at *Ndee* conceptions of place as useful methodology in reference to forming better understandings of the intricacies and interrelations of *Ndee* knowledge systems. To do this I will (1) provide a brief background of *Ndee* communities in the US Southwest; (2) describe some issues underlying *Ndee* thought and western archaeological reasoning; (3) discuss archaeological and *Ndee* conceptions of place; and (4) discuss how *Ndee* understandings of place can serve as useful pathways to Indigenize archaeological method and theory.

Background: Western Apache

The Western Apache are usually divided into five geographic groupings. Goodwin (1942) identifies San Carlos, White Mountain, Cibecue, Southern, and Northern Tonto. The name Western Apache was coined by anthropologists to designate those Apaches "whose twentieth-century reservations are in Arizona and their immediate historical predecessors" (Basso 1983:487). These groups can be further divided into a series of territorial units of differing size and organization including "groups," "bands," and "local groups" (Goodwin 1942:6). Although the five Western Apache groups intermarried to a certain degree, "they considered themselves quite distinct from one another" (Basso 1970:5).

The White Mountain Apache group are considered one of the largest, most powerful bands of the Western Apache (Goodwin 1942:12). Their territory ranged over an extensive area bound by the Pinaleño Mountains on the south and the White Mountains to the north. The San Carlos Apaches (Gillespie 2001:2) traditional territory extended into the foothills of the Catalina Mountains and on both sides of the San Pedro River (Basso 1970:1). The territory of the Cibecue Apache extended north from the Salt River to above the Mogollon Rim and "whose western boundary marked by the Sierra Ancha Mountains, which together with the Mazatzal and East Verde River, defined the area of the Southern Tonto" (Basso 1983:463). The Northern Tonto territory extended to the upper Verde River area and north to the San Francisco Mountains (Basso 1983:463). This chapter focuses on the White Mountain Apache community and how ties to place not only resonate from traditional and contemporary homelands but also how

84 · Nicholas C. Laluk

place-based knowledge functions at other realms within White Mountain reasoning that can help inform archaeological method and theory.

Ndee Conceptual Tools

Richard Perry states that "The Apache past belongs to the people themselves. Our attempt to uncover and interpret it involves a certain audacity" (1991:x). This statement is simultaneously a claim to Apache sovereignty and a recognition of the challenges of interpretation. Western Apache ties to place are ancient and intergenerational. Knowledge passed down from the creator since time immemorial helps guide and maintain *Ndee* understandings of the collective universe. For me, as an Indigenous archaeologist I continue to cultivate, utilize, and call upon learned knowledge from *Ndee* family and friends in my own research and everyday life practices. For example, my colleague and friend Benrita Burnette and I (Laluk and Burnette 2021) have written about the deeper components of relationality and archaeological practice centered around reciprocity and community well-being through the use of yellow cattail pollen as archaeological methodology.

Such tools as yellow pollen, however, are not just for indigenizing archaeological research projects, they are institutions given by creator that help to inform and navigate everyday life. Can traditional western tools of archaeological methods align with such goals? This is quite different than many tools utilized by non-*Ndee* archaeologists including trowels, which are not necessarily useful beyond use as digging instruments utilized during archaeological projects. Moreover, the deeper issues associated with such tools are rarely addressed. For example, how often do we think about how destructive a simple tool of metal and wood has been to Indigenous communities worldwide? The trowel has been a powerful instrument of settler colonialism for years because it is through the use of such a tool that such desecration and extraction have occurred within many communities worldwide. In my own *Ndee* language we do not even have a term for trowel. The closest term I could come up with is the phrase for a small shovel—*be'okaahá ásts'iséhi.*

My point is whether we talk about tools, methods, practice, or theory there remain ongoing structures of power that prevent the consideration of the ways Indigenous people themselves "Indigenize" their own ways of knowing in reference to the practice of archaeology and heritage management and preservation within their own contexts. Here, we could ask the question of whether this practice of "Indigenizing" in Indigenous contexts is truly "Indigenizing" because it is empirical knowledge handed down by creator and is just plain reality for many people growing up in Indigenous communities. How then can we empower Indigenous toolsets not only as archaeological method and theory, but as distinctive forms of knowledge, recognized at the same level of equality and usefulness as non-Indigenous forms of knowledge, and capable of contributing to the challenges of the modern world?

Speaking to this point of what counts as knowledge, Wildcat states "in our Native traditions, it is not romanticism to refer to mountains, plants, animals, rivers and so forth as our teachers or elders—it is realism" (2005:420). This realism is the main point I am trying to get at in this chapter. Indigeneity is grounded in realism and not in some abstract or romanticized notion of how to integrate Indigenous knowledge into archaeological method and theory. This might be useful in some contexts, but Indigenous knowledge standing on its own with its own power to drive and assert Tribal self-determination in archaeological research is important.

For example, in my own research I have written about *Ndee* concepts such as *Gozhǫǫ*—beauty, balance, and harmony—that drive my interests to constantly strive for sovereignty-driven research that helps my own community maintain and arrive at states of *Gozhǫǫ* (Laluk 2021). In my mind this simple *Ndee* tenet looks beyond simple linear, materialist, and objective questions that are often brought on by archaeological research. It reaches toward the core of collective understandings of what my own community strives for in reference to cultural heritage resource management. How do we arrive at states of beauty? Does this research contribute to ecological balance between cultural heritage resources and the community? How do we achieve balance? How does this research contribute to ongoing community harmony? Such questions demonstrate how such *Ndee* tenets as *Gozhǫǫ* are useful as theory within *Ndee* contexts but how do we continue to stress and Indigenize the archaeological record through Indigenous knowledge systems?

The Archaeology of Place

Binford (1982) provides an influential example of the archaeological approach to "place." He suggests that "if archaeologists are to be successful in understanding the organization of past cultural systems they must understand the organizational relationships among *places*, which were differentially used during the operation of past systems" (Binford 1982:5). This framework has been particularly well received for its utility in describing the complexity of the land-culture interactions of Native American communities related to group size and seasonality. Other anthropological work involving the concept of place appears to be tied to cultural landscape approaches to the past through experience and phenomenology (Anschuetz et al. 2001; Ferguson and Colwell-Chanthaphonh 2006; Knapp and Ashmore 1999; Stoffle et al. 1997; Tilley 1994; Zedeño et al. 1997).

Bender (1993) offers a key insight in linking the concept of "landscape" to the "western gaze." She reminds us that this gaze is a historically defined way of viewing the world and that it creates an artificial separation between nature and people. Casey (1996) has argued that "place is the most fundamental form of embodied experience—the site of a powerful fusion of self, space, and time." Similarly, Whitridge emphasizes the experiential, describing "place" as a "qualitative, historically emergent, experientially grounded mode of inhabiting or dwelling in the world that invests particular locations with personal and collective significance" (2004:214). Kearney and Bradley (2009:79) extend this perspective to encompass the story of place. They hold that place is a continual narrative that exists in the here and now, and that is embodied in emotional engagements derived from people's connections to their spirit ancestors.

I am inspired by Bowser's (2004:1) observation that archaeologists are seeking to expand upon new ways of anthropological thinking and knowing and that "place" is assuming a central role of developing archaeological method and theory. Moreover, I agree with Golledge and Stimson that "place is seen as the focus of human intentions" (1997:387). This resonates with my own *Ndee* culture—place-based knowledge systems such as ties to the landscape act as integrative frameworks defining *Ndee* culture and history and act as resources for present-day *Ndee* concerns and well-being.

More recently, Eiselt (2012) has embraced these recognitions of place as embodied experience and as the focus of human intentions in her study of Jicarilla Apache enclaves in northern New Mexico. Using the concepts of Jicarilla cosmogeography and practices of placemaking Eiselt defines cosmogeography as "a system of territorial organization in which the concept of space depends on the coordination of the body with astronomical or geographic markers" (2012:145). Her argument considers concepts of power as the basis for Tribal boundaries, moiety divisions, and sacred geography defined through reference to the human body (Eiselt 2012:166). This approach contributes to the archaeological use of place because it strengthens large-scale regional identity of Jicarilla occupations of large portions of New Mexico through the innovative use of multiple concepts to explain the Jicarilla embodied experience.

In sum, based upon these concepts, it seems feasible to suggest that various scholarly perceptions of the concept of "place" involve some type of human relationship, interaction, or experience with the natural environment that transcends time and space. This resonates with *Ndee* philosophy. The interrelatedness of all things and the reciprocal nature of these relations are integral to understanding basic underpinnings of *Ndee* conceptions of the past and present. Moreover, the basic application of *Ndee* knowledge—rationalizations and worldviews—pragmatic thinking, and the creative modification or thinking beyond research goals can illuminate much about the *Ndee* past and contribute to stronger collaborative relationships between Indigenous groups and non-Indigenous researchers.

Ndee groups in the US Southwest have their own unique senses of the environment and landscape. A sense of place is integral to how *Ndee* people view themselves and how individuals should act in *Ndee* society. These perceptions are tied to everyday ordinary life. Basso (1996) suggests that stories are an important component of *Ndee* identity and well-being. The connection between natural topography and *Ndee* social reasoning drives much of *Ndee* moral responsibility. Certain land formations can (like arrows) be shot and upon hearing about or viewing these places an *Ndee* person can be reminded of how to act in their society (Basso 1996:59). However, contemporary forms of *Ndee* placemaking can also reach other forms of *Ndee* reasoning brought on by simple naming. Therefore, such a rational, place-based approach stressing *Ndee* knowledge systems and concerns regarding the interpretation of their past, present, and future is an appropriate methodological and theoretical framework to discuss *Ndee* culture and history. Place-based epistemologies underpin and epitomize *Ndee* belief systems and worldviews bound by the inseparability of land and mind manifested by an overall sense of place.

Place as Method and Theory

In their discussion of quantitative research Walter and Anderson suggest that "probably the most important element of this methodology is that it *abstracts*" (2013:11). In reference to such abstraction the authors also state "it also seems to downplay the importance of 'place,' central to many expressions of Indigeneity" (2013:11). As an Indigenous scholar, I often think about "abstraction" and the work it does to permit comparisons across different cultural contexts. But is abstraction a result of marginalization or even the deeper sociocultural effects of ongoing settler-colonial policies during periods of increased Euro-American interactions? How do we balance such abstractions with specificity and the effective representation of Indigenous people? Basso states "places possess a marked capacity for triggering acts of self-reflection, inspiring thoughts about who one presently is, or memories of who one used to be, or musings on who one might become" (Basso 1996:107). If we consider such self-reflection in combination with the ongoing abstraction of Indigenous notions of place by western research methods and practices, then we see how concepts of space and time are not only viewed quite differently, but how Indigenous and non-Indigenous conceptions of place might be viewed differently.

Placemaking as methodology for understanding and knowledge building is something that is ongoing in many Indigenous communities. For example, in my own community contemporary place-names recall recent events that relate to off-reservation places and foreground community issues. The community of Rainbow City that was burnt over during a large wildland fire in the 1990s is referred to as "ground zero" due to buildings and residences being burnt to their foundations. Another area where a Tribal member takes care of the homeless is referred to as "Caesar's Palace." Finally, an area near the only supermarket on the reservation is referred to as "Times Square." Contemporary *Ndee* inscriptions of place often demonstrate a combination of humor, irony, and satire. They function to bind space and time as understood by community practice as well as to acknowledge broader affiliations of places beyond reservation boundaries. As Basso suggests "Apache constructions of place reach deeply into other cultural spheres, including conceptions of wisdom, notions of morality, politeness and tact in forms of spoken discourse, and in certain conventional ways of imagining and interpreting the Apache Tribal past" (1996:xv).

Here lies a theater within the mind, places drawing from outside influences to an extent, but grounded in *Ndee* place-based experience and mentality. Images and names of popular places within the United States are utilized as devices to tell a story that is understood at the community level and beyond. Drawing on the ancient tradition of storytelling and placemaking, contemporary *Ndee* people focus on simple and pragmatic forms of placemaking that potentially reach the deeper core of *Ndee* Indigeneity grounded in contemporary reality. Because within *Ndee* reasoning *where* events happened matter as much or are more important than *when* events happened, we can see how the tool of placemaking can help archaeologists better understand *Ndee* conceptions of Indigeneity and how place as method forces thought processes beyond western linear conceptions of time and space.

We can broaden understandings of *Ndee* conceptions of place that are grounded in lived, everyday, experiential knowledge that call upon storytelling through the use of place to accomplish awareness and deepen ties to reservation lands. For example, in discussing the ongoing influence of Vine Deloria Jr.'s work and potential for Native American recolonization of the land Wildcat states "his hope was that once Indians adopted corporate structures to accomplish a wide range of goals, they would adapt these structures to fit their own worldviews." Here, if we view such corporate structures as those that are Tribally-driven—reintroduction of bison into the environment (Wildcat 2005:426) we can better inform archaeological method and theory at levels of epistemology that center important points of Tribal values in the past and present. Going back to my example of the *Ndee* use of contemporary western place-names to ground our own realities and experiences we can see how a reference to a place like ground zero might reach the deeper meanings adapted to *Ndee* understandings of lived reality. Large-scale wildland fires occurring on or near Tribal trust lands have been extremely devastating and detrimental to overall community well-being. The Rainbow Fire, which burned many structures and homes to their foundations a couple decades ago speaks to this point. *Ndee* suffering is present, and this presence conveyed in place-name form brings that devastation to life in both the *Ndee* and western worlds. In this sense, Tribal corporate structures Deloria Jr. is referring to can also be those place-names used to Indigenize understandings of community and events defining such communities. As Basso suggests in reference to the *Ndee* past and place-based understandings "It was like that. The people who went many places were wise" (1996:123). This statement hits the core of my argument here. Places—local and distant—ground realities in the present and make people wiser.

Now can these Indigenous ideas about place be a useful methodology for archaeologists? If you experience such places across intratribal contexts regardless of time and space, you can become wiser and thus more Indigenized in your own thought processes in a sense. Contemporary *Ndee* placemaking does not necessarily have to be anchored to a topographical place linked to stories of social community-based learning. What is important is the story itself and what meaning is shared even if certain cultural practices are not practiced as frequently as in the past. Respect and remembering are critical here. Basso makes this point in describing his struggles to speak the *Ndee* language. He writes he had not foreseen "that my failure to pronounce the stubborn Apache place-name would be interpreted by him as displaying lack of respect" (Basso 1996:10). Here Basso hits on a very important insight—communication can only take place in a context of mutual respect. In my own research (Laluk 2021) I have talked about the importance of getting beyond surficial or superficial understandings of respect. In reference to *Ndee* conceptions of place such respect carries over into recognizing place as method and theory within archaeological discourse. *Ndee* place-based understandings are not solely tied to topography within reservations or traditional *Ndee* homelands. *Ndee* lived realities are constantly informed by thought processes and everyday experiences that engage with wide realms of place-based knowledge. This hits on what Wildcat calls having a "synthetic attentiveness"—"to the web of complex relationships that constitute our experience" (2005:429). Tying such attentiveness and respect back to *Ndee* conceptions of wisdom is critical here for archaeologists trained in western methods to see the bigger interworking connections of the past and present through an informal theory of the mind. For example, Basso notes that the "capacity for prescient thinking is produced and sustained by three mental conditions, described in *Ndee* as *bíni' godilkǫǫh* (smoothness of mind), *bíni' gontł'iz* (resilience of mind), and *bíni' gonłzil* (steadiness of mind)" (1996:130). Like the deeply intertwined components of *Gozhǫǫ*—beauty, balance, and harmony—these conditions must be constantly worked at. This suggests how an *Ndee* place-based theoretical framework can be used to extend archaeological method and theory. If archaeologists ground various realms of experience to *Ndee* place reasoning, then we can see a pathway that links past and present in a continuous process. If we explore the deeper interconnected meanings of place-names like Ground Zero, Caesar's Palace, and Times Square we can foreground issues of community and individual trauma, suffering, and settler colonialism. Looking through such issues through lenses of the three *Ndee* mental conditions that bring one to prescient thinking or wisdom we can move beyond surficial understandings of such place-names toward a consideration of the social, moral, and political understandings of community. As archaeologists, if we come across an area in the future—a housing foundation destroyed by wildland fire—we might map, record, and interpret the area. But without the place-name and an understanding of an *Ndee* theory of the mind, how do we begin tying the place back to *Ndee* culture and identity?

I have argued (Laluk 2017) that if we define theory as the explanatory framework used to account for facts (Johnson 2010), then we can strengthen our empirical observations through Indigenous place-based theories of looking at the world. Thinking about contemporary Indigenous place-names can help western archaeologists build capacity and wisdom by experiencing various meanings of place bound to simple place-names. In discussing the *Ndee* theory of the mind Basso states, "if your mind is not smooth you will fail to see danger" (1996:126). He goes on stating "you must make your mind steady. You must learn to forget about yourself" (1996:127). Both these statements drive theory in very rational ways that can help archaeologists destabilize their own thought process as to what constitutes archaeological method and theory, particularly when working with Indigenous communities. Avoiding danger is such an everyday strategy of basic human survival, but taking this statement further, how do archaeologists avoid such danger in the form of speculation and misinterpretation of place-names? Moreover, in reference to the second statement, forgetting about yourself allows individual thought processes to be more attentive and respectful in grasping what types of Indigenous knowledge persist as practical experiential method and theory within Indigenous contexts. Putting aside learned academic theoretical discourse, research questions, and agendas for short or longer periods allows the mind to operate and become wiser in the *Ndee* sense because obstacles blurring better understandings of *Ndee* place-based knowledge are cleared from the path of Indigenized wisdom. My point here is that, as archaeologists, we need to be able to recognize such Indigenization of society in the present because it not only demonstrates an intergenerational commitment to the past through place-based understandings but can better inform on issues, circumstances, and overall pragmatic rationalizations of lived everyday experiences of the past.

Conclusion

Place is a key concept in contemporary archaeology. It has historically been approached through formal, spatial perspectives as well as experiential and pragmatic ones. I have argued that it can be Indigenized through a consideration of the ongoing interactions of people and land over time and space. I agree with Atalay that "our [Indigenous] voices are increasingly needed in conversations about the way knowledge is produced and shared, the way institutions think and operate, and how we can design and develop institutions that are more relevant for and in line with the goals and needs of a changing world" (2019:515). Continuing to foreground such voices is an ongoing process but respecting and effectively recognizing Indigenous knowledge as archaeological method and theory is necessary for ongoing Indigenization of the discipline. Ultimately Indigenizing archaeology through Indigenous method and theory can not only disrupt power relations but can contribute to overall sovereignty-driven research that foregrounds Indigenous knowledge passed down from generation to generation since the beginning of time. Place as method and theory comes from millennia of practical and rational understandings of the world. Forming new understandings of the intricate network of place-based realities from distinct and diverse Indigenous ways of knowing can help archaeologists do better archaeology through Indigenous experience-based knowledge. This is how *Indigenization* can contribute to a socially relevant archaeology.

References

Aguilar, Joseph R.
2019   Asserting Sovereignty: An Indigenous Archaeology of the Pueblo Revolt Period at Tunyo, San Ildefonso Pueblo, New Mexico. PhD dissertation, University of Pennsylvania, Philadelphia.

Anschuetz, Kurt F., Richard H. Wilshusen, and Cherie L. Scheick
2001   An Archaeology of Landscapes: Perspectives and Directions. Archaeological Research 9(2):157–211.

Atalay, Sonya
2006   Indigenous Archaeology as Decolonizing Practice. American Indian Quarterly (2006):280–310.
2012   Community-Based Archaeology: Research with, by and for Indigenous and Local Communities. Berkely: University of California Press.
2019   Can Archaeology Help Decolonize the Way Institutions Think? How Community-Based Research is Transforming the Archaeology Training Toolbox and Helping to Transform Institutions. Archaeologies 15(3):514–535.

Basso, Keith
1970   The Cibecue Apache. New York: Holt, Rinehart, and Winston.
1983   Western Apache. *In* Handbook of North American Indians: Southwest, vol. 10. Alfonso Ortiz, ed. pp. 462–488. Washington D.C.: Smithsonian Institution.

1996   Wisdom Sits in Places. Albuquerque: University of New Mexico Press.

Bender, Barbara, ed.

1993   Landscape: Politics and Perspectives. Providence: Berg.

Binford, Lewis R.

1982   The Archaeology of Place. Anthropological Archaeology 1(1):5–31.

Bowser, Brenda J.

2004   Prologue: Toward Archaeology of Place. Archaeological Method and Theory 11(1):1–3.

Campbell, Wade

2021   Na'nilkad bee na'niltin—Learning from Herding: An Ethnoarchaeological Study of Historic Pastoralism on the Navajo Nation. Kiva 87(3):295–315.

Casey, Edward

1996   How to Get From a Space to a Place in a Fairly Short Stretch of Time. Phenomenological Prolegomena. *In* Senses of Place. Stephen Feld and Keith H. Basso, eds. pp. 13–52. Santa Fe: School of American Research Press.

Deloria, Vine Jr.

2004   Marginal and Submarginal. *In* Indigenizing the Academy: Transforming Scholarship and Empowering Communities. Devon Mihesuah, and Angela Wilson, eds. pp. 16–30. Lincoln: University of Nebraska Press.

Eiselt, Sunday

2012   Becoming White Clay: A History and Archaeology of Jicarilla Apache Enclavement. Salt Lake City: University of Utah Press.

Ferguson, T. J., and Chip Colwell-Chanthaphonh

2006   History is in the Land: Multivocal Tribal Traditions in Arizona's San Pedro Valley. Tucson: University of Arizona Press.

Gillespie, William B.

2001   Apaches and Mount Graham: A Review of the Historical Record. Ms. On file, Coronado National Forest Supervisors Office. Tucson: Heritage Program.

Golledge, R. G., and R. J. Stimson

1997   Spatial Behavior: A Geographic Perspective. New York: Guilford.

Gonzalez, Sara L.

2016   Indigenous Values and Methods in Archaeological Practice: Low-impact Archaeology through the Kashaya Pomo Interpretive Trail Project. American Antiquity 81(3):533–549.

Goodwin, Grenville

1942   Social Organization of the Western Apache. Chicago: University of Chicago Press.

Johnson, Matthew

2019   Archaeological Theory: An Introduction. Chichester: John Wiley & Sons.

Kearney, Amanda, and John J. Bradley

2009   "Too Strong to Ever Not be There": Place Names and Emotional Geographies. Social and Cultural Geography 10(1):77–94.

Knapp, A. Bernard, and Wendy Ashmore

1999   Archaeological Landscapes: Constructed, Conceptualized, Ideational. *In* Archaeologies of Landscape: Contemporary Perspectives. Bernard A. Knapp and Wendy Ashmore, eds. pp. 1–30. Oxford: Taylor and Francis.

Laluk, Nicholas C.

2017   The Indivisibility of Land and Mind: Indigenous Knowledge and Collaborative Archaeology within Apache Contexts. Social Archaeology 17(1):92–112.

2021   Changing how Archaeology is done in Native American Contexts: An Ndee (Apache) Case Study. Social Archaeology 21(1):53–73.

Laluk, Nicholas C., and Benrita Burnette

2021   We Know Who We Are and What Is Needed: Achieving Healing, Harmony, and Balance in Ndee Institutions. Advances in Archaeological Practice 9(2):110–118.

Perry, Richard J.

1991   Western Apache Heritage: People of the Mountain Corridor. Austin: University of Texas Press

Schneider, Tsim D.

2021   The Archaeology of Refuge and Recourse: Coast Miwok Resilience and Indigenous Hinterlands in Colonial California. Tucson: University of Arizona Press.

Schneider, Tsim D., and Katherine Hayes

2020   Epistemic Colonialism: Is it Possible to Decolonize Archaeology? American Indian Quarterly 44(2):127–148.

Stoffle, Richard, David B. Halmo, and D.E. Austin

1997   Cultural Landscapes and Traditional Cultural Properties: A Southern Paiute View of the Grand Canyon and Colorado River. American Indian Quarterly 21(2):229–249.

Supernant, Kisha, Jane Eva Baxter, Natasha Lyons, and Sonya Atalay, eds.

2020   Archaeologies of the Heart. New York: Springer International Publishing.

Thompson, F. Kerry, and Ora Marek-Martinez

2021   Engaging Archaeology as Social Justice for Navajo Communities. In Trowels in the Trenches: Archaeology as Social Activism. Christopher P. Barton, ed. pp. 211–222. Gainesville: University Press of Florida.

Tilley, Christopher

1994   A Phenomenology of Landscape: Places, Paths and Monuments. Oxford: Berg.

Trigger, Bruce G.

1989   A History of Archaeological Thought. Cambridge: Cambridge University Press.

Watkins, Joe

2000   Indigenous archaeology: American Indian Values and Scientific Practice, vol. 1. Walnut Creek: Altamira Press.

Walter, Maggie, and Chris Andersen

2013   Indigenous Statistics: A Quantitative Research Methodology. Walnut Creek: Altamira Press.

Whitridge, Peter

2004   Landscapes, Houses, Bodies, Things: "Place" and the Archaeology of Inuit Imaginaries. Archaeological Method and Theory 11(2):213–250.

Wilcox, Michael

2010 Saving Indigenous Peoples from Ourselves: Separate but Equal Archaeology is not Scientific Archaeology. American Antiquity 75(2):221–227.

Wildcat, Daniel R.

2005 Indigenizing the Future: Why we Must Think Spatially in the Twenty-First Century. American Studies, 46(3/4):417–440.

Zedeño, M. Nieves, Diane Austin, and Richard Stoffle

1997 Landmark and Landscape: A Contextual Approach to the Management of American Indian Resources. Culture and Agriculture 19(3):123–129.

7

Living Our Relationships in the NAGPRA Process

ASH BOYDSTON-SCHMIDT

When discussing the Native American Graves Protection and Repatriation Act (NAGPRA 1990) in the classroom, theoretical, and conference settings, it is often met with an air of finality. "NAGPRA was passed, the work was done, that is that" appears to be the attitude of several archaeologists, museum professionals, and other professions that encounter NAGPRA in any capacity. This could not be further from the truth. In reality, the NAGPRA process needs to be living and breathing with room to grow and evolve to fit the needs of Indigenous peoples and communities. NAGPRA, at its core, is a relationship. It is a relationship between Indigenous peoples, Tribal governments, the US federal government and institutions that fall within the law. It is a relationship of past, present, and future. It is a relationship of life, death, grief, healing, and it is a relationship of Spirit. To view NAGPRA as anything other than a dynamic, changing process is to not understand NAGPRA at its core.

Introduction to the Author

You must know me to know my work. I was not raised in a traditional household; I was not raised with my tribe. I was raised apart but in the heart of another Nation. I grew up surrounded by spirit in the people and places and relationships, and through this I have been led to my current life path. I am a descendant of the Apsaalooke people, The Crow Tribe of Montana. However, I was raised in Oklahoma, in the heart of the Chickasaw Nation, among many Chickasaw and Choctaw people. Because of this I identify as a descendant and with a more "pan-Indian" identity. My family's history is difficult and often complicated, which I believe is one of the reasons I feel so called to the work of the complexities and tangled histories involved with NAGPRA. These complex relationships are present everywhere throughout Indian Country, and they live with us as we navigate them.

First, I must acknowledge and express gratitude to those that came before and laid the groundwork for NAGPRA, those that continue the work, and those whom I work adjacent to and alongside. I am constantly learning from you all, and I am ever grateful to have so many teachers. Thank you for having the strength to work in any capacities with NAGPRA. Your strong spirits have helped to guide the next generations into continuing the work. It is because of you that I am continuously working to fully understand where I have come from, my process, and where I am now going.

Second, I must acknowledge and express gratitude for those who have not yet started within this work but who will further the process.

Young Bones

Young bones carry the burden now
clad in suits and khaki pants
they bend under the weight tossed to them

Told here, take this
do what you can to make it just
our birthright, camped out here in the open . . .

. . . Yet council fires burn brighter before us
blazing far past the firelines, those invisible walls
for young bones carry our memories too

Rebecca Hatcher Travis (2008)

NAGPRA as a Living Relationship

As previously stated, NAGPRA is more than legislation set forth by the US federal government. It is a living relationship; it needs to breathe and be able to evolve with time; "all relationships have a natural history. People have a history in a place and a history of a relationship to each other" (Cajete 2000:77). NAGPRA's history is what set forth the relationship as it is today. The history of the desecration of Indigenous burial grounds, sacred and cultural sites, and the abuse to Indigenous peoples by the US federal government and the field of anthropology and archaeology is what started this relationship. It has since evolved and taken many different forms but has been established into what we put forth as NAGPRA processes today. The establishment of this relationship defines legal boundaries but does not explicitly define boundaries beyond legal ones. This falls to specific circumstances of localized NAGPRA processes. As each situation involving NAGPRA is different and unique, the relationships and issues will be different and unique. Growing and changing with the process is necessary in order to engage with it.

One of the Main Issues with Federal Agency NAGPRA Work

One of the main issues with NAGPRA is the lack of regular introspection and comprehensive looks into past practices. NAGPRA is critiqued and examined by Tribal offices, archaeologists, museum professionals, academics, and many others regarding public museums, academic institutions, and other institutions subject to the law. However, NAGPRA is not often critiqued and examined by governmental agencies and entities, whether this be from lack of funding, personnel, time, or a combination of several other reasons. When these reviews do happen in the federal sphere they typically only happen from a governmental perspective, asking what could be done to improve the governmental agencies' stance or position, not asking what can help Indigenous peoples. This is a break in the relationship that is NAGPRA. To proceed in the spirit of the law, effort must be made to listen to Indigenous peoples as to what the issues as they stand are and how they can be bettered. If NAGPRA is not doing its utmost for Indigenous peoples, then NAGPRA is not working. If any part of a relationship is broken, it ceases to function as it should. However, relationships can be bruised and remain functioning in some capacity. We must examine and look at the differences between these bruises and breaks, and how the NAGPRA process is affected by both.

A report was published in 2010 from the Government Accountability Office examining the previous twenty years of NAGPRA across several government agencies. The main tasks of this report were to determine "(1) extent to which agencies have complied with their NAGPRA requirements, (2) actions taken by National NAGPRA, and (3) extent of repatriations reported by agencies" (GAO 2010). This report found that all eight key agencies examined were out of compliance, and that none of the agencies could be confident in their compliance with inventory and summary requirements. The report gave recommendations to each agency, and all agencies addressed and began to implement these recommendations. However, in a recent report from 2022 that featured testimony on the implementation of the 2010 recommendations, many of these implementations still have not been fully engaged and several issues remain. These issues include "(1) consulting with tribes and Tribal organizations, (2) better protecting Native American cultural items, and (3) addressing challenges in the limited scope of the law and enforcement" (GAO 2022). Additionally, the GAO made forty-one recommendations to these agencies in recent reports from 2018, 2019, and 2021 (GAO 2022). So far thirteen recommendations have been implemented, but twenty-eight remain open (GAO 2022). Both reports highlight the breaks in NAGPRA relationships, and while efforts are being made to improve, these breaks are still present. Joe Watkins wrote in a review of the 2010 report, "Because human remains and sacred objects evoke such strong emotional reactions, I doubt the stake holders will ever be fully pleased with the way NAGPRA is managed" (Watkins 2011). I agree but would like to expand on this statement. Tribal Nations may never be fully happy with the management of NAGPRA, but this is a part of the relationship. Growing, adapting, and improving NAGPRA processes and implementation means that there will always be something that is needing to be adapted and improved. This is a part of the living relationship of NAGPRA.

There has been movement to address some concerns with the NAGPRA process from a federal perspective in recent months. In late 2022 the Department of the Interior (DOI) initiated the rulemaking process for a proposed rule to improve the implementation process of the law (87 Federal Register 2022:63202). The proposed changes would help to provide guidance to museums and federal agencies in adhering to timelines to facilitate repatriation (87 Fed. Reg. 63202). Additional proposed changes explain the processes of NAGPRA in accessible language with clearer timelines and terms in an effort to reduce ambiguity (87 Fed. Reg. 63202). The proposed changes also emphasize consultation at every step and "defer to the customs, traditions, and Native American traditional knowledge of lineal descendants, Indian Tribes, and Native Hawaiian organizations" (87 Fed. Reg. 63202). During the notice and comment period for this proposed rule, DOI has planned for Tribal & Native Hawaiian consultation sessions and public listening sessions (87 Fed. Reg. 63202). This is not a procedure that is done with every proposed rule. Additionally, as of January 10, 2023, the notice and comment period has been extended to the last day of January (88 Federal Register 2023:1344). This is a relatively common occurrence with notice and comment for proposed rules, but the effort is there to ensure that adequate time has been given for comment and feedback. It would not be surprising if there is another extension before the closure of notice and comment. Even though heavily bureaucratic, this process is a part of the living relationship and will hopefully go forward to help heal some of the breaks in the living relationship.

Project Overview

As I work toward a master's in Museum Studies, my work will focus on a comprehensive history and study of the NAGPRA process and compliance of the Chaco Culture National Historic Park with the National Park Service (NPS). This comprehensive history will be a dynamic, living document. As NAGPRA work continues, it will need to be updated and expanded on. Engaging in this work will need to be approached from a multifaceted view; because of the nature of the US federal government, it can be difficult to operate outside of any federal standards and parameters. However, even though the basis of the project will be defined by federal standards, it will be rooted in a reciprocal relationship approach. This project is looking at the history of the NAGPRA process of a specific park service unit, but it will also be incorporating and centering Indigenous perspectives of this history, and how it has affected and continues to affect the Tribal Nations connected with Chaco Canyon. Sonya Atalay describes ways of incorporating different sources of knowledge and methods that can assist in guidance of this project, "Braided knowledge involves multiple forms of braiding: understanding how western and Indigenous knowledge complement each other, as well as ways that community and university knowledge can be integrated" (Atalay 2019). Braiding Knowledge is to live within a relationship between western and Indigenous ways of knowing. This specific circumstance uses documentation from western sources while further expanding on the story with oral histories and accounts from Indigenous peoples and others involved. Whereas Atalay refers to community and university knowledge being integrated, this project integrates Indigenous methodologies, truths, and histories with federal documentation and information. I will be engaging in oral history and account interviews from the peoples previously involved with the NAGPRA compliance efforts, including previous or still serving TPOs/THPOs (Tribal Preservation Officers/Tribal Historic Preservation Officers) and other Tribal members involved who wish to participate, previous park and museum staff, and anyone else that may not fall under any one category of work.

The Why

Why is a comprehensive history and study of this particular NAGPRA compliance effort necessary? It has never been done for Chaco Canyon. There is no complete history of what happened at Chaco Canyon with NAGPRA. Through several conversations with current park staff, and those now retired, it became apparent that there is currently not a single, concise place in which to orient oneself to the previous and ongoing NAGPRA processes and past actions. Understanding past NAGPRA at Chaco would currently require several days or even weeks in the archives reading Tribal consultation meeting minutes, various NAGPRA related forms, correspondence, National NAGPRA Review Committee meeting minutes, various publications, and so on. It would also require tracking down specific individuals and hoping that they still retained the information. With how frequently NPS staff and Tribal staff and officers can change, having a reference timeline and framework for the work that has already taken place can be beneficial for all parties involved. There are pages and pages of studies and writings on Chaco Canyon culture, economy, social structures, and spiritual beliefs. These all address what people (mainly non-Indigenous archaeologists and anthropologists) think happened at Chaco centuries ago. But there is considerably less on what did happen at Chaco in more recent history, the NAGPRA process and implementation being an example of this recent history. In many ways, Chaco set the standards for NAGPRA compliance on the governmental agency side in the early days when the National Park Service was trying to navigate through the brand-new legislation of NAGPRA. I would like to acknowledge the staff that took NAGPRA seriously in the early days when many other individuals and institutions were resistant. While Chaco park and museum staff had already dipped their toes into repatriation and collaborative work before the enactment of the law, navigating the new legislation was going to be very different from the elective efforts they had engaged in thus far. Chaco Culture National Historic Park completed all initial required inventories and notices before 2000, which is considered exceptionally fast as compared to other institutions and governmental agencies. This swiftness is one of the reasons Chaco is considered to have set standards in the

NAGPRA process. While Chaco recorded their efforts in official documentation, reports, and consultation meeting minutes, this does not tell the whole story of the NAGPRA process. Speaking to Indigenous peoples on their oral history and accounts on this process is essential for understanding the full story of what happened. Hearing directly from those involved, especially from Indigenous voices, will help tell to ensure that there is not a dominant federal perspective.

Part of the story that is vital to understanding the process is knowing why particular affiliations were determined, what methods were used to determine affiliation, and how Tribal consultation has been conducted. The early days of NAGPRA were very different from how many NAGPRA compliance situations are handled now. This includes determining affiliations, approaching Tribal consultation, and building relationships. Michael Schillaci and Wendy Bustard expand on some of the history and explanations surrounding the early cultural affiliations with Chaco in a coauthored article. While their insight into those early days of NAGPRA at Chaco provide a basic timeline and framework for the cultural affiliations, there are a lot of nuances in between the lines. The story is complex, with issues that go back to time immemorial. As they themselves put it, "How the park went about making its determinations of cultural affiliation is poorly understood and has provoked controversy and disputes" (Schillaci and Bustard 2010:358). As Chaco sets many standards for NAGPRA compliance from a governmental agency aspect, knowing the history and context behind these standards can assist in providing the ability to examine and determine if this is the most appropriate way for government organizations to be conducting NAGPRA compliance today. With the previous controversies and disagreements on affiliation of NAGPRA at Chaco, examining the process of affiliation is an important aspect of this study. A comprehensive history lives within the relationship between the past, present, and future of NAGPRA within NPS. Without a comprehensive look, it is difficult to understand the relationships in motion, and how they may need to grow and change.

This is what leads to the comprehensive study. We need to understand how the National Park Service as a whole operates under NAGPRA, but to do that we must start at one of the beginnings. We need to understand the National relationships, how they affect the local relationships, and vice versa. The gaps are in understanding and resources and how NAGPRA has been treated across the board. As with many things in the US federal government, there are the standards and practices set forth, and then there is the practical application and the reality of the situation. In understanding how NPS conducts NAGPRA processes, Tribal governments can have a better look at what they specifically feel are the gaps for their specific situations. In understanding past and present practices, we can work toward a future in which NAGPRA processes truly work and serve Indigenous peoples as living relationships, not as stagnant policy.

A Clarification on Affiliation

There are many peoples who descend from Chaco Ancestors and the Greater Chaco region. This comprehensive history and study will not be determining, confirming, or denying affiliations in any way. That would be inappropriate and unacceptable. The history and study are to report on what happened in the NAGPRA process, how affiliations were determined, and the results and actions that stemmed from these determinations.

The How

In engaging in this work, I will be drawing on my past experiences working with NAGPRA. I have previously worked in the theoretical parts of NAGPRA, as well as in the physical process. Humility and respect are the two biggest lessons I have ever learned within this work. This process is long, and it is complicated. It is not easy to get it all right, and there will be shortfalls along the way. Listen, graciously accept feedback, apologize if needed and appropriate, adjust, and then go forward with the work. The process is more than completing the inventory, summary, and notice to meet federal requirements. The process includes the relationship building that comes with Tribal consultation. As Shawn Wilson writes in *Research is Ceremony*, "research by and for Indigenous peoples is a ceremony that brings relationships together" (Wilson 2008:8). In this context, the research is the process, and it is understanding the framework of the specific NAGPRA situation of the given work that is being done. The relationships come together with time and effort and are essential to moving forward. Non-Indigenous peoples who may be involved in this work must build relationships; it is not enough to simply send an email or make a phone call and then consider the interaction to be done. The relationship must be built, and continuously supported and attended to. Much like our everyday relationships. Likewise, Indigenous peoples involved in the work must also engage in relationship building. Margaret Kovach in *Indigenous Methodol-*

ogies states "simply because a researcher is Indigenous (or following Indigenous framework) does not automatically translate into community trust. Trust needs to be earned internally" (Kovach 2009:147). While having Indigenous peoples in positions to be a part of the NAGPRA process is a step toward healing, we are working in paradigms that require self-checking, and self-accountability. We are Indigenous peoples, but we are also working with and in some cases for the institutions that perpetuated colonial violence against Indigenous peoples. It is in some ways a paradoxical situation. We work to bring home our ancestors and cultural and sacred objects, but we also operate within the system that has fostered the violence of the removal of our ancestors and cultural and sacred objects. So, we must work to build, nurture, and responsibly go forward with our relationships not only to these institutions but also to the Indigenous peoples we work in conjunction with through consultation and repatriation efforts.

When first approaching a NAGPRA process, research is necessary to understand what has and has not been done with not only the physical process, but with consultations, publications, and previous staff as well. This is what I previously referred to as the framework and is what will give insight to the relationships that have already been formed. For example, you do not want to come into a Tribal consultation or situation and not know what has been asked or worked through before. Tribal governments can have high turnover due to election cycles and other intertribal reasons; preparing and knowing all you can to answer questions and not have to ask repetitive questions can go a long way with the NAGPRA process and relationship building. This relationship building with a community, Tribal leaders, and liaisons, and with the process itself, is how the work is furthered.

On the physical aspects of the process, thorough and careful work is required. Whether this is working with ancestors and their belongings, sacred objects, or objects of cultural patrimony, they should all be treated with respect and attention. Many of the early inventories and summaries that were completed to reach compliance missed an extremely large amount that should have been included. This was for many reasons, but the results were that objects and ancestors remained out of sight from the NAGPRA process. Many secondary inventories and summaries are being done to right this wrong, and through these efforts more detailed practices are being observed. For example, when working with any object that may be in question of whether it is possibly subject to NAGPRA, best practices would be to flag the object for consultation. It should also be stated that there are many objects that may not be recognized as potentially subject to NAGPRA unless a Tribal member identifies them. Much information is kept with specific knowledge holders, and as such many objects cannot be identified without them. These identifications can only happen through the relationships that have been fostered and built. The relationship is essential to building the trust to ask and bring these knowledge holders into the process. This process cannot be completed without them.

Additionally, with this secondary effort to expand inventories and summaries, photographs should be considered as well. Not only photographs of ancestors, but photographs of sacred and cultural objects too. Again, there may be objects that can only be identified by specific knowledge holders, and photographs of these objects should be kept in mind. If the ancestors or objects are included in Tribal consultation, any photographs should also be included. Unfortunately, there are situations in which these photographs have been published either prior to NAGPRA or prior to realizing they apply to the law. In this situation I would suggest compiling the publications or places where the photographs may appear into a list that can be presented at a Tribal consultation. In many cases, these publications and other places where the photographs may appear can be very niche and known mainly to academic circles or specialized fields of study. Doing as thorough of a job as you can to find all materials that relate to ancestors and objects subject to NAGPRA is living within the relationship and ensuring genuine effort to move the process forward.

With all of this being said, have care for yourself. This work can be difficult and will stay with you. Breaks are necessary; it is not something you can grind away at. If you are Indigenous and working with NAGPRA, you need to take your appropriate precautions and ensure you do what you need to after engaging with the process. If you are non-Indigenous and you are working with, around, or adjacent to Indigenous peoples, you need to have care as well. It may not be in your immediate world view, but you have a responsibility in this too. Ask what is appropriate in order to protect others and respect cultural boundaries. Non-Indigenous people involved with NAGPRA often forget about this step, but it is truly important to the process and the relationships within the process.

Responsibilities in Relationships

As many Indigenous peoples know, all living things are imbued with spirit. NAGPRA is a living process and has spirit. As Gregory Cajete writes in

Native Science, "no division exists between science and spirituality" (Cajete 2000:69). NAGPRA exists within the US legal system, while holding spirit. It is not separate. Thus, we have responsibilities to this spirit and the relationships it exists within. This responsibility for NAGPRA does not fall solely to Indigenous peoples. Within this relationship, it falls to everyone involved to hold themselves accountable. You are accountable for not only the physical care of these ancestors, and objects, but you are also responsible for your words, for your actions, and how you explain the objects and situations surrounding them. Careless language is not appropriate. If you are to work with NAGPRA or with anything relating to our ancestors, and our traditional, ceremonial, and sacred objects, you must be aware of these responsibilities. For Indigenous peoples, these are our relatives, our cousins, and we must love and care for them. We are not like many of our non-Indigenous colleagues. We cannot leave our work at work. It lives with us. We cannot remove ourselves from this process, and we cannot live subjectively in a relationship. This goes for non-Indigenous peoples involved in this work as well. To live this relationship, you cannot remove yourself from this process. You are a part of this process. Borrowing again from Wilson, "when talking about our research we came to realize . . . we belong to it, we're not alone here, so we have to realize that our relationship has to be built on that notion firstly . . . It is clear that the nature of the research that we do as Indigenous people must carry over into the rest of our lives. It is not possible for us to compartmentalize the relationships we are building apart from the other relationships that make us who we are" (Wilson 2008:91).

Upright

Turtle, flipped on her back
strains to right herself
as we struggle to regain our history, our place
to right ourselves in this modern world

She bends a strong neck
rocks back and forth
tipping slightly side to side
barely making progress in her silent fight

As we work to gather our past, our bones
from curious collectors

museum back rooms and
musty archives

Her foot brushes the ground
fighting against the shape of her shell
as we battle against
ignorance and greed

Turtle claws her way over
at last!
she stands
four feet meet solid ground

Following in her way
we continue, we press on
in the struggle to stand
upright, feet firm on Mother Earth

   Rebecca Hatcher Travis (2008)

Conclusion

In undertaking any work within NAGPRA, you must be mindful of your relationships and the responsibilities within them. You must foster them, and actively learn and adapt with them. NAGPRA is a process, not a linear set of tasks to be completed. In entering this work, you must be mindful of your relationships, how you are living, and how you fulfill your responsibilities to the relationships and the process. NAGPRA work will never be easy and may not truly be done for generations, but it is necessary not only from a decolonial perspective, but from a re-Indigenizing one as well. We are in a time of reckoning for many colonial institutions with repatriation and decolonization, but as we move forward in the process, we must keep in our minds that this work is living in the cycle, it is living the relationships.

References

87 Federal Register 63202
2022   Native American Graves Protection and Repatriation Act Systematic Process for Disposition and Repatriation of Native American Human Remains, Funerary Objects, Sacred Objects, and Objects of Cultural Patrimony. Proposed Rule.

October 18, 2022. pp. 63202–63260. https://www.federalregister.gov/documents/2022/10/18/2022-22376/native-american-graves-protection-and-repatriation-act-systematic-process-for-disposition-and.

88 Federal Register 1344

2023   Native American Graves Protection Act Systemic Process for Disposition and Repatriation of Native American Human Remains, Funerary Objects, Sacred Objects, and Objects of Cultural Patrimony. Proposed Rule. January 10, 2023. p. 1344. https://www.federalregister.gov/documents/2023/01/10/2023-00360/native-american-graves-protection-and-repatriation-act-systematic-process-for-disposition-and.

Atalay, Sonya

2019   Braiding Strands of Wellness: How Repatriation Contributes to Healing through Embodied Practice and Storywork. The Public Historian 41(1):78–89.

Cajete, Gregory

2000   Native Science: Natural Laws of Interdependence. Santa Fe: Clear Light Books.

Kovach, Margaret

2009   Indigenous Methodologies. Toronto: University of Toronto Press.

Native American Graves Protection and Repatriation Act (NAGPRA)

1990   101st United States Congress. 25 U.S.C. ch. 32 § 3001 et seq.

Schillaci, Michael, and Wendy Bustard

2010   Controversy and Conflict: NAGPRA and the Role of Biological Anthropology in Determining Cultural Affiliation. Political and Legal Anthropology Review 33(2):352–373.

Travis, Rebecca Hatcher

2008   Picked Apart the Bones. Ada, Oklahoma: Chickasaw Press.

U.S. Government Accounting Office (GAO)

2010   Native American Graves Protection and Repatriation Act: After Almost 20 Years, Key Federal Agencies Still Have Not Fully Complied with Act. Report to Congressional Requesters. pp. 10–768.

2022   Native American Issues: Federal Agency Efforts and Challenges Repatriating Cultural Items. Report and Testimony for the U.S. Government Accounting Office. pp. 22–105685.

Watkins, Joe

2011   Taking an Account of NAGPRA: Review of Government Accounting Office's Report. American Anthropologist, New Series 113(2): 348–349.

Wilson, Shawn

2008   Research Is Ceremony: Indigenous Research Methods. Black Point, Nova Scotia: Fernwood Publishing.

8

Truth and Reconciliation in Archaeology

HONEY CONSTANT-INGLIS

I do not remember the weather, the things we did, or what we saw during my first-grade trip to Wanuskewin. However, I do remember walking down into a large theater and taking a seat. I sat staring up at a well-lit stage and saw a men's Fancy dancer with golden yellow regalia and thought to myself, "Wow. This is my culture. This is me." At such a young age, I did not understand what identity was, let alone how to differentiate culture and heritage. I knew I was different from others in my French immersion classroom, but beyond my darker complexion, I could not pinpoint why. When looking back on this memory, I see that moment of recognition started me on this journey. Honey Constant-Inglis *nitisîyikâson, ninêhiyawiskwêwin pakitahwâkan-sâkahikanihk ohci niya*. I am proud to identify as a Plains Cree woman from Sturgeon Lake First Nation. As an Intergenerational Indian Residential School survivor, I use archaeology as a form of healing and reconnecting to stolen heritage. These methods led me through my undergrad and have continued into my current studies at the University of Saskatchewan where my master's thesis is to design archaeological interpretive programming from an Indigenous perspective for Wanuskewin Heritage Park.

Wanuskewin and the Opimihaw valley always silently played a role in my journey as an Indigenous Plains archaeologist. Spiritually speaking, the spirit of the Opimihaw valley is strong and it inspired my spirit when I visited as a child and again as an undergraduate student during my field school experience. Wanuskewin was the first safe space where I was able to explore both my identity as an Indigenous person and my science of archaeology. Wanuskewin is a place where Indigenous people can see themselves in the artwork, the stories, and the land. I imagine my younger self to be like an ember and Wanuskewin held me up with kindling. These are the experiences that led me to become an interpretive guide and master's student at Wanuskewin.

Background

Wanuskewin Heritage Park is located ten kilometers north of the city of Saskatoon. It was established as a Provincial Heritage Property in 1983, and then a National Historic site by Her Majesty Queen Elizabeth II in 1987. The interpretive center opened in June of 1992 and has been a center of education ever since. Wanuskewin sits over the Opimihaw valley and has a record that dates back at least 6,000 years (Walker 1988). Wanuskewin became a potential United Nations Educational, Scientific and Cultural Organization (UNESCO) World Heritage Site in December 2017, and it was one of my first days as an interpretive guide with Wanuskewin. To be considered for a UNESCO World Heritage Site designation, Wanuskewin needed to demonstrate why the park was unique to the rest of the world and how it was a value to humanity now and into the future (United Nations 2019).

There are many facets to the Wanuskewin story such as the archaeological record, interpretive programming, bison and grassland restoration, and tourism; but there are also many facets that are harder to communicate. This includes the Northern Plains Indigenous worldviews, belief systems, and Natural Laws in creation. For UNESCO consideration, the park's evidence of its value is in the extensive archaeological record supported by cultural and reconciliation connections starting in 1932. Wanuskewin is unique as it has nineteen precontact and two post-contact sites, including two bison jumps, a bison pound, habitation sites, processing sites, a petroglyph site, the most northerly documented medicine wheel on the plains, and archaeological evidence of every culture group of the Northern Plains. Wanuskewin and the Opimihaw valley was and continues to be a gathering place in Central Saskatchewan.

Wanuskewin's structure allows self-determination within its operation through the 1997 Wanuskewin Heritage Park Act (Wanuskewin Heritage Park 2020). The Wanuskewin Heritage Park Authority (WHPA) is built of three central guiding bodies: (1) A Board of Directors of both Indigenous and non-Indigenous descent. (2) The Elder's Council who represent the surrounding cultural groups and various Indigenous communities of Saskatchewan. The Elders' considerations are equal to those of the Board of Directors and the Elders support the park, staff, and guests spiritually and provide guidance as needed. (3) The CEO is responsible for the overall operation of the park and is supported by the various departmental directors, managers, and coordinators (Wanuskewin Heritage Park 2020; Dr. E. Walker, personal communication 2021).

Since 1992, Wanuskewin has been a dedicated center of education where Indigenous and non-Indigenous peoples come together to learn about the Northern Plains Indigenous peoples. My research expands on the importance of including Indigenous peoples and knowledge systems in public archaeology, which has had a positive impact on Truth and Reconciliation education at Wanuskewin for the past twenty-nine years. Wanuskewin's story weaves 6,000 years of human occupation of the Opimihaw valley and that of the past, present, and future Northern Plains Indigenous peoples (Walker 1988:88–89). Wanuskewin provides the public community and Saskatchewan educators with a broader view of the past, as told by the descendants of the archaeological record and this has positively affected Indigenous communities, youth, and education in Saskatchewan.

My journey is one such specific story. My research question will answer "How can archaeology informed by Indigenous knowledge and practice impact Truth and Reconciliation education?" From that ember of my younger self, I have become a steady flame and it is my hope that these moments of recollection, recognition, and reconciliation will stoke the fires of other Indigenous youth, communities, and fellow archaeologists. Through traditional storytelling and ways of knowing alongside Saskatchewan's curriculum, Wanuskewin's interpretive programs demonstrate how archaeology contributes to recovering, preserving, and promoting Indigenous cultures. The continued commitment to sacred promises made with the Elder's Council and the preservation of the archaeological record has solidified the park's position as a leader in Truth and Reconciliation through archaeology.

Archaeologies through the Lens of Wanuskewin

Indigenous archaeology is about intent and relations; it is better defined as archaeology done by, for, and with Indigenous communities (Nicholas and Andrews 1997). For me, Indigenous archaeology needs to have all three components to be considered a meaningful effort of reconciling archaeology. This methodology is meaningful because it "intersects with Indigenous values, knowledge, practices, ethics, and sensibilities, and through collaborative and community-originated or -directed projects, and related critical perspectives" (McNiven 2016:28). A project for the sake of research is not for a community's benefit, and a project for community's benefit is not for the sake of research. ". . . a great deal of the objection of Native people to archaeology relates to power imbalances and the related lack of respect that has characterized much of archaeological practice . . . Management of one's own cultural heritage is an important part of self-determination and sovereignty" (Atalay 2010:48). A project done by, for, and with Indigenous communities should be focused on recovering, preserving, and promoting our cultural heritage within our communities. The goal of Indigenous Archaeology is to be more responsible, reflective, and relevant for the Indigenous communities (McNiven 2016).

Built from the archaeological record of the Opimihaw valley through excavations and investigations, Wanuskewin has incorporated Indigenous archaeological methods since its inception. My journey to becoming a master's candidate in archaeology and ultimately writing the words you are reading is because of Dr. E. Walker, Senator Hilliard McNab, the original Elders, and the community members who created a space like Wanuskewin. Wanuskewin and my thesis heavily employs public archaeology as an active vehicle to deliver topics like Indigenous heritage, preservation of grasslands, bison restoration, and the archaeological record of the Opimihaw valley.

Public archaeology allows public interaction with the field of archaeology while centering on the local community. At Wanuskewin, "the value of public archaeology is essential, not only as a tool of communication and understanding, but also as a tool of opinion that can make a difference at the local level" (Almansa Sánchez 2010:9). As an interpretive guide, I need to deliver information in a way that is accessible across all ages, language barriers, and varying levels of interest. In the case of Wanuskewin, public archaeology is the interpretation delivered by professional and student archaeologists to engage the public and Saskatchewan educators in meaningful learning experiences that are true to the archaeological record and Indigenous ways of knowing. In a sense, as a non-profit organization Wanuskewin utilizes public archaeology as a political tool to involve the public with the park and with calls to support campaigns like the Thundering Ahead fundraising campaign.

Thundering Ahead was an ambitious capital campaign that raised forty-million dollars to fund four pillars: (1) strengthening and expanding the interpretive center as a center of excellence, (2) repatriating plain's bison to the park, (3) preserving the Opimihaw valley as an ecological island,

and (4) pursuing UNESCO World Heritage Site designation (Wanuskewin Heritage Park 2015). As of December 2019, Wanuskewin welcomed six young female bison from Grasslands National Park and five adult bison (one bull and four pregnant cows) who are descendants of the Yellowstone National Park herd (Wanuskewin Heritage Park 2020). Welcoming the bison back to the land continues grasslands restoration efforts and is a historical step toward cultural revitalization and Truth and Reconciliation in Saskatchewan. Preserving the Opimihaw valley as an ecological island promotes education surrounding the largest and most endangered biome in North America, the Great Plains. With guidance from the Elder's Council, Wanuskewin acts as stewards of the natural landscape and archaeological record as the city of Saskatoon continues to expand its city limits (Wanuskewin Heritage Park 2015).

The Wanuskewin Story

Wanuskewin, *wânaskêwin* in Cree, means "seeking peace of mind" or "peaceful gathering place." This name was chosen to reflect the archaeological record and the spirit of the valley. The physical history of the valley starts with a glacier receding approximately 11,500 years before present (BP) that resulted in the creation of Glacial Lake Saskatoon (Rutherford 2004). Glacial Lake Saskatoon soon evolved into a system of braided rivers, one of which became what we know as the Opimihaw Creek that cut and shaped the valley. This river meandered back and forth, creating flat areas in the bottom of the valley that were suitable for habitation sites and acted as protection from Saskatchewan's winter winds. Archaeological investigations are not new to the Opimihaw valley with the first visit being in 1932, but excavations have been ongoing annually from 1982 until 2019; this makes Wanuskewin the longest running archaeological research dig in Canada (Walker 1988:76). From this research, there is a higher percentage of Middle Precontact (6,000–2,000 BP) dates within the valley (Burdeyney 2019). The presence of these dates may suggest the valley was a refuge and served as an ecological island for the people of the area. In 1876, Treaty 6 was signed at Fort Carlton and the mobile people of the Plains were removed from the valley and placed into reserve systems (Wanuskewin Heritage Park 2020).

Mike Vitkowski had farmed and raised cattle on the land that would become Wanuskewin from 1934 until his retirement. Mike was said to be a short stocky man and a bit of a recluse who limited access to the land.

One invited guest was Dr. E. Walker, who had become close friends with Mike (Dr. E. Walker, personal communication 2021). Walker had helped move cattle across the landscape and often brought surface finds to the old man, relaying that he had something special on his hands, but Mike would brush it off, as many of our quiet grandfathers would. As Dr. Walker tells these stories of old Mike, I feel the love and care the man had for this place. I feel the spirit of Mr. Vitkowski some days, especially when I take on that stewardship role at the park.

During Mike's time on the land, there was very little known regarding the complete depth of the archaeological record. The story of how Wanuskewin came to be started in the late 1970s—Walker was working in Texas and continued to have phone calls with Mike. The old man would ask when Walker was going to return home, until one day, Mike says, "I'm retiring, and I want the land to go to someone who is going to take care of it" (Dr. E. Walker, personal communication 2021). As Walker says, "that was our first Wanuskewin miracle . . . the old man was listening the whole time" (Dr. E. Walker, personal communication 2021) Thus started the most unconventional endeavor for the late 1970s . . . raising money to buy the land and establishing Wanuskewin Heritage Park.

Walker connected with prominent community members of Saskatoon, and they realized that this is about Indigenous heritage, and the Indigenous peoples needed to be at the table. This was a radical concept for Saskatchewan in the 1970s; Indigenous communities were battling and healing from living and intergenerational trauma from Canada's Indian Residential Schools, the Sixties Scoop, and various health and socioeconomic crises related to the reserve living systems. Saskatchewan was one of the last provinces to close their Residential Schools in 1996 and had been home to the horrific "Starlight Tours." The Starlight Tours were instances where the Saskatoon Police Service would arrest predominantly Indigenous men for alleged drunken behavior, drive them out of the city, and leave them stranded in freezing Saskatchewan winter temperatures (Louttit 2013). There was enough tension that initially made Indigenous communities at the time hesitant to any community-based projects, but we are a resilient and loving people who live within the natural law and hold teachings of the seven generations close.

Walker reached out to one of his close friends, Senator Hilliard McNab, a nêhiyaw (Cree) man from George Gordon First Nation. I have already introduced Hilliard to you, and you know him by his traditional name, which translates to "the one who hovers above the ground," *opimihaw* (Dr.

E. Walker, personal communication 2021). Hilliard was instrumental in getting Wanuskewin to where it is today. He helped connect more Elders with Walker and established Wanuskewin's first Elder's Council. Some of the original Elders included Lawrence Tobacco, Philomene Gamble, Senator Ernie Mike, and Jim Canepotatoe (*kâ-nîpitêhtêw*) (Dr. E. Walker, personal communication 2021).

Before the Indigenous community would agree to walk with Wanuskewin, they held space for discussion and ceremony. They held a sweat ceremony in the valley, and after their final round, the Elders and Walker poured out of the lodge and laid on the cool grass in silence until one Elder spoke; Tobacco said, "We don't know what you mean by a heritage park, but we think it was meant to happen all along" (Dr. E. Walker, personal communication 2021). In my time at Wanuskewin, I have witnessed Lawrence Tobacco's words come true time and time again. I heard Walker refer to these moments as our "Wanuskewin miracles" where the spirit of the valley takes care of itself. Those early Elders knew that Wanuskewin would be a good space for Indigenous youth to learn about themselves and for non-Indigenous peoples to learn something about the treaties and obligations.

In the 1980s, Wanuskewin Heritage Park was established as a non-profit organization born out of the community. This means that Wanuskewin is not a municipal, provincial, or federal park, but rather a unique standalone structure. The structure of the WHPA allows for the spirit of the valley and our Indigenous and non-Indigenous communities to gather and work toward "advancing the appreciation and understanding of the Northern Plains Indigenous peoples," while "being a living reminder of the people's sacred relationship with the land" (Wanuskewin Heritage Park 2020). The interpretive center opened June of 1992 and has been delivering interpretive programs related to the archaeological record, the land and its resources, and cultural teachings like Elder Mary Lee's *Tipi Teachings* ever since.

Archaeological Programming from the Indigenous Perspective

I grew up in Saskatchewan, where it is not always a safe place to be Indigenous. My journey has had many bumps and bruises, but it led me to where I am today. As an Indigenous woman, I see my life experiences as part of my research and key points to my mission. I have always seen archaeology as a way of reconnecting to my culture and reclaiming my heritage. From my experience as an interpretive guide, I have learned that how we tell a story carries more weight than most people realize. Sometimes, there are folks who do not want their perceptions of Indigenous peoples or history challenged, especially when it is uncomfortable for them to learn the truth. Reconciling archaeology at its core is about reconciling the lost pieces of heritage, and correcting oppressive narratives. At Wanuskewin I am using archaeology to tell the story of the Northern Plains Indigenous peoples— as we see ourselves.

My thesis contributes to the overall mission of Wanuskewin, demonstrates archaeology as a vehicle for learning, and provides space for Indigenous peoples to reconnect and reclaim their culture in a way that is unique to the Opimihaw valley. The program balances archaeology and *nêhiyaw* worldviews while presenting the story of the people and their connection to the land. There have been two previous theses on creating archaeological programming informed by Indigenous peoples (Fedorak 1994; Karner 2008), but, for Wanuskewin this is the first time archaeological programming is informed directly by an Indigenous archaeologist.

It is essential to my journey as a Plains archaeologist that my *nêhiyawêwin* (Cree) language and Indigenous ways of knowing are present in my research. The content of the program explores the lifestyles and settlement patterns in the valley, the use of natural resources for tools, shelter, food, and hunting, and the traditional values and belief systems that influence how people fit into the world around them. This program is land-based and explores concepts like sacred relationships to land, innovation of the Plains, and *wâhkôhtowin*. wâhkôhtowin, a nêhiyawêwin word which means kinship according to direct translations, but hidden in the language, means "all my relations." This is a teaching of kinship that goes beyond bloodlines. wâhkôhtowin relates to connections and relationships between everything in creation. Creating an interactive archaeological program that encompasses land, relationships, and reconciliation through the lens of an Indigenous worldview creates a culturally informed learning environment that benefits Indigenous learners (Ministry of Education 2018).

It is my experience that bridging my Indigenous ways of knowing with archaeology was only constrained in the existing framework of my stakeholders. Interviews with teachers provided the much-needed insight to the challenges of the education system as a whole. Despite the "Inspiring Success" budget to increase cultural education in the classroom, more often than not teachers are left struggling to meet their land-based outcomes meaningfully with the limited budget across all teachers in the school division (Constant-

Inglis 2022). This limitation constrained the creation and implementation of my programming materials for the pre- and post-learning activities. In addition, this informed my program delivery logistics and how Wanuskewin would price an interpretive program currently. Identifying the budget constraints for learning resources, field-trip costs, and any additional expenses were a limiting factor to overall program development.

Through intergenerational resiliency there will always be smart, innovative, and willing Indigenous teachers who can meet their outcome requirements and honor their Indigenous ways of knowing regardless of their increasing constraints. During my research it became abundantly clear that funding, access to Elders or Knowledge Keepers, and accessible land is not always available immediately during times of need, or available long-term (Constant-Inglis 2022). This would be the biggest barrier to long-term Indigenous Archaeology in education as it currently stands. During my research, the various stakeholders were enthusiastic and engaged in the content and programming and expressed excitement for long-term access. Stakeholders include the teachers, students, school division administration, and Wanuskewin's administration. The only limiting factor had been pre-existing education provincial budgets.

Although there is no specific method of Truth and Reconciliation education, I understand this to be an effort to decolonize the curriculum by Indigenous and non-Indigenous educators. Reconciling education identifies the gap between Indigenous and non-Indigenous learners and develops culturally relevant learning styles and outcomes. Implementing the new education framework in 2018 is one way the Ministry of Education in Saskatchewan has answered the Truth and Reconciliation Commission's Calls to Action. This includes funding and implementing Elder-in-Residence, Knowledge Keeper, and Cultural Advisor positions within the schools (Ministry of Education 2018).

The need for archaeology to reconcile comes from the messy past left to us by those archaeologists who came before us. We are constantly living in the cycle known as the seven generations. This teaching, as I understand it to be, is the cause and effect that our actions have on those generations yet to come. Imagine three people to your left, three people to your right, and you are in the middle, all standing in a row. The left represents the generations that came before you: parents, grandparents, and great-grandparents. To the right are those who will come after: children, grandchildren, and great-grandchildren. Those early archaeologists are on our left side of our seven generations. "The power to control Native American sites, ancestral remains, and other aspects of tangible and intangible cultural heritage was taken over by archaeologists who came to see themselves as stewards of the archaeological record" (Atalay 2010:48). Their methods and actions have rippled outward and archaeologists today, both Indigenous and non-Indigenous, are left to experience their lasting implications. As Eddy outlines beautifully in chapter 1 of this volume, we are haunted (Eddy 2023)

As Vine Deloria Jr. relates, the perception of anthropologists, and subsequently archaeologists, were not seen favorably in Indigenous communities (Deloria 1988). During my undergraduate career, I would share with my peers and community members that I was working toward an archaeology degree; often, I was met with harsh reactions and genuinely curious why's. I chose archaeology after I visited a prominent museum at sixteen years old. The museum portrayed Indigenous people as a concept of the past and not how I knew the people to be. It did not reflect our stories, our smiles, or our spirits. I researched their curator education requirements and there it was—Masters of Archaeology.

Much like Truth and Reconciliation, there is always going to be a dark past and to some, it may not make sense why I would choose a field that historically disenfranchised Indigenous peoples of their heritage and culture. By continuing the work of Dr. Walker and Wanuskewin, I am reconciling this field for myself, our communities, and future Indigenous archaeologists. I am aware that I have limited time in the physical world, but what I create could ripple out and amplify through the next generations. It is our time as the next generation of archaeologists to incorporate various methods of Indigenous Archaeologies to create more accessible spaces for reconciliation in archaeology. Truth and Reconciliation is about acknowledging truths and moving forward with intention (Truth and Reconciliation Commission of Canada 2015). There is always a responsibility to learn, understand, and move forward in allyship and wâhkôhtowin.

When the Truth and Reconciliation Commission (TRC) released their final report in 2015, I was nineteen years old. My fundamental undergraduate years were developing as the 94 Calls to Action were being implemented. From 2008 until 2015, the TRC collected and compiled historical and oral records on the operation of Canada's Indian Residential School System from 1885 until 1996. The TRC "hopes to guide and inspire First Nations, Inuit, and Métis peoples and Canadians in a process of truth and healing leading toward reconciliation and renewed relationships based on mutual understanding and respect" (Truth and Reconciliation Commission of Canada 2015).

The TRC had individual reports of each Residential School across Canada and included findings from survivor testimonies and any surviving documentation from these schools. One reason I am so adamant about the 94 Calls to Action is because I clung to these reports as means to understanding my family's history and myself. The intention of the Residential Schools was to disrupt the traditional practices of Indigenous communities, which included banning Indigenous languages and tangible and intangible cultural practices. Residential Schools have effectively disrupted Indigenous cultural heritage and well-being to the point that many peoples are feeling its effects years later, including myself. I grew up in an era of Indigenous activism, where Indigenous communities witnessed the Oka Crisis, Idle No More, and more recently Stop Line Three, Black Lives Matter, and Stop Asian Hate.

The TRCs 94 Calls to Action are aimed at varying governing bodies to make change for the betterment of Indigenous well-being. Although some calls are directly aimed at the federal and provincial government, the various church affiliations, or post-secondary institutions, these calls to action are still applicable to the field of archaeology. In 2007, the United Nations General Assembly passed a framework for the United Nations Declaration on the Rights of Indigenous Peoples (UNDRIP). This framework is intended to provide "minimum standards for the survival, dignity and well-being of the indigenous peoples of the world" (United Nations 2016). In my research, I incorporate specific Calls to Action and articles as I interpret their relation to my thesis and mission. I encourage you to reflect on these documents and read into the intentions of each Call to Action.

Conclusion

Wanuskewin stands as a National Historic site, born from the community in Central Saskatchewan and has been consistently innovating public and Indigenous archaeology since its inception in the 1980s. With fundraising to support the creation, the interpretive center sits over the Opimihaw valley, a center of education for Indigenous and non-Indigenous alike. The goal of Wanuskewin is to advance the appreciation and understanding of Northern Plains Indigenous people through its extensive archaeological record and cultural programming. As a heritage park built from 6,000 years of human occupation, Wanuskewin has completed over forty years of archaeological excavations and simultaneously established themselves as leaders in Truth and Reconciliation. Wanuskewin's work and collaboration has influenced multiple industries like archaeology, Indigenous activism, education, tourism, and more recently bison and grassland restoration. It has been through meaningful partnerships and grassroots initiatives that this radical prairie endeavor is aiming at UNESCO world heritage designation.

After all these considerations in my thesis and how I approach Indigenous Archaeology, ultimately all it takes is one person, one safe space, to create a lasting impact on somebody's spirit. For me, that person was Dr. Walker and Wanuskewin. From a small ember of a child to a steady flame, Dr. Walker and Wanuskewin are the kindling to my journey. I have no words to describe where I started from and to where I am now. I personally find it hard to vocalize, but the difference is like night and day. It is through constant support and wâhkôhtowin that I find safety in my position. It takes one mentor, one space, one project, to change the cycle. I challenge you to carry the teaching of the seven generations: whose safe space will you be?

It is my mission to reconcile myself, my research, and the field of archaeology as an Indigenous archaeologist. This includes being vocal throughout my journey as many of us experience the world with similar bumps and bruises. I could speak for ages and still not precisely convey the entire Wanuskewin story, but I invite you to visit and join our interpretive programs, listen to the land, and feel the spirit of the valley for yourself. These moments of recollection, recognition, and reconciliation come to life through Indigenous Archaeologies and that is the echo of Lawrence Tobacco's words, *it's always meant to happen*.

êkosi (That is all).

References

Almansa Sánchez, Jamie
2013   To Be or Not to Be? Public Archaeology as a Tool of Public Opinion and the Dilemma of Intellectuality. Archaeological Dialogues 20(1):5–11.
Atalay, Sonya L.
2010   Chapter Four: Raise Your Head and Be Proud Ojibwekwe. *In* Being and Becoming Indigenous Archaeologists. George Nicholas, ed. pp. 45–54. Walnut Creek: Taylor & Francis.
Burdeyney, Kathryn
2019   Phytolith Analysis at Wanuskewin Heritage Park. Master's thesis, Department of Archaeology and Anthropology, University of Saskatchewan, Saskatoon.

Constant-Inglis, Honey
2023 Archaeological Interpretive Design For Wanuskewin Heritage Park from The Indigenous Perspective. Master's thesis, Department of Anthropology, University of Saskatchewan. Saskatoon.

Deloria, Vine, Jr.
1988 Custer Died for Your Sins: An Indian Manifesto. Norman: University of Oklahoma.

Eddy, Zoë
2023 Story of Your/My/Our Skull: The Museum as a Haunted and Haunting Space. *In* Indigenizing Archaeology: Applying Theory into Practice. Emily Van Alst and Carlton Shield Chief Glover, eds. pp. 16–37. Gainesville, FL: University Press of Florida.

Fedorak, S.
1994 Is Archaeology Relevant. An examination of the roles of Archaeology in Education. Master's thesis, Department of Archaeology and Anthropology, University of Saskatchewan, Saskatoon.

Karner, M.
2008 Teaching with Archaeology: Grade 6 Science and Grade 9 Social Studies. Master's thesis, Department of Archaeology and Anthropology, University of Saskatchewan, Saskatoon.

Louttit, Ernie
2013 Indian Ernie: Perspectives on Policing and Leadership. Saskatoon: Purich.

McNiven, Ian. J.
2016 Theoretical Challenges of Indigenous Archaeology: Setting an Agenda. America Antiquity 81(1):27–41.

Ministry of Education
2018 Inspiring Success First Nations and Métis PreK-12 Education Policy Framework. Electronic Document. https://www.saskatchewan.ca/residents/education-and-learning/first-nations-and-metis-education#inspiring-success, accessed March 31, 2020.

Nicholas, George P., and Thomas D. Andrews
1997 Indigenous Archaeology in the Post-Modern World. *In* At the Crossroads: Archaeology and First Peoples in Canada. George P. Nicholas and Thomas D. Andrews, eds. pp. 1–18. Burnaby, BC: SFU Archaeology Press.

Rutherford, Jocelyn Sian
2004 Hillslope Sediments and Landscape Evolution in Wanuskewin Heritage Park: A Geoarchaeological Interpretation. Master's thesis, Department of Archaeology and Anthropology, University of Saskatchewan, Saskatoon.

Truth and Reconciliation Commission of Canada
2015 Our Mandate. Electronic Document. http://www.trc.ca/about-us/our-mandate.html, accessed October 12, 2020.

United Nations
2016 United Nations Declaration on the Rights of Indigenous Peoples. Electronic File.

https://www.un.org/development/desa/indigenouspeoples/declaration-on-the-rights-of-indigenous-peoples.html, accessed October 20, 2019.

2019 About World Heritage. UNESCO. Electronic File. https://whc.unesco.org/en/about/, accessed November 21, 2019.

Walker, Ernest

1988 The Archaeological Resources of the Wanuskewin Heritage Park. *In* Out of the Past: Sites, Digs, and Artifacts in the Saskatoon Area. Urve Linnamae and Tm E. H. Jones, eds. pp. 75–89. Saskatoon: Saskatoon Archaeological Society.

2021 Overview and Intent of Wanuskewin Heritage Park: Visitor Services Training. Wanuskewin Heritage Park, Saskatchewan. April 19, 2021. Personal Communication.

Wanuskewin Heritage Park

2015 Case for Support. Saskatoon: Wanuskewin Heritage Park.

2019 Our Story. Electronic Document. https://wanuskewin.com/our-story/, accessed November 15, 2019.

2020 We're Back. Electronic Document. https://wanuskewin.com/bison/, accessed March 29, 2020.

III

RETELLING INDIGENOUS STORIES

Excavating Our Braids, by Kay Kakendasotkwe Mattena.
Mixed media on canvas. 2023.

9

Indigenizing Rock Art Research

Indigenous Archaeological Methods to (Re)Contextualize and (Re)Claim Rock Art Sites

EMILY C. VAN ALST

Historically, rock art has been studied from a western art historical perspective, images carved by ancestors seen by western researchers as photographs. But for many Indigenous communities, rock art is much more than art; it is knowledge, history, community, and most importantly, it is part of a deep relationship with the land and the ancestors before us. For many Indigenous people, rock art sites are places of stories, images, and ancestors that still play an active role in communities (Brady and Taçon 2016). Indigenous-made rock art must be contextualized within its communities' traditional understandings to gain a fully culturally grounded interpretation (Norder 2012). Methodological practices of rock art research have been limited in their scope.

Ultimately, a large part of the lack of Indigenous interpretations is due to the lack of access created by colonial policies designed to destroy the relationship between Native people and sacred places (Silliman 2005; Supernant et al. 2020; Watkins 2003). Many rock art sites are situated in landscapes that are sacred to Indigenous and descendant communities (Gillette et al. 2014). Today, this relationship is still under threat, as seen in clashes between the US government and Native communities protecting their cultural heritage such as Bears Ears, Standing Rock, and Oak Flat, all sacred sites that are also places of natural resource extraction. Linea Sundstrom notes that "in the Northern Plains, some sacred sites are clearly associated with natural resources. Put any other way, some kinds of natural resources are more likely than others to contain sacred sites" (Sundstrom 2003:285). Noting this connection further illustrates that rock art and other sacred sites are threatened, making the need for Indigenous-based preservation efforts all the more salient. The lack of access has resulted in the lack of Indigenous-centered interpretations of these sites, further dividing archaeologists and Native communities. Research on rock art panels is hampered by narrow western bias by focusing on the art without considering the essential knowledge imbued within the sacred sites.

Within the past two decades, Indigenous archaeology has become an ever-emerging theoretical and methodological paradigm bridging a perceived gap between Indigenous knowledge and western archaeological thought (Pyburn 1999). Through community-based practices and Indigenous ontological and epistemological understandings of cultural heritage, a more equitable archaeological practice can occur (Atalay 2012; Nicholas 1997). Indigenous archaeology also calls for self-determination, community engagement, and centering Native American voices within archaeological methods (Supernant et al. 2020). Following this trend, this proposed methodology calls for the interpretation of rock art through the lens of Indigenous knowledge while taking advantage of existing western scholarship and recent methodological advances. This Indigenous-focused methodology calls on archaeologists, Indigenous and non-Indigenous, to create long-term relationships *with* Indigenous communities, establish and regain the correct cultural context of the images *for* Indigenous communities, and collaborate *with* Indigenous communities to create Indigenous-centered preservation efforts with the ultimate goal of reclaiming rock art sites. It should be noted that correct cultural context means one that is focused on particular Indigenous interpretations. Noting that rock art exists for Native communities as different things and that the actual term *rock art* may fall short in terms of describing the images created on stone surfaces (Montgomery and Fowles 2020; Moro Abadía and Porr 2021; Schaafsma 2013). These three methodological areas of focus will hopefully result in Indigenous communities regaining self-determination over their cultural heritage.

Background

Western Methods

Rock art researchers continually wrestle with the question, what do rock art images mean? To answer this question, researchers have used varying methodologies, theories, and histories, most of which have largely ignored Indigenous knowledge about these places and images. Rock art research methodology in North America has mainly focused on four main areas, which have been described as "informal, formal, dating, and analogy" (Chippindale and Taçon 1998). Informal and analogy methods as more interpretive methods and formal and dating methods such as data collecting, together with all four methods, contextualize the images and dig at the question of what the images mean. Field methods can vary based on the type of rock art, whether it be petroglyphs (images that are carved, incised, scratched, or abraded) and/or pictographs (painted images using natural pigments). Field methods include photography, mapping (including Geographic Information Systems [GIS] and Photogrammetry), drawing, surveying, recording the images and the environment, and identifying associated archaeological materials (Smith et al. 2012; Blundell et al. 2010; Brady and Taçon 2016; McDonald and Veth 2012). But more recently, archaeologists have begun to consider Indigenous knowledge about rock art (extracted from ethnography) a formal method in the interpretation of images versus an informal one (Moro Abadía and Porr 2021). Many archaeologists use a combination of these informal and formal methods to contextualize and interpret the images.

Indigenous Ontology

Ontology is defined as the state of being within the world (Alberti 2017). Ontology is a crucial aspect of an Indigenous method of archaeology. By understanding that Indigenous people have different conceptions of being and living, archaeologists can begin to think about how material culture can be interpreted with an Indigenous worldview. Indigenous people have consistently recognized that knowledge flows from the past to the present to the future. Indigenous practices of (re)turning to and (re)establishing our relationships with the land, kin (human and non-human), and our heritage will be the driving force behind these proposed methodological steps to study rock art imagery better. A large part of the theoretical and physical displacement of Indigenous people from sacred sites is how rock art research is done, explicitly ignoring Indigenous understandings of rock art. Creating a divide between rock art and the land it rests on. When in fact, much of Indigenous relationality and ontology is grounded in relationships with the land. Margaret Spivey-Faulkner (Pee Dee) (2021) argues that western ontologies are focused on time and chronology, while Indigenous ontologies are focused on the importance of space and place. This distinction between the two ontological backgrounds is essential to (1) understand the importance of the landscape, and (2) provide a further context of rock art images. Not only is place important, but non-human actors are active parts of Indigenous culture and worldviews (Rutecki 2018; Watts 2013), so conceptions of ancestors and non-human community members are critical in the analysis of these sites.

Indigenous groups worldwide are connected to their homelands through this natural/cultural relationship that constitutes a vital part of their lived experience. As much colonial policy was designed to remove and destroy that relationship, rock art preserves salient knowledge that may have been lost due to these policies. To preserve that knowledge, maintenance by Indigenous people, including creating and preserving the images, must be done as a community. One way to better comprehend rock art is to understand it as not a single creator but a community of artists. Some scholars who work on the Northern Plains (my research area) have suggested creating images as a group activity (Amiotte 1987; Mackie 2015). Mackie's work measured hand sprays in Wyoming to determine that men, women, and children all created imagery together, suggesting a social activity. This type of relationship has been increasingly noted in rock art research done elsewhere within the past two decades (Alberti and Fowles 2018; Ambrosino 2017; Bradley 1991; Kinahan 1999; Sundstrom 2003). For example, Paul Taçon (2019) shows the importance of the physical location of images for understanding the relationship between images and people. Josie, an Aboriginal Australian woman whose community maintains their sites, spoke to Taçon about how in her youth, she would go with the two creators of the images to learn how to preserve the site. She contextualizes the physical space to tell stories and show the younger generation how to maintain rock art and emphasizes the importance of visiting the physical place as a community to maintain the relationship between the community and the site. In these two examples, creation and preservation are done by a group, not an individual Indigenous artist. This is in stark contrast with western art historical methods and thought among researchers.

Relationships

Defining Your Community

Many Indigenous folks, those in and around archaeology, are aware of the challenges between western archaeological traditions and Indigenous concepts of cultural heritage. Building and the process of rebuilding relationships is a crucial first step in any archaeological project, especially when working in North America. If you are conducting an archaeology project in the United States or Canada, you are digging on Native American / First Nations land. This means that you *must* define your community (Pyburn 2003). Who are you working with? Is it one person, one family, one extended family, or the entire tribe? Defining who you will work with is a critical first step. Many archaeologists working within community-based archaeological practices have noted that it is first crucial to define the community you wish to research with (Atalay 2012; Gould and Pyburn 2018; Nicholas 2019). By building relationships with local communities and including these communities in every step of the archaeological process, Indigenous people gain a voice in the research. Defining precisely who you are working with is an essential first step to understanding exactly who you are working with. For those who already have an established community (here, I define community as the member of an extended family circle that I practice ceremony with), such as many Indigenous archaeologists, define who your community is and who you are related to through kinship or familial ties. Those who are outside of the community you wish to work with may establish a relationship with that community through a particular Tribal office (that is, the Tribal Historic Preservation Officer [THPO]), or maybe community members who were asked to consult on the project you are working with. Many times, depending on the project you are working with, at the very least you should have contact with the THPO, Tribal council members, and/or Elders and knowledge keepers that are part of the community. This may be your only connection to the community or an introduction but over time these relationships can develop into stronger relationships or relationships with other community members.

Even if an Indigenous archaeologist is a community member, they still must build and maintain those relationships. The simplest definition of Indigenous archaeology is the archaeology with, by, and for, Indigenous people (Nicholas and Andrews 1997). This author emphasizes the importance of archaeologists working *for* Indigenous communities. As noted in *Transforming Archaeology*, "the Society of American Archaeology identifies stewardship as the central principle of archaeological ethics" (Atalay et al. 2016). This means that archaeologists have an explicit goal of being stewards of archaeological material. Still, I argue that this includes the descendant and Indigenous communities that archaeologists work, for especially in North America, as the majority of the archaeological material is created by Native American ancestors.

Relationship building between archaeologists and Indigenous people forces archaeologists to reflect on their position between western archaeology and Indigenous communities, and I argue that archaeologists must work *for* Indigenous and descendant communities. Working *by* or *with* Indigenous people has allowed archaeologists to opt-out of working in the community's interest, where mandated consultation becomes the only way archaeologists are actively working with Indigenous people. This way, Native people have a better understanding of how archaeological research benefits their community. Though admittedly, as a graduate student, community-based work is challenging as one has to balance the needs of a community with the requirements the institution/university has for the student. Nevertheless, to create a truly community-based project, archaeologists must work for the betterment of the community, which includes working with Indigenous communities at every step of the archaeological process: creating research questions, conducting methods, writing, and disseminating the knowledge found together. Archaeologist Sara Gonzalez describes in her work with the Kashia Band of Pomo Indians that fieldwork moved "from generating *knowledge about* the Kashaya to creating *knowledge with* the tribe," (Gonzalez 2016:541). If you have done community-based research correctly, you have generated knowledge with the community you are working with and for.

Establishing a Rock Art Methodology

Visiting Circles, Visiting Sites, and Indigenous Interpretations

Anthropology has always had its hand in how Indigenous people and their culture have been collected and interpreted. Archaeology has equally helped in this systematic process. Archaeology, at the end of the day, has been a scientific method of colonialism used to study the deep past, and in North America, mostly studying Indigenous people from a western worldview. Much of sociocultural anthropological research and early anthropological research is related to ethnography (written description of cultural practices within communities). Much of the knowledge anthropologists and archaeologists know about Indigenous people comes from early ethnohistorical and ethnographic records; these have, of course, ignored, silenced, and erased certain information related to marginalized peoples within these records (Blackmore 2018). To give Indigenous people a voice, I argue that the next step of Indigenous-centered rock art method is speaking with Indigenous communities and allowing Indigenous people the right to speak or not about their own cultural heritage (Tuck and Yang 2014). This is critical for Indigenous people, but I argue it is also crucial for researchers to have more knowledge regarding interpreting or reinterpreting material culture made by the community's ancestors.

After defining your community, it is crucial to gain IRB (institutional review board) approval if you are conducting systematic interviews (or interviews with more than one person). Many college/university institutions do not require an IRB approval if you are obtaining knowledge from one member of a particular group of people but in ethical good practice, you should seek IRB approval from both the institution and Tribal IRB (Van Alst and Cory 2018). IRBs are a western way of protecting human subjects in scientific and social scientific research, though it was created for biomedical research specifically. IRBs have been utilized by Tribal communities as well to protect individuals from outside research. Though some researchers may conduct research with just an institution's approval (the college or university the researcher is working for), to respect Tribal sovereignty and to repair the uneasiness some Tribal members may feel about an outsider researcher conducting this type of work, you should seek approval by Tribal IRB (Ketchum and Meyers 2018). IRB documents should be submitted well in advance of the research you want to conduct as you want approval from both your institution's IRB as well as the Tribal government you will be working with. Though not explicitly asked for by university IRB in some cases, more universities are asking for IRB approval by the Tribal community you choose to work with. But as an Indigenous archaeologist, I can speak from experience that the methods such as visiting circles described below are not within the protocol of western IRB; therefore a very explicit methodological breakdown of your process should be included in the IRB submission. In addition to the digital paperwork (such as consent forms and a list of questions asked), Tribal IRB may ask you to physically meet in person to discuss your research with Tribal members and Elders. This practice of visiting allows community members to establish a better relationship with you as the researcher, showing that you are not using the community to extract research for your professional benefit.

Ethnographic research has historically been the anthropologist recording the customs of a particular group of people. Within my own research, I push back on this. Though as an Indigenous archaeologist I have questions to ask my community, they are culturally aware (using Lakota language when necessary), and they are questions that my family is also interested in answering. Though as an archaeologist I am interested in the temporal aspect of how long we have done a particular ceremony or created rock art, these questions don't have specific answers I am looking for and therefore asking a question about how long we have done something for is irrelevant as "we have always done this" (Van Alst 2016). Being culturally aware of how Indigenous communities understand things like time or space or something that is sacred is critical when developing questions. In terms of the moment of interviews with my community, I utilize First Nations scholar Shawn Wilson's method. He explains the importance of *talking circles* in research with Indigenous communities in Canada to allow for a more community-based interview approach (Wilson 2008:41). *Visiting* is a term commonly used by Native American people to describe talking with a group of people over the kitchen table. I call them visiting circles, as visiting is an integral part of relationship building with community members. The kitchen table in my Auntie's house becomes a salient physical space where all household members catch up, gossip, and share knowledge. In research, I utilize my Auntie and Uncle's kitchen table as a physical space to interview them about the cultural knowledge they share. It is fundamental that the place in which interviews take place can be done in a space that makes my family comfortable. In my experience, interviews take place after mealtimes as people are already gathered around the kitchen table.

Interviews are critical when practicing rock art research methods. Much of western rock art research focuses on the images (measuring, photographic, and so on), but the interpretation is based on older ethnographic material and associated archaeological material. This leaves a disconnect between the images, the interpretation, and the Indigenous people whose ancestors created the images. If rock art researchers continue to interpret with a culturally grounded approach, the images will only be interpreted as art, when the images could be much more. Interviews (1) Allow Indigenous people to have a voice in how their cultural heritage is viewed, discussed, and interacted with, and (2) Allow interpretation to be culturally specific and not just from a western archaeological perspective.

Because rock art is inherently tied to place and the land, it is critical to employ a method that is founded on giving Indigenous people a voice in interpretation and their relationship with the land. Many anthropologists have employed the ethnographic method of cultural mapping as a way to understand people's relationships to their landscape because "cultural mapping explores people's historical and contemporary relationships with local environments. It entails 'going on a walkabout' with informants in the places that they consider to be important, and collecting social, histori-cal, and ecological data" (Strang 2010:132). Other anthropologists have em-ployed similar methods to understand plants and landscapes fundamental to descendant communities (Alexiade 1996; Osterhoudt 2017; Basso 1996). By employing the visiting circle for initial interviews and interviewing throughout the visitation of the rock art site and walking the land on which the rock art is situated on, archaeologists can have a better grasp of how the landscape and rock art connect.

Indigenous interpretations of rock art can help researchers gain a more holistic understanding of the images by providing insight into gender and ontological understandings of landscape (Norder 2018). And as seen above, allowing Elders and other community members to speak about their heri-tage without the guidance of the archaeologists allows for a better inter-pretation of the images. Though the formal methods mentioned above are helpful in understanding archaeological questions about rock art, these questions may not be the same questions the community is interested in. Australian archaeologist Jo McDonald argues that as archaeologists, we can photograph and use soil samples to date occupation, but it isn't until talking to contemporary communities that "we can fully understand a rock art panel" (2016). As many archaeologists who study rock art seem to be missing the critical knowledge to fully interpret Indigenous images; this is an important note. By asking questions focused on cultural knowledge with my family, we can get to culturally informed interpretations together. Indigenous perspectives can illuminate the significant spiritual, cultural, and social importance of the images because Indigenous ancestors created those images their descendants are now interpreting.

Reclaiming Rock Art Heritage

What does reclamation mean and look like in a settler-colonial Nation, where Native American cultural heritage is constantly at threat of being destroyed (Nicholas 2020)? As noted before, many spiritual and cultural sites of Indigenous heritage are at risk, and rock art is explicitly at risk of settler vandalism and erosion related to climate and environmental changes (Agnew et al. 2015). Very few rock art preservation and manage-ment projects have been done with Indigenous communities. One example is Sonya Atalay (Anishinaabe) who worked with the Saginaw Chippewa Indian tribe to protect a sacred petroglyph site called Sanilac, in Michi-gan (Atalay et al. 2016). She argues that there is much we know from an archaeological perspective, but "the meaning of the petroglyphs as used by present-day Anishinaabe and passed down from our ancestors also provides valid and important truths" (Atalay et al. 2016). This approach by scholars acknowledges the previous work done by archaeologists and acknowledges that Indigenous communities have had an active role in the past, present, and future. It weaves together western scientific approaches to preservation and Indigenous knowledge-based preservation practices. Community knowledge about rock art sites can add to archaeologists' interpretations without taking away from rock art research. This grounds interpretation in Indigenous understandings of rock art, moving beyond understanding it as more than art but also as knowledge and history. Rock art scholar Janette Deacon (2006) argues that in South Africa, for communities to access their rock art and preserve it, they have to be able to govern it and control tourism and non-Indigenous people visiting the area. Part of self-determination is communities' ability to make decisions for themselves, especially within research (Smith 2013). Part of self-determination allows for the reclamation of Indigenous voices, material culture, and even identity. And in the United States, reclamation includes land back. In their groundbreaking essay *Decolonization is not a Metaphor*, Tuck and Yang (2012) argue that decolonization is a repatriation of the land. I argue that because rock art should and cannot be moved from its original place, the only way to repatriate this part of our cultural heritage that rock art and, by extension, the land where rock art rests, must be rematriated (Newcomb 1995). As to acknowledge women's knowledge and a reclamation of the land which is Mother Earth. This would give Indigenous communities full self-determination over this aspect of their cultural knowledge and heritage.

Conclusion

To finish my chapter, I reflect on Terry Thomas's speech in episode four of the groundbreaking Native American-focused television show *Rutherford Falls*. Terry, a member of the fictional Northeast tribe the Minishonka, reflects on his role and purpose when he asks the reporter if he has "ever heard of the Seven Generations?" Terry explains that it is a practice to ensure that the Earth and our language, and our people will not only exist but thrive seven generations from now, that the decisions we make today will have an impact long after we're gone. As an Indigenous archaeologist, I must make sure our culture survives for the next seven generations. I think about how rock art is so much more than art but is the knowledge that ancestors created so that knowledge that may have been lost through colonial violence and destruction could survive; seven generations back is when much of the rock art imagery I look at was created. Allowing Indigenous voices to be the root of interpreting rock art allows for a more holistic interpretation of this particular aspect of material culture. Interpretation also must include landscape approaches and ontological frameworks to contextualize the imagery (Norder 2012). Lastly, an Indigenous interpretation allows for Indigenous created and preserved rock art to survive for the next seven generations, and archaeologists must ground interpretation and preservation efforts in Indigenous ontological understandings of place, space, and knowledge.

References

Agnew, Neville, Janette Deacon, Nicholas Hall, Terry Little, Sharon Sullivan, and Paul Taçon
2015   Rock Art: A Cultural Treasure at Risk. Los Angeles: Getty Conservation Institute.

Alberti, Benjamin
2017   Archaeologies of Ontology. Annual Review of Anthropology 45:163–179.

Alberti, Benjamin, and Severin Fowles
2018   Ecologies of Rock and Art in Northern New Mexico. *In* Multispecies Archaeology. Suzanne E. Pilaar Birch, ed. pp. 133–153. Abingdon, UK: Routledge.

Alexiades, Miguel N., ed.
1996   Selected Guidelines for Ethnobotanical Research: A Field Manual. Bronx, New York: New York Botanical Garden.

Ambrosino, Gordon R.
2017   Rock Art, Ancestors and Water: The Semiotic Construction of Landscapes in the Central Andes. Thesis, Department of Anthropology, La Universidad de Los Andes.

Amiotte, Arthur
1987   The Lakota Sun Dance—Historical and Contemporary Perspectives. *In* Sioux Indian Religion. Raymond J. DeMallie and Douglas R. Parks, eds. pp. 75–89. Norman: University of Oklahoma Press.

Atalay, Sonya
2012   Community-Based Archaeology: Research With, By, and For Indigenous and Local Communities. Berkeley: University of California Press.

Atalay, Sonya, Shannon Martin, and William Johnson
2016   Final Report: Education, Protection and Management of ezhibiigaadek asin (Sanilac Petroglyph Site). Intellectual Property Issues in Cultural Heritage.

Atalay, Sonya, Lee Rains Clauss, Randall H McGuire, and John R Welch (eds)
2014   Transforming Archaeology: Active Practices and Prospects. New York: Routledge.

Basso, Keith
1996   Wisdom Sits in Places: Landscape and Language Among the Western Apache. Albuquerque: University of New Mexico Press.

136 · Emily C. Van Alst

Blackmore, Chelsea

2018 Queering the Archaeology of Complexity: Gender, Class, and Sexuality among the Ancient Maya. Unpublished. Santa Cruz: University of California.

Blundell, Geoffrey, Christopher Chippindale, and Benjamin Smith, eds.

2010 Seeing and Knowing: Understanding Rock Art With and Without Ethnography. Walnut Creek: Left Cost Press.

Brady, Liam M., and Paul S. C. Taçon, eds.

2016 Relating to Rock Art in the Contemporary World: Navigating Symbolism, Meaning, and Significance. Boulder, Colorado: University of Colorado Press.

Bradley, R

1991 Rock Art and the Perception of Landscape. Cambridge Archaeological Journal 1: 77–101.

Chippindale, Christopher, and Paul S. C. Taçon (editors)

1998 The Archaeology of Rock-Art. Cambridge University Press.

Deacon, Janette

2006 Rock Art Conservation and Tourism. Journal of Archaeological Method and Theory 13(4):376–396. DOI:10.1007/s10816-006-9024-y.

Gillette, D. L., M. Greer, M. Helene Hayward, and W. Breen Murray, eds.

2014 Rock Art and Sacred Landscapes. New York: Springer-Verlag.

Gonzalez, Sara L.

2016 Indigenous Values and Methods in Archaeological Practice: Low-Impact Archaeology Through the Kashaya Pomo Interpretative Trail Project. American Antiquity 81(3):533–549.

Gould, P. G., and K. A. Pyburn, eds.

2018 Collision or Collaboration: Archaeology Encounters Economic Development. New York: Springer.

Ketchum, Scott, and Richard Meyers

2018. "Recognizing and Respecting Tribal IRBs." Anthropology News, July 11, 2018. DOI: 10.1111/AN.908.

Kinahan, John

1999 Towards an Archaeology of Mimesis and Rainmaking in Namibian Rock Art in The Archaeology and Anthropology or Landscape: Shaping Your Landscape. Peter J. Ucko and Robert Layton, eds. pp. 336–357. London: Routledge.

Mackie, Madeline E.

2015 Estimating Age and Sex: Paleodemographic Identification Using Rock Art Hand Sprays, an Application in Johnson County, Wyoming. Archaeological Science: Reports 3:333–341.

McDonald, Jo

2016 Our Rock Art, Our Heritage. Presented at TedxPerth. Perth, Western Australia.

McDonald, Jo, and Peter Veth, eds.

2012 A Companion to Rock Art. West Sussex, UK: Wiley-Blackwell.

Montgomery, Lindsay M., and Severin Fowles

2020 An Indigenous Archive: Documenting Comanche History through Rock Art. The American Indian Quarterly 44(2):196–220.

Moro Abadía, Oscar, and Martin Porr, eds.

2021 Ontologies of Rock Art: Images, Relational Approaches, and Indigenous Knowledges. Abingdon, UK: Routledge.

Newcomb, Steven

1995 "PERSPECTIVES: Healing, Restoration, and Rematriation." News & Notes Spring/Summer: 3.

Nicholas, George P.

2019 Listening to Whom and For Who's Benefit: Promoting and Protecting Local Heritage Values. *In* Archaeologies of Listening. Peter R. Schmidt and Alice B. Kehoe, eds. pp. 155–176. Gainesville: University Press of Florida.

2020 Considering the Denigration and Destruction of Indigenous Heritage as Violence. *In* Critical Global Perspectives on Cultural Memory and Heritage: Construction, Transformation and Destruction. V. Apaydin, ed. pp. 131–154. London: UCL Press.

Nicholas, G. P., and T. A. Andrews, eds.

1997 At a Crossroads: Archaeology and First Peoples in Canada. Burnaby (BC): Archaeology Press.

Norder, John

2012 The Creation and Endurance of Memory and Place Among First Nations of Northwestern Ontario, Canada. International Journal History Archaeology 16:385–400.

2018 Listen for the Echo of Drums Across the Water: Rock Art Sites as Engaged Community Research in Ontario, Canada. *In* Engaging Archaeology: 25 Case Studies in Research Practice. Stephen W. Silliman, ed. pp. 71–78. Hoboken, New Jersey: Wiley-Blackwell.

Osterhoudt, Sarah R.

2017 Vanilla Landscapes: Meaning, Memory, and the Cultivation of Place in Madagascar. Bronx, New York: The New York Botanical Garden.

Pyburn, K. Anne

1999 Native American Religion vs. Archaeological Science: A Pernicious Dichotomy Revisited. Special issue edited by Merilee Salmon. Science and Engineering Ethics 5(3):355–366.

2003 Engaged Archaeology: Whose Community? Which Public? In New Perspectives in Global Public Archaeology. Katsuyuki Okamura and Akira Matsuda, eds. pp. 29-41. London: Springer.

Rutecki, Dawn

2018 Religious Foodways: Intertwined Subsistence and Religious Practices at Spiro Mounds, OK. Indiana University: ProQuest Dissertations Publishing.

Schaafsma, Polly

2013 Images and Power: Rock Art and Ethics. New York: Springer-Verlag.

Silliman, Stephen

2005 Culture Contact or Colonialism? Challenges in the Archaeology of Native North America. American Antiquity 70(1):55–74.

Smith, Benjamin, Knut Helskog, and David Morris (editors)

2012 Working with Rock Art: Recording, Presenting and Understanding Rock Art Using Indigenous Knowledge. Johannesburg: Wits University Press.

Smith, Linda T.

2013 Decolonizing Methodologies: Research and Indigenous Peoples. London: Zed Books.

Spivey-Faulkner, S. Margaret

2021 Juggling Sand: Ethics, Identity, and Archaeological Geophysics in the Mississippian World. Archaeological Science Reports 36:102882.

Strang, Veronica

2010 Mapping Histories: Cultural Landscapes and Walkabout Methods. *In* Environmental Social Sciences: Methods and Research Design. E.A.S. Shankar Aswani and Ismael Vaccaro, eds. pp. 132–156. Cambridge: Cambridge University Press.

Sundstrom, Linea

2003 Sacred Islands: An Exploration of Religion and Landscape in the Northern Great Plains in Islands on the Plains: Ecological, Social, and Ritual Use of Landscapes. Salt Lake City: The University of Utah Press.

Supernant, Kisha, Jane Eva Baxter, Natasha Lyons, and Sonya Atalay

2020 Archaeologies of the Heart. New York: Springer International Publishing.

Taçon, Paul

2019 "This is my Father's Painting": A First-Hand Account of the Creation of the Most Iconic Rock Art in Kakadu National Park. Rock Art Research 36(2):199–213.

Tuck, Eve, and K. Wayne Yang

2012 Decolonization is Not a Metaphor. Decolonization: Indigeneity, Education & Society 1(1):1–40.

2014 R-Words: Refusing Research. *In* Humanizing Research: Decolonizing Qualitative Inquiry with Youth and Communities. D. Paris and M. T. Winn, eds. pp. 223–247. Thousand Oakes, CA: Sage Publications.

Van Alst, Emily

2016 Iglake S'a: Maintaining a Hunter-Gatherer Lifestyle within Lakota Culture in the 21st Century on Pine Ridge Indian Reservation. Thesis for the Department of Anthropology, Yale University.

Van Alst, Emily C., and Mackenzie J. Cory

2018 Bureaucracy and Community: Addressing the Need for an Archaeological IRB at Indiana University. Presented at the 2018 Central States Anthropological Society Spring Meeting.

Watkins, Joe E.

2003 Beyond the Margin: American Indians, First Nations, and Archaeology in North America. American Antiquity 68(2):273–285.

Watts, Vanessa

2013 Indigenous Place-Thought and Agency amongst Humans and Non-humans (First Woman and Sky Woman go on a European Tour!). DIES: Decolonization, Indigeneity, Education and Society 2(1):20–34.

Wilson, Shawn

2008 Research is Ceremony: Indigenous Research Methods. Nova Scotia: Fernwood Publishing.

10

Storywork as Method and Theory in Indigenous Archaeology

ASHLEIGH BIGWOLF THOMPSON

I grew up most of my childhood away from Anishinaabe aki (land). Therefore, when I returned to Minnesota for college and reconnected with my Ojibwe family, language, culture, and community, I gained a sense of belonging and purpose I did not realize was missing. Yet, after graduating college, I moved to Tohono O'odham and Pascua Yaqui lands to attend the University of Arizona for graduate school. It was a difficult decision to leave Anishinaabe aki because I knew that by leaving, those rekindled connections to community and culture would be altered, and they were. I could no longer make a weekend trip to visit the rez, practice Ojibwemowin in person once a week at a language table, or participate in cultural activities with other Anishinaabe. Thus, to stay connected, I read, listened, and watched Anishinaabe storytellers in my free time and spoke to people from home on the phone. In addition, I focused my graduate school assignments on topics that were related to issues in Anishinaabe aki and sought research that would connect me to my community. Furthermore, being accountable to the community of which I am a member is important to me, especially as an early-career scholar who works within the field of Indigenous archaeology. Therefore, I did my thesis and dissertation research in collaboration with my community, the Red Lake Ojibwe, to study our traditional foodways. For my research, I thought about how to Indigenize the field of anthropology and do research grounded in Anishinaabe philosophy. One theme that repeatedly caught my attention was Anishinaabe storytelling and its importance to Anishinaabe epistemology. For example, stories—whether personal, traditional, or sacred—are how Anishinaabe keep and share knowledge. If I wanted to do anthropological research grounded in Anishinaabe theory, incorporating Anishinaabe stories into both the theoretical framework and methodology was one way to accomplish this goal.

The reasons for writing a chapter about this topic are multifold. For one, as an early-career Indigenous scholar, practical ways to Indigenize research were, and continue to be, helpful in re-envisioning how research can be more relevant to Indigenous researchers and communities. For example, anthropology and archaeology are criticized by Indigenous people for being useless to Indigenous communities. To this point, in a chapter devoted to critiquing anthropologists, Dakota scholar Vine Deloria, Jr. writes, "The massive volume of useless knowledge produced by anthropologists attempting to capture real Indians in a network of theories has contributed substantially to the invisibility of Indian people today" (1969:81). He goes on to say, "Over the years anthropologists have succeeded in burying Indian communities so completely beneath the mass of irrelevant information that the total impact of the scholarly community on Indian people has become one of authority" (Deloria 1969:86). Although *Custer Died for Your Sins: An Indian Manifesto* in which this critique is included was published over fifty years ago, Indigenous archaeology as a subfield of the discipline did not gain popularity until the 1990s, and archaeological research that uses storywork as method and theory is scant (Nicholas 2008).

Another reason for writing on this topic is that texts that legitimize Indigenous ways of knowing benefit those communities and scholars who collaborate with them. In academic institutions and western culture, western ways of knowing are viewed as more authentic and more legitimate than Indigenous ways of knowing. For example, Roger Echo-Hawk, who integrates Indigenous oral tradition with archaeology, states, "twentieth-century American archaeology has displaced Native American oral traditions as the source of valid knowledge about ancient human circumstances" (2000:285). Western science is favored over Indigenous knowledge, but it is also used to disprove knowledge Indigenous communities have developed and carried since time immemorial (Echo-hawk 2000). Even within legislation meant to protect Indigenous sovereignty over Indigenous cultural material, western knowledge takes precedent, which can have consequences for Native American communities. For example, the Native American Graves Protection and Repatriation Act (NAGPRA) is one piece of legislation that allows, under specific contexts, Native American control over Indigenous burial sites, human remains, and cultural items in the United States. Enacted in 1990, the goal of NAGPRA is to reconcile archaeology and American Indian requests for repatriation of human remains and associated sacred objects found on federal lands or kept in museums that receive federal funding (Iraola 2003). One issue with NAGPRA is that important scientific study trumps repatriation. For example, remains and cultural items must be returned to Tribes that are found culturally affiliated "unless such items are indispensable for the completion of a specific scientific study, the outcome of which would be of major benefit to the United States." This exception to the rule is a significant piece of the legislation because it could potentially dismiss Native knowledge, despite how important the remains or cultural items are to Indigenous peoples (Pensley 2005). An additional example of decentering Indigenous knowledge in favor of western science is in the case of The Ancient One. In 1996, remains of a 9,000-year-old man—one of the earliest, most complete, and best-preserved human remains—were found in the Americas (Echo-Hawk and Zimmerman 2006). The legal fight for the remains of The Ancient One resulted in a years-long court battle (Nash and Colwell 2020). In 2004, the courts decided that the remains could not be linked to contemporary Native Americans, so Tribes could not rebury him as they wished. A scientific study was allowed to continue on The Ancient One's body until DNA evidence proved he was Native American (Watkins 2003). Bruning (2006) argues that even if The Ancient One were found to be Native American and affiliated with the Umatilla Tribe, it might have been possible for scientists to study him despite his affiliation because of the importance of the study.

Lastly, this chapter addresses how storytelling can be used within the field of archaeology. Indigenous storytelling in archaeology is discussed by some scholars such as Atalay (2019), Echo-Hawk (2000), and Nicholas and Markey (2015). Still, considering Indigenous archaeology's rising popularity in recent years, archaeological research that uses storywork as method and theory has not received as much attention as one would expect. Therefore, I hope that this chapter will serve undergraduate and graduate students, community members, and people working with Indigenous cultural resources interested in incorporating the rich storytelling traditions of Indigenous peoples into their research.

Indigenous and Anishinaabe Knowledge: Storywork

The Ojibwe word for knowledge, *anishinaabe-gikendaasowin*, is the "knowledge, information, and synthesis of our personal teachings" (Geniusz 2009:11). The Anishinaabe are gifted this knowledge through several means, including ceremony and spirits, the land, more-than-human kin, Elders and knowledge keepers, personal experience, and stories. The foundation of *anishinaabe-gikendaasowin* is *gaa-izhi-zhawendaagoziyaang*, which translates to that which is "given to us in a loving way by the spirits" (Geniusz 2009:67). Therefore, knowledge and stories are spiritual gifts. To this point, Simpson writes of the importance of spiritual knowledge: "within Nishnaabeg epistemology, spiritual knowledge is a tremendous, ubiquitous source of wisdom that is the core of every system in the physical world" (2014:12). Thus, unlike western science, Indigenous knowledge does not separate spirituality from knowledge. Rather, Anishinaabe acknowledges that the world is imbued with spirit. In addition, Indigenous knowledge is not Indigenous knowledge "unless it comes through the land" (Simpson 2014:9). Land includes more-than-human relatives such as water, plants, animals, rocks, and every being with spirit. Traditionally, Anishinaabe learn from these relatives through observation and stories (Dumont 1999; Peacock and Wisuri 2009).

Furthermore, Indigenous people recognize that place-based knowledge is localized and observations from living in homelands over generations form localized knowledge, which helps Indigenous peoples thrive in their homelands (Deloria Jr. et al. 1999). For example, Cordova says, "the idea of being a part of a bounded space becomes the ground upon which a very intimate knowledge and understanding of the homeland is acquired" (2007:188). Indigenous knowledge is contextualized by where it originates, and stories are bound to place.

Oral tradition is fundamental to Indigenous knowledge systems. Vansina provides definitions of oral history and oral tradition:

> The sources of oral historians are reminiscences, hearsay, or eyewitness accounts about events and situations which are contemporary, that is, which occurred during the lifetime of the informants. This differs from oral traditions in that oral traditions are no longer contemporary. They have passed from mouth to mouth, for a period beyond the lifetime of the informants. (1985:12)

Therefore, oral tradition spans generations, whereas oral histories originate within the storyteller's lifetime. The oral tradition serves to transmit knowledge that is different from the western tradition of writing knowledge and disseminating information through text. Deloria writes, "the non-Western, tribal equivalent of science is the oral tradition, the teachings that have been passed down from one generation to the next over uncounted centuries. The oral tradition is a loosely held collection of anecdotal material that, taken together, explains the nature of the physical world as people have experienced it and the important events of their historical journey"

(1997:36). Thus, oral tradition is an Indigenous method of teaching and transmitting Indigenous knowledge. Not only does oral tradition carry knowledge, but it is vital to passing on Indigenous culture, language, and identity. Lakota anthropologist, Medicine, writes that "Indigenous cultures of North America and elsewhere have had, as part of their heritages, strong emphasis on oral history and traditions. These have persisted despite strong efforts directed toward acculturation to the dominant society via educational endeavors and language and religious suppression" (2001:313). Medicine writes that oral traditions persist in Native cultures, yet persistence goes both ways: Indigenous cultures persist *because of* oral tradition. In addition, oral traditions "are powerful means of cultural transmission; they evoke respect and identity among Indians today" (Medicine 2001:73). Not only do oral traditions teach, but they sustain Indigenous identities in the modern world. They are honored by many Native peoples and continue to help teach Native ways, values, and histories.

The oral tradition is used by many Indigenous peoples to share knowledge, including the Anishinaabe (Archibald 2008; Kovach 2009; Qwul'sih'yah'maht 2015; Wilson 2008). Within the oral tradition, storytelling, in particular, is of the utmost importance. For example, Peacock and Wisuri state that "the Ojibwe are a story people, and stories have been the most common means by which the history and culture have been passed down through the generations" (2009:28). Thus, stories are the most prevalent method to share Ojibwe knowledge, values, and protocols, and in traditional settings, storytelling is done orally and in person rather than through written texts (Peacock and Wisuri 2009; Doerfler et al. 2013). Among the Ojibwe, there are different types of stories, including *dibaji-mowinan* (personal stories) and *aandisokaana* (sacred stories) (Simpson 2017:32). Both types of stories relay ideas, values, and meaning; however, determining the interpretations of lessons and metaphors within stories is left to the listener to decide (Simpson 2017). In Anishinaabe culture, anyone can share personal stories, but within Ojibwe epistemology, some protocols control what contexts specific knowledge, especially sacred or ceremonial knowledge, is shared. In addition, Elders are regarded with the utmost respect and reverence because of the wisdom and stories they carry (Johnston 1975; McNally 2009).

Within academic contexts, storytelling is vital to Anishinaabe research:

Anishinaabeg stories are roots; they are both the origins and the imaginings of what it means to be a participant in an ever-changing and vibrant culture in humanity. In the same vein, stories can serve as a foundation and framework for the field of Anishinaabeg Studies, providing both a methodological and theoretical approach to our scholarship. They embody ideas and systems that form the basis for law, values, and community. Stories are rich and complex creations that allow for the growth and vitality of diverse and disparate ways of understanding the world. (Borrows 2013: xii)

Therefore, for research grounded in Anishinaabe philosophy, stories can serve as a method and theory, guiding how research is conducted and information is interpreted. In addition, stories can also be a method in their own right (Archibald 2008; Atalay 2019; Cajete 2000; Gross 2010). For example, the process of receiving and sharing stories is a standard method for Indigenous people to relay information through time and space. Importantly, there are certain times of year and contexts in which some types of sacred and traditional stories are told, which differ depending on the community (Archibald 2008). For people who work with Indigenous knowledge, it is essential to understand the storytelling protocols of the communities they work with to do research respectfully and ethically (Archibald 2008). Archibald's research on Indigenous Storywork is a helpful guide for researchers seeking to use storywork as part of their methodology. In her book, *Indigenous Storywork: Educating the Heart, Mind, Body, and Spirit*, Archibald outlines seven principles of storywork: "The principles of respect, responsibility, reciprocity, reverence, holism, interrelatedness, and synergy helped me get to the 'core' of making meaning with and through stories" (2008:140). These principles, which she explores more deeply in her book, are helpful to those wishing to incorporate storywork into their research and use storywork as theory and method. Furthermore, she provides ethical considerations for using storywork, including gaining permission from the communities that researchers collaborate with, maintaining respectful cultural protocols, and verifying information shared through storytelling with the storyteller, among other lessons she learned working with stories (Archibald 2008).

Storywork as Theory and Method

Indigenous storywork can be used to create theory, method, or both in research with Indigenous communities. Considering the audience of this volume, it is useful to define theory because theoretical frameworks are often an unfamiliar concept for undergraduate students and community members. Therefore, first, I build on Smith's definition to define theory:

> [Theory] helps make sense of reality. It enables us to make assumptions and predictions about the world in which we live. It contains within it a method or methods for selecting and arranging, for prioritizing and legitimizing what we see and do. Theory enables us to deal with contradictions and uncertainties. Perhaps more significantly, it gives us space to plan, to strategize, to take greater control over our resistances. (Smith 2012:40)

Thus, contained within theory is how we conceptualize reality, methods of research, and organization of knowledge. Simpson states that "a 'theory' in its simplest form is an explanation of phenomenon" (Simpson 2017:151). Therefore, a theory is a framework used to organize the information researchers gather. Different theories have different research approaches and impact the way research is conceptualized, executed, and interpreted.

In archaeology, using Indigenous knowledge to create theory is not common practice, but there are some examples of integrating Indigenous philosophies into interpretative frameworks (Cipolla et al. 2018; Laluk 2017). One example of using Indigenous theory in archaeology is found in Laluk's research (2017). Laluk spoke with Apache cultural experts about the difficulties of finding a theoretical framework for an Apache archaeological project, writing, "tribal cultural experts questioned why there is a need for theory and why couldn't I just write about what people told me?" (2017:101). At first, this incident seemed strange compared to Simpson's work, an Anishinaabe intellectual, who writes, "theory isn't just for academics; it's for everyone" (2017:151). Were these Apache cultural experts saying that the Apache does not have theory? With more thought, it became clear that it isn't that they do not need or have theory. Instead, it is more likely they do not classify research the same way western academia does. For example, Simpson writes regarding Anishinaabe people that "our theoretical understandings were constructed differently than western theory: they are woven into doing, they are layered in meaning, they can be communicated through story, action, and embodied presence" (2017:56). In other words, if Indigenous philosophy views phenomena holistically rather than compartmentalizing knowledge, then knowledge and all of its parts—philosophy, axiology, methodology, and theory—are enacted at once without being separated. This is why the Apache consultants did not see a need to choose a theory and explain it; Indigenous theories are layered into doing the research and guiding Indigenous thought, actions, and research, even if they are not explicitly laid out.

However, in academia, research through western institutions requires that theory and method are explicitly stated. Thus, there is a need for Indigenous frameworks, and these can be helpful in interpreting data for collaborative, Indigenous projects (Hart 2010; Wilson 2008). One example of a collaborative Indigenous archaeological approach is by Cipolla et al. (2018). Using Mohegan philosophy by interpreting humans as part of the land and not a part of it and the idea that the past is in the present, their team was able to interpret Mohegan sites more completely, enriching their interpretations (Cipolla et al. 2018). For example, Mohegan collaborators recognized that certain sites were valuable and occupied by Mohegan people despite the absence of human-modified objects because Mohegan oral history and contemporary knowledge revealed their significance. In addition, the research team incorporated culturally meaningful plants into their project due to their cultural significance to the Mohegan, which widened the scope of their archaeological project and brought meaningful insights. For projects that incorporate Indigenous philosophies into interpretive frameworks, the research is more complete because it utilizes Indigenous ways of knowing, providing information not available within the scope of western research paradigms. In turn, this knowledge provides new perspectives on anthropology. Furthermore, by using an interpretative framework that comes from the people one works with, the research can be more accurate to the community's worldview and philosophy, creating relevance and accuracy in the research and its interpretations for both community members and researchers.

Methodologically, storytelling is used and adapted in various ways in Indigenous research (Archibald 2008; Atalay 2019; Doerfler et al. 2013). Atalay, an Anishinaabe archaeologist, developed a research approach she calls braided knowledge that blends Indigenous philosophies with western knowledge to decolonize research. She states,

> Braided knowledge involves multiple forms of braiding: understanding how western and Indigenous knowledge complement each other, as well as ways that community and university knowledge can be integrated. As we consider health, well-being, and repatriation or other aspects of reclaiming through community-based heritage work, the braiding involves bringing intellectual learning together with embod-

ied practices (hands-on physical learning) and with emotional and spiritual understanding. (Atalay 2019:82)

Therefore, braiding knowledge offers an approach to research that holistically integrates different knowledge systems, accounting for other aspects of data that are intentionally omitted from western, positivistic forms of research such as the emotional and spiritual nature of knowledge that is prevalent in Indigenous epistemologies (Cajete 2000; Deloria 1992; Harris 2005). Braiding knowledge can be used by researchers who wish to decolonize their research by incorporating culturally appropriate theory and methods into their approaches, such as storywork.

Case Study: Red Lake Ojibwe Foodways and Food Sovereignty

The Ojibwe are also known as the Chippewa, and more broadly, Anishinaabe. The Ojibwe people began their migration to the Great Lakes region 1500 years ago because of food shortages and conflict in what is now the northeast United States (Treuer 2015). Anishinaabe people were told by spiritual leaders to move west to where food grows on water, a reference to wild rice. Today, there are seven Ojibwe reservations in Minnesota and many more Anishinaabe communities spread across the Great Lakes region. The Red Lake Band of Chippewa referred to in this chapter as the Red Lake Ojibwe, are located in northern Minnesota. Currently, Red Lake has ~17,000 Tribal members, and about half of those live on the Red Lake reservation.

Desiring a project grounded in Indigenous archaeology and wanting to work within my own community, I approached the Red Lake Tribal Historic Preservation Office (THPO) about doing my master's research in collaboration with the Tribe. When I asked what topic would be useful to study, they suggested a project investigating Red Lake Ojibwe traditional foodways. They envisioned a project that employed interviews as part of the methodology to preserve Tribal members' stories and knowledge about traditional foods, especially Elders' knowledge. Therefore, using interviews, as well as ethnographic and other historical material, I outlined seven major traditional foodways of the Red Lake Ojibwe and their significance to the community. For both the methodology and theoretical framework for this research grounded in Indigenous archaeology, storywork played a central role.

Situating my project within Indigenous archaeology allowed me to incorporate Indigenous knowledge into the research design, using storywork as method and theory (Thompson 2019). Methodologically, I interviewed community members to hear their personal stories to learn about traditional foodways and these foods' importance to the community. Although interviews are not the same as storytelling, braiding knowledge makes space for a hybrid of Indigenous and western methods (Atalay 2019). Using a hybrid method of storytelling and interviewing made this project more culturally relevant because it draws on Ojibwe traditional knowledge. Furthermore, by asking community members about foodways, I incorporated information that is not readily found in the archaeological record. For example, within traditional archaeology, researchers have to make the best educated guesses for answering questions related to "why" (for example, why are these foodways important to Ojibwe culture?). Yet, when using living knowledge from the community one works with, answering "why" isn't hypothetical. Rather, the community can tell us the answer themselves. This is one of the major differences between analyses of traditional archaeological data and knowledge shared by community members. Additionally, this research has been critiqued for not being an archaeological project, and I agree that it is not archaeology in the traditional, positivistic sense of the discipline. When people think of archaeology, excavation and artifacts are often what come to mind. Yet, within Indigenous archaeology, projects are designed using the values and wishes of the communities we work with. Even though I sought an archaeological project for my master's research, the THPO desired that I use interviewing and storywork as my methodology. As a result, rather than "things" or material culture as the subject of study, Indigenous knowledge and practices were centered instead.

The project's theoretical framework drew on teachings from the Anishinaabe *Deer Clan Story* for conceptualizing, executing, and analyzing data (Thompson 2019). This traditional story has many cultural teachings contained within it, including lessons of reciprocal relationality with more-than-human kin, humans as responsible caretakers of the earth, and humans as part of—rather than apart from—the land (Simpson 2013). These teachings guided how I formulated my interview questions and interpreted data. The teaching that we are all related helps researchers understand Ojibwe foodways better. Particularly, food is not just food but comes from our relatives, which is helpful when conceptualizing how interviewees discuss food. For example, understanding food as kin makes food more than subsistence; food is about relationships to the land and our more-than-human relatives. The second teaching, Ojibwe as keepers of the earth, means there are consequences when the Red Lake Ojibwe are not keeping balance and harmony with the land. One example of this is when Tribal members overfished Red Lake walleye and the population crashed in the 1990s. A few of the people I interviewed told me that if they had treated the lake and fish with respect, the collapse would not have occurred. This understanding of Ojibwe as stewards of the earth helped to interpret interviewees' thoughts regarding how interviewees conceptualize themselves and their relationships with more-than-human kin within Ojibwe worldview. The third teaching, the land is us, means that Red Lake Ojibwe come from the land and so does every living being. Moreover, what Red Lake Ojibwe do to the land inevitably impacts everyone, humans and more-than-human relatives. This teaching is interrelated with the other two teachings and was used to understand Ojibwe foodways and their significance to Red Lake, as well as the community's own role in their food system.

Methodologically, interviewing community members was the main source of knowledge. I spoke with Tribal members who live on the Red Lake Indian Reservation. Using word-of-mouth and the guidance of the THPO, I was able to find community experts who participate in traditional foodways to interview. For this project, interviewees were over the age of fifty, half were men and half were women, and they practiced traditional foodways to varying degrees. Although a handful of interviewees is not a representative sample of the Red Lake Ojibwe, who number in the thousands, the people interviewed are recognized as cultural experts in the community, and therefore, the information they shared carries validity and reliability. Furthermore, stories may not have much clout in a positivist research paradigm but are a valid form of knowledge within Ojibwe theory. Interviews were conducted as one-on-one interviews between the interviewee and me. These lasted one to two hours and took place at the interviewee's residence or a Tribal building. All interviews were recorded using an audio recorder and documented with interview notes. Interview questions revolved around the three main research questions: (1) What traditional foods do Red Lake Ojibwe harvest and consume? (2) Who, when, where, and how are these foods collected, harvested, grown, and consumed by the Red Lake Ojibwe? and (3) Why are these foods important to Ojibwe culture and lifeways?

The interviews were transcribed verbatim by me. Although it would have been quicker to send them to a transcription service, transcribing them myself allowed me to be more familiar with the content and search for key themes across the interviews. In addition, English was the primary language used in the interviews, but *Ojibwemowin* (the Ojibwe language) was also spoken, so I translated Ojibwe words and phrases. The first two research questions have answers that are easily organized by foodway type. The last question, why are traditional foodways important to Red Lake Ojibwe, are organized by common themes I found throughout the interviews.

I identified seven major traditional foodways of the Red Lake Ojibwe, including maple sugar harvesting; agriculture; berry picking; wild rice harvesting; hunting, snaring, and collecting eggs; other wild foods gathering; and fishing (Thompson 2019). In addition, community members explained the importance of traditional foodways and Red Lake Ojibwe food sovereignty. These foodways are significant because of their contribution to Ojibwe people's health, their medicinal and ceremonial importance, the wellness of future generations of Ojibwe, and for cultivating respectful relationships with the land and more-than-human kin. After examining in their entirety the interviewees' thoughts and responses to the interview questions, I made three observations about Red Lake Ojibwe foodways that identify the significance of traditional Ojibwe foods. First, traditional foods are a continuation of Ojibwe ancestral ways. Continuation of ancestral foodways is continuation of culture and helps the Ojibwe fulfill their obligation of taking care of the land. Second, although there have been changes to Red Lake Ojibwe foodways, these changes are adaptations that help cultural traditions to continue, and Ojibwe people survive. Finally, traditional foodways are a way of cultural survivance for Red Lake Ojibwe. Anishinaabe scholar Gerald Vizenor says that "survivance is an active sense of presence, the continuation of native stories, not a mere reaction, or a survivable name" (1999:viii). In Red Lake traditional foodways, survivance is a main theme and a way of resistance to colonization. Colonization introduced many hardships to the Red Lake Ojibwe, which all of the interviewees discuss. These adversities include health problems related to nutrition, materialistic and selfish values, and loss of culture. Yet, by participating in traditional foodways and passing this knowledge on to the future generations, the Red Lake Ojibwe are able to fight for their health, values, and culture. They practice survivance when they practice traditional foodways.

As a result of using method and theory grounded in Ojibwe philosophy, the research is more complete and relevant to the community because it incorporates Ojibwe knowledge into the research design, providing information not available through material culture such as cultural understandings of food and their importance. Moreover, by using theory that originates from the people I collaborate with, the research is situated within the Ojibwe worldview, creating accuracy in how foodways are understood from an Ojibwe perspective.

Conclusions

Considering the diversity across Indigenous Country and the growing number of Indigenous archaeological projects, there are countless opportunities to braid Indigenous and western knowledge together in future research. In the case of the Red Lake Ojibwe Traditional Foodways and Food Sovereignty project, braiding together storytelling with interviewing methods and incorporating Ojibwe theory adapted from a traditional Anishinaabe story provided new insights about foodways and their importance to the community. I hope that future Indigenous scholars or researchers who work with Indigenous communities can also develop ways to do research that is in line with their community's knowledge, ethics, and worldview.

References

Archibald, Jo-Ann
2008   Indigenous Storywork: Educating the Heart, Mind, Body, and Spirit. Vancouver: University of British Columbia Press.
Atalay, Sonya
2019   Braiding Strands of Wellness: How Repatriation Contributes to Healing through Embodied Practice and Storywork. The Public Historian 41(1):78–89.
Borrows, John
2013   Maajitaadaa: Nanaboozhoo and the Flood, part 2. *In* Centering Anishinaabeg Studies: Understanding the World Through Stories. J. Doerfler, J. N. Sinclair, and H. Stark, eds. pp. ix–xiv. Lansing: Michigan State University Press.
Bruning, Susan B.
2006   Complex Legal Legacies: The Native American Graves Protection and Repatriation Act, Scientific Study, and Kennewick Man. American Antiquity 71(3):501–521.

Cajete, Gregory
2000   Native Science: Natural Laws of Interdependence. Santa Fe: Clear Light Books.
Cipolla, Craig N., James Quinn, and Jay Levy
2018   Theory in Collaborative Indigenous Archaeology: Insights from Mohegan. American Antiquity 84(1):127–142.
Cordova, Viola F.
2007   How It Is: The Native American Philosophy of V.F. Cordova. Tucson: University of Arizona.
Deloria Jr., Vine
1969   Custer Died for Your Sins: An Indian Manifesto. New York: Macmillan.
1992   Relativity, Relatedness and Reality. Winds of Change 7(4):34–40.
1997   Red Earth, White Lies: Native Americans and the Myth of Scientific Fact. Golden: Fulcrum Publishing.
Deloria Jr., Vine, Barbara Kristen Foehner, and Sam Scinta
1999   Spirit & Reason: The Vine Deloria, Jr., A Reader. Golden: Fulcrum Publishing.
Doerfler, Jill, Niigaanwiwidam James Sinclair, and Hedi Kiiwetinepinesiik Stark
2013   Centering Anishinaabeg Studies: Understanding the World Through Stories. Lansing: Michigan State University Press.
Dumont, James
1999   Anishinaabe Izhichigaywin. *In* Sacred Water: Water for Life. Lea Foushee, Renee Gurneau, and Edward Benton-Banai, eds. pp. 13–57. Lake Elmo: North American Water Office.
Echo-Hawk, Roger
2000   Ancient History in the New World: Integrating Oral Traditions and the Archaeological Record in Deep Time. American Antiquity 65(2):267–290.
Echo-Hawk, Roger C., and Larry J. Zimmerman
2006   Beyond Racism: Some Opinions about Racialism and American Archaeology. American Indian Quarterly 30(3/4):461–485.
Geniusz, Wendy
2009   Our Knowledge is Not Primitive: Decolonizing Botanical Anishinaabe Teachings. Syracuse: Syracuse University Press.
Gross, Lawrence W.
2010   Some Elements of American Indian Pedagogy from an Anishinaabe Perspective. American Indian Culture and Research Journal 34(2):11–26.
Harris, Heather
2005   Indigenous Worldviews and Ways of Knowing as Theoretical and Methodological Foundations Behind Archaeological Theory and Method. *In* Indigenous Archaeologies: A Reader on Decolonization. Margaret M. Bruchac, Siobhan M. Hart, and H. Martin Wobst, eds. pp. 63–68. Walnut Creek: Left Coast Press.
Hart, Michael Anthony
2010   Indigenous Worldviews, Knowledge, and Research: The Development of an Indigenous Research Paradigm. Indigenous Voices in Social Work 1(1):1–16.

Iraola, Roberto

2003 A Primer on the Criminal Provisions of the Native American Graves Protection and Repatriation Act. American Indian Law Review 28(2):431–445.

Johnston, Basil

1975 Ojibway Heritage. New York: Columbia University Press.

Kovach, Margaret

2009 Indigenous Methodologies: Characteristics, Conversations and Contexts. Toronto: University of Toronto Press, Scholarly Publishing Division.

Laluk, Nicholas C.

2017 The Indivisibility of land and mind: Indigenous knowledge and collaborative archaeology within Apache contexts. Social Archaeology 17(1):92–112.

McNally, Michael D.

2009 Honoring Elders: Aging, Authority, and Ojibwe Religion. New York: Columbia University Pres.

Medicine, Bea

2001 Oral History as Truth: Validity in Recent Court Cases. *In* Learning to be an Anthropologist and Remaining "Native." Sue-Ellen Jacobs, ed. pp. 312–316. Urbana: University of Illinois Press.

Murray, Tim

2011 Archaeologists and Indigenous People: A Maturing Relationship. Annual Review of Anthropology 40:363–378.

Nash, Stephen E., and Chip Colwell

2020 NAGPRA at 30: The Effects of Repatriation. Annual Review of Anthropology 24:225–239.

Nicholas, George

2008 Native Peoples and Archaeology. *In* Encyclopedia of Archaeology. D. Pearsall, ed. pp. 1660–1669. New York: Academic Press.

Nicholas, George, and Nola Markey

2015 Traditional Knowledge, Archaeological Evidence, and Other Ways of Knowing. *In* Material Evidence: Learning from Archaeological Practice. Robert Chapman and Alison Wylie, eds. pp. 287–307. New York: Routledge.

Peacock, Thomas, and Marlene Wisuri

2009 Ojibwe Waasa Inaabidaa: We Look in All Directions. Minnesota Historical St. Paul: Society Press.

Pensley, D. S.

2005 The Native American Graves Protection and Repatriation Act (1990): Where the Native Voice is Missing. Wicazo Sa Review 20(2):37–64.

Qwul'sih'yah'maht (Robina Anne Thomas)

2015 Honoring the Oral Traditions of the Ta't Mustimuxw (Ancestors) through Storytelling. *In* Research as Resistance: Revisiting Critical, Indigenous, and Anti-Oppressive Approaches. 2nd edition. Susan Strega and Lesslie Brown, eds. pp. 177–198. Toronto: Canadian Scholars Press Inc.

Simpson, Leanne Betasamosake

2013   The Gift is in the Making: Anishinaabeg Stories. Winnipeg: Highwater Press.

2014   Land as Pedagogy: Nishnaabeg Intelligence and Rebellious Transformation. Decolonization: Indigeneity, Education, & Society 3(3):1–25.

2017   As We Have Always Done: Indigenous Freedom through Radical Resistance. Minneapolis: University of Minnesota Press.

Smith, Linda Tuhiwai

2012   Decolonizing Methodologies. 2nd edition. London: Zed Books.

Thompson, Ashleigh

2019   Red Lake Ojibwe Foodways and Food Sovereignty: An Analysis. Master's thesis, School of Anthropology, University of Arizona, Tucson, Arizona.

Treuer, Anton

2015   Warrior Nation: A History of the Red Lake Ojibwe. St. Paul: Minnesota Historical Society Press.

Vansina, Jan

1985   Oral Tradition As History. Madison: The University of Wisconsin Press.

Vizenor, Gerald

1999   Manifest Manners: Narratives on Postindian Survivance. Lincoln: Bison Books.

Watkins, Joe

2003   Beyond the Margin: American Indians, First Nations, and Archaeology in North America. American Antiquity 68(2):273–285.

Wilson, Shawn

2008   Research Is Ceremony: Indigenous Research Methods. Winnipeg: Fernwood.

11

Histories within Radiocarbon

CARLTON SHIELD CHIEF GOVER

This chapter outlines how I conducted my MA thesis research at the University of Wyoming. Throughout this chapter, I will mention critiques about my work, how I could have done better, and clarify my data. Unlike the previous authors in this volume, you'll notice that I will not be citing much Indigenous Archaeology theory literature. I was in the University of Wyoming's Anthropology Graduate Program, the only Indigenous archaeology graduate student and the only graduate student working on Plains Village archaeology. I was not exposed to Indigenous Archaeology until my doctoral program at the University of Colorado Boulder.

Background

My MA thesis is titled *Dating Apps in Archaeology: Matching the Archaeological Record with Indigenous Oral Traditions through Glottochronology, Summed Probability Distributions, and Bayesian Statistical Analysis* (Gover 2019). Three hypotheses drove my thesis research:

1. The Chaticks-si-Chaticks (Pawnee) and Sahnish (Arikara) are descendants of the Central Plains tradition and Initial Coalescent Variant populations.
2. Oral tradition accounts of Northern Caddoan migration into the Central Plains from the Southeast of Nebraska are factual.
3. Ethnogenesis of the Chaticks-si-Chaticks (Pawnee) and Sahnish (Arikara) begins in the sixteenth century.

I investigated the relationship between Pawnee and Arikara oral traditions, regarding migration and ethnogenesis, and the archaeological record. The two most critical sources of information for my thesis were Indigenous oral traditions and radiocarbon dates from Dr. Robert Kelly's

National Science Foundation-funded radiocarbon project: "Populating a Radiocarbon Database for North America." Robert Kelly collected all the radiocarbon data through his NSF grant, which are now uploaded to the Canadian Archaeological Radiocarbon Database (CARD). With CARD, you can replicate, and improve upon, my research methodology with your Nation's oral traditions.

My thesis research was rooted in conversations with my dad when we drove all around Wyoming, Montana, and Utah in my youth. In Pawnee society today, it is common knowledge that the Pawnee, Arikara, and Wichita are all related and were once one people. In particular, the Skiri Band of Pawnee and the Arikara were "one people" in the not-so-distant past. If you ask a Skiri, they'll tell you the Arikara split off from them, but if you ask an Arikara, they'll say that the Skiri split off from the Arikara. During my undergraduate program in anthropology, I began looking for articles on Pawnee and Arikara ancestry in the archaeological record, and being unable to find conclusive information, I decided to pursue the research myself as a Master's thesis project.

Since there wasn't an official timestamp or date for when the Pawnee, Arikara, and Wichita diffused in the oral traditions, I did not know where to focus my archaeological investigation in the literature. Initially, I revitalized a Culture History approach. I started with "historic" Pawnee, Arikara, and Wichita material culture, worked my way back in time, and used a comparative ceramic analysis as the foundation of my research to connect archaeological cultures. I had initially intended to work backward through time. I avoided becoming a dedicated ceramicist by taking the following steps in my research:

1. Start with Oral Traditions: Analyze Pawnee and Arikara oral traditions for geographic localities within stories about migration and ethnogenesis.
2. Linguistic Analysis: Investigate glottochronological and impressionistic dates for separation time-depth within the Caddoan Language Family.
3. Investigate the Archaeology: Research Central Plains archaeological cultures' cultural taxonomy and general characteristics. Identify relationships between oral traditions, linguistic analysis, and the archaeological record.
4. Identify Population Trends: Create Summed Probability Distribu-

tions (SPDs) of radiocarbon dates in the Central Plains for the last four thousand years to investigate population trends and migration.

5. Creating Precision in Chronology: Develop Bayesian chronological models for precise chronological ordering of archaeological cultures to identify cultural continuity.

The purpose of this chapter is to provide a methodology for those interested in dating oral traditions and investigating the time-depth separation between populations. Since my MA thesis, I have published work with more robust Bayesian and statistical methods. The data and the code have changed, but the general methodology has not. In the text I reference, I refer to the Nations I investigated with their contemporary names in their language. For brevity and clarity's sake, in this chapter, I use "Pawnee," "Arikara," and "Wichita" rather than "Chaticks-si-Chaticks," "Sahnish," and "Kirikir?i's."

Step 1. Starting with Oral Traditions

Long ago in every city of Pawneeland, when night fell among the earthlodges and the camps, people would gather to tell stories. There would follow long hours of narrative cinematic journeying. Every evening distant stars would waft through the dark above the storytellers of Pawneeland.

(Roger Echo-Hawk 2018:iii)

Oral traditions were the foundation of this research. *Ancient History in the New World: Integrating Oral Traditions and The Archaeological Record in Deep Time* by Roger Echo-Hawk (2000) is a primary source for using Indigenous oral traditions in archaeological research. Roger lives in the greater Denver metro area. During my Master's research at the University of Wyoming, I met with him monthly to discuss my research and his work with oral traditions. Roger is also a citizen of the Pawnee Nation of Oklahoma, and his research continues to investigate and collect Pawnee and Arikara oral traditions.

For my thesis, I collected oral traditions from Pawnee and Arikara sources (Echo-Hawk 2000, 2018; Hyde 1974; Parks 2001a, 2001b; Weltfish 1965; Wood 1955). There was limited literature on Wichita oral traditions, and I had difficulty contacting a representative from the Wichita and Affiliated Tribes to verify the validity of the available literature. Therefore, I did not feel comfortable investigating Wichita oral traditions without the ability to verify the legitimacy of the source material. I did verify Pawnee and Arikara oral traditions source materials with Roger Echo-Hawk, John Michael Knife Chief, Matt Reed, Marti Only-A-Chief, and Herb Adson.

I did not personally conduct archival research. Without Roger Echo-Hawk's (2000, 2018) decades-long investigations into collecting oral traditions, I would not have had access to the information I used for this research. That will not always be the case for other Indigenous Nations to have an accessible library of collected ethnographic accounts.

I investigated accounts that identified places, settlement patterns, and relative chronologies for events in oral traditions. In the thesis, I presented four Arikara and seven Pawnee oral traditions that provide the following relative chronology of migration:

> Both Nations acknowledge a shared origin southeast of the Central Plains along the Missouri and Mississippi Rivers where they were part of the same population in the distant past. An ancestral Sahnish population was the first to splinter off from this ancestral population and migrate into Nebraska and Northern Kansas. An ancestral Skidi population later followed the ancestral Sahnish (Arikara) into Nebraska where they lived together for some time before the Skidi displaced the Sahnish into the Dakotas. Ancestral South Band Chaticks-si-Chaticks (Pawnee) populations, along with the ancestral Kirikir?i's (Wichita), followed the Mississippi River to the Missouri River and migrated into Nebraska at a time when there were only the Skidi residing in the area. War ensued between the Skidi and the South Bands with the victorious South Bands settling in Nebraska and Northern Kansas. (Gover 2019:10–11)

Rivers, such as the Missouri, Mississippi, and Loup, were critical geographic markers for identifying where and when Pawnees and Arikara moved across the Plains. Additionally, one oral tradition noted a change in living structures that were instrumental in identifying connections to archaeological cultures.

> A Skidi oral history states the Skidi Federation was founded along Beaver Creek (also known as Wild Licorice Creek) near Genoa, Nebraska (Echo-Hawk 2018). Before the federation was formed, the people lived in small, scattered hamlets with square-shaped structures;

afterwards, they adopted the circular earthlodge (Echo-Hawk 2018; Hyde 1974). (Gover 2019:9–10)

What the oral traditions lacked in terms of information were dates and times when migrations or changes in living structures occurred. However, the oral tradition provided relative chronological information that I could put in order of occurrence. Still, nothing could provide a period to narrow down my investigation into archaeological cultures I should explore.

I highly advise anyone looking into oral traditions to not only investigate the Nation(s) that is the focus of your work. One of my regrets that I am now correcting is not investigating oral traditions from the Indigenous Nations that were neighbors to the Pawnee and the Arikara. I should have also investigated Ponca, Omaha, Mandan, Hidatsa, Apache, and Ioway oral traditions. Since these Nations were geographical neighbors to the Pawnee and Arikara, they have oral traditions about their history on the Plains and when and where they met ancestral Pawnees and Arikaras. Investigating their oral traditions could provide more information and a more holistic history of the Central Plains before European contact.

Step 2. Linguistic Analysis

Since the Pawnee and Arikara oral traditions did not contain Gregorian calendar dates, I used glottochronological data on the Caddoan Language Family to help me isolate a period to look at in the archaeological record. Linguistic separation should result from population diffusion. Growing up, I was always told that Arikara, Pawnee, and Wichita languages were all in the same language family. Pawnee, Arikara, and Wichita are Northern Caddoan Languages within the Caddoan Language Family (Hyde 1974; Parks 1979, 2001c; Weltfish 1965). With the confirmation that the Pawnee, Arikara, and Wichita languages are related, I investigated the time depths in the separation of each language through glottochronological analyses.

I learned about *glottochronology* in my Linguistic Anthropology Theory course. The final research paper I submitted for the Linguistic Anthropology Theory course became integral to the linguistic section of my thesis. Glottochronology comprises a mathematical formula to calculate the rate of change between languages within a language family (Lees 1953). A few scholars had done glottochronological analyses on the Caddoan Language

160 · Carlton Shield Chief Gover

Table 11.1. "Table 1. Impressionistic and glottochronological dates for time depths of separation of the Caddoan language family (Parks 2001b:85; Parks 1979)" (Gover 2019:12)

Language pair/dialect pair	Swadesh and Weltfish 1955 Glottochronological *Years of separation*	Parks 1979 Glottochronological *Years of separation*	Parks 1979 Impressionistic *Years of separation*
Pawnee-Arikara	500	300	500
Pawnee-Kitsai	-	1,200	1,000–1,200
Arikara-Kitsai	-	1,200	-
Pawnee-Wichita	1,400	1,900	1,200–1,500
Arikara-Wichita	2,000	2,000	-
Kitsai-Wichita	-	1,950	1,200–1,500
Pawnee-Caddo	3,300	-	-
Arikara-Caddo	3,500	-	-
Wichita-Caddo	3,000	-	-
South Band-Skidi	-	-	200–300

Family, and I created a table putting their results together (Parks 1979, 2001c).

Now glottochronology is not perfect. It relies on the incorrect assumption that the rate of language change is constant; it is not (Parks 1979). Identifying that the separation between Pawnee and Arikara was roughly 400 ± 100 years ago (Gover 2019), I focused my archaeological investigation into the past one thousand years.

Step 3. Investigate the Archaeology

The oral traditions provided geographical locations and settlement pattern clues to *where* I should investigate, and the linguistic analysis gave me direction as to *when*. The archaeological cultures that I identified as ancestral to Pawnee and Arikara based on the oral traditions and linguistic data were the Initial Coalescent Variant, Extended Coalescent Variant, the Central Plains tradition, and the Lower Loup Phase. I was not the first archaeologist to postulate the ancestry and relationship between these archaeological cultures (Echo-Hawk 2018, 2000; Johnson 1998, 2007; Krause 2001; Parks 2001a, 2001b; Roper 2006a, 2006b, 2014; Steinacher and Carlson 1998; Zimmerman 1990). Using the information about these archaeo-

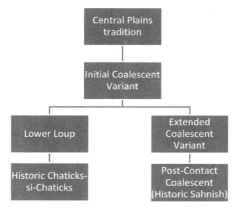

Figure 11.1. "Figure 3. Sequence of archaeological cultures in the Late Prehistoric and Protohistoric Central Plains. In descending order, ancestral cultures to descendant cultures (Echo-Hawk 2000, 2018; Johnson 1998, 2007; Krause 2001; Parks 2001a, 2001c; Roper 2006b; Steinacher and Carlson 1998; Zimmerman 1990)." Gover 2019:18.

logical cultures, I created Figure 11.1 to illustrate the relationship between each archaeological culture.

Then I investigated where each archaeological culture was on the landscape when they existed and their settlement patterns. To synthesize the archaeology background section, I summarized the archaeological cultures on page 16 of my thesis (Gover 2019).

By looking at the time frames for these archaeological cultures, I noticed a significant transition occurring in the fifteenth century. The glottochronology suggested language separation was occurring between the Pawnee and Arikara in the same period. Additionally, the Central Plains tradition has a settlement pattern comprised of square-shaped earthen dwellings in small, semi-permanent hamlets across Nebraska and Kansas (Echo-Hawk 2000; Hedden 1994; Page 2009; Roper 2006a; Scheiber 2006; Shield Chief Gover et al. 2021; Steinacher and Carlson 1998; Wedel 2001, 2010). Following the Central Plains tradition (CPt) was the Initial Coalescent Variant (ICV) culture comprised of large earth lodge villages in Northern Nebraska and South Dakota (Fox 1980; Johnson 1998, 2007; Shield Chief Gover et al. 2021; Tiffany et al. 2011). Even without the radiocarbon analyses, I identified a relationship between the oral traditions, the linguistic analyses, and the archaeological record. I created Table 11.2 to summarize the proposed relationships between the archaeological record and oral traditions.

Table 11.2. "Table 3. Summary of proposed direct relationships of historic tribes to archaeological cultures based on oral tradition accounts. * Demarks Chaticks-si-Chaticks (Pawnee) band level identity" (Gover 2019:22)

Archaeological culture	Phase	Tribal oral tradition suggesting relationship	Evidence for relationship
Central Plains tradition	Itskari	Skidi*	Geographical location, settlement pattern
—	Nebraska	South Bands*	Geographical location
Initial Coalescent Variant	Cambell Creek	Sahnish Skidi*	Geographical location, settlement pattern

To partially test my second hypothesis: *Oral tradition accounts of Northern Caddoan migration into the Central Plains from the Southeast of Nebraska are factual*, I used a "course-grain" approach in summed probability distributions (SPDs) of radiocarbon data to identify population trends in the Central Plains to detect possible migrations.

Step 4. Identify Population Trends

I used Summed Probability Distributions of radiocarbon dates to investigate migration and population trends. Specifically, I used the rcarbon package (Bevan and Crema 2018) in Rstudio (RStudio Team 2015), which is an open-sourced program freely available to anyone. Summed Probability Distribution plots have become frequently used as proxy records for demographic trends in "prehistory" (Buchanan et al. 2008; Fiedel and Kuzmin 2007; Freeman, Baggio, et al. 2018; Freeman, Byers, et al. 2018; Gamble et al. 2005; Kuzmin and Keates 2005; McKechnie 2015; Peros et al. 2010; Shennan and Edinborough 2007; Story and Valastro 1988; Williams 2012). To identify a Northern Caddoan migration into the Central Plains from a Southeastern origin along the Missouri River, I created three SPDs that divided the Central Plains into three sections: Southern, Central, and Northern. These sections were based on state boundaries along a north-to-south orientation. Below is how I explained the selection for my radiocarbon data:

> The dates used in this study span the past four-thousand years. From four-thousand to one-thousand years ago, radiocarbon dates (n = 559) were used regardless of taxonomic designation. For the past one-thousand years, I used only dates (n = 462) from the Central Plains

tradition, Initial Coalescent Variant, Extended Coalescent Variant, and Lower Loup phase sites. I excluded dates from other archaeological cultures for the past one-thousand years to capture the population trend in the central plains as it relates to proposed Northern Caddoan ancestors. The purpose of this analysis is to identify population growth in the central plains around the tenth century AD as a result of Northern Caddoan ancestral populations migrating in.

To examine population trends in the central plains for evidence of migration mentioned in the Northern Caddoan oral histories I divided the dates into three regions: Southern: 502 dates (Kansas and Missouri dates), Central: 347 dates (Nebraska, Iowa, NE Colorado, and S.E. Wyoming dates) and Northern: 172 dates (South Dakota and North Dakota dates). The dates in this study are associated with occupation events and are used as a proxy for population. (Gover 2019:24–25)

There was bias in my data selection because I had already assumed that CPt was ancestrally Northern Caddoan. I should have included all the radiocarbon data for the past 1kya regardless of taxonomic designation. So I wholly ignored Oneota occupations in Nebraska, Kansas, and Iowa, which are contemporaneous to CPt (Shield Chief Gover et al. 2021). But Oneota site locations and the settlement patterns do not align with the Pawnee and Arikara oral traditions, which is why, at the time, I believed they could be excluded. I am correcting this oversight in my current research.

Still, my SPDs (Gover 2019:28) did show a statistically significant population increase in the Central Plains beginning around AD 950 with a general trend northward. The SPDs also show what appears to be a sharp population decline beginning after AD 1250 (Gover 2019:28). In my thesis, I explained this to be the abandonment of Kansas and Nebraska and migration into South Dakota by ancestral Pawnees and Arikara (Gover 2019), which I believe is partially the case. I later realized that the SPDs also show a change in settlement pattern. The SPDs do not show population counts; they illustrate trends in human activity through radiocarbon data. I explained the math behind my Rstudio code and provided the codes I ran, so please refer to the thesis to understand the values. But a radiocarbon date from a CPt hamlet does not represent the same amount of people as a radiocarbon date from an ICV town. So as CPt populations transition into ICV lifeways, a radiocarbon date changes from representing a dozen or so people in CPt to hundreds if not thousands of people in ICV. Therefore, the

164 · Carlton Shield Chief Gover

"decline" shown in my SPDs beginning in the thirteenth century AD also shows the transition from CPt to ICV, which begins in the early 1300s and does not necessarily illustrate the region's abandonment. Therefore, it is critical to understand the archaeology behind the radiocarbon data when interpreting SPD plots.

Still, even though the SPDs could demonstrate population trends in the Central Plains, they were too coarse in time scale and unrelated to specific archaeological cultures. I could argue that there was a migration into the Central Plains from a southerly origin. Still, I needed precision in the chronological ordering of my investigated archaeological cultures to identify cultural continuity.

Step 5. Creating Precision in Chronology

To identify cultural continuity between archaeological cultures, I used Bayesian statistical analysis of radiocarbon data to create a precise chronology of archaeological cultures. For my thesis, I used the OxCal v4.3 program (Bronk Ramsey 2009), which used the IntCal13 calibration curve (Reimer et al. 2013). OxCal is another open-sourced platform that is freely available. OxCal has been updated since the approval of my thesis, and there is a new calibration curve: IntCal20 (Reimer et al. 2020). One of the cool things about OxCal is that the creator of the program moderates a Google Group called "OxCal," where you can ask for assistance in developing and running your Bayesian models.

Bayesian is a powerful tool and is especially predisposed to approaches in Indigenous archaeology because of its ability to incorporate non-quantitative archaeological data into a model (Hill et al. 2018), such as oral traditions. Bayesian statistical methods have been specifically produced for archaeological research communities, such as OxCal, over the past three decades (Bronk Ramsey 2008, 2009; Buck and Meson 2015). Also, the literature is specifically written to introduce scholars to the Bayesian methods in archaeology (Bronk Ramsey 2008; Buck and Juarez 2017; Buck and Meson 2015). However, the power of Bayesian statistics is that it allows scholars to collate information from an array of sources such as expert opinion, prior knowledge, and prior scientific data (Bronk Ramsey 2008, 2009; Buck and Juarez 2017; Buck and Meson 2015). OxCal is a tool well-suited for incorporating Indigenous knowledge into Bayesian statistical modeling.

I divided each archaeological culture into its taxonomic phases for my Bayesian models. I did this because each "phase" within an archaeological culture is geographically bounded within Great Plains' taxonomy. The Great Plains archaeological taxonomy is a mess, so I understand if you're not a plains archaeologist and are confused by "phases" being geographically bounded.

By separating radiocarbon data by individual phases, I interpreted the directionality of the Central Plains' ancestral Pawnee and Arikara populations. The scale of the SPDs was just too great to see precisely where populations were coming from. Still, with a Bayesian chronology, I could more precisely associate where and when people were moving across the landscape. The following is how I explained my model and my data selection:

> For my model (Appendix 2), I analyzed 392 radiocarbon dates from 151 archaeological sites that belonged to Central Plains tradition phases, Coalescent Variant phases, or Lower Loup Phase archaeological sites. The Lower Loup Phase is the archaeological culture understood to represent protohistoric Chaticks-si-Chaticks populations (Roper 2000) and Post-Contact Coalescent phases are historic Sahnish archaeological cultures (Johnson 2007). The St. Helena Phase radiocarbon record consists of only one usable date and therefore the phase was omitted from this analysis. Table 4 illustrates the distribution of radiocarbon dates used for my analysis by archaeological culture and Figure 8 illustrates the distribution of radiocarbon dates used for this analysis geographically.
>
> I organized my model (Appendix 2) so that radiocarbon dates belonging to a specific archaeological phase are grouped as single sequence. Archaeological phases in the late prehistoric Central Plains are primarily determined by pottery types that have temporal and spatial boundaries (Grange 1968; Johnson 1998, 2007; Krause 2001; Parks 2001a, 2001b; Roper 2006a, 2006b; Steinacher and Carlson 1998; Zimmerman 1990). This basis for archaeological phase taxonomy makes pottery typologies one of my two main informative priors that I use to construct my model (Figure 9). Sequences in my model are constructed to be "overlapping" so that each phase is treated independent from one another. This was done due to the archaeological evidence of taxonomic phases overlapping in time.

The temporal dynamic between archaeological phases constitutes my second informative prior for the construction of my Bayesian statistical model (Figure 9). For my model twelve "sequences" were constructed: Nebraska (CPt), Steed-Kisker (CPt), Smokey Hill (CPt), Solomon River (CPt), Upper Republican (CPt), Itskari (CPt), Anoka (ICV), Arzberger (ICV), Cambell Creek (ICV), Extended Coalescent, Lower Loup, and Post-Contact Coalescent. The models' sequences are constrained by "start" and "end" Boundaries that are used in calculating the start and end of a sequence (Bronk Ramsey 2009). "Start" and "End" Boundaries are based on the calibration of individual radiocarbon dates belonging to a sequence (Bronk Ramsey 2009). This function allows me to identify when archaeological phases appeared and disappeared from the archaeological record. (Gover 2019:32–34)

Figure 11.2 and Table 11.3 show the results of the Bayesian analysis for my MA thesis. Figure 11.2, which is Figure 9 in my thesis (Gover 2019:36), does not effectively illustrate the temporal relationship between archaeological cultures and their phases. I should have created three figures: one comparing archaeological cultures with one another, that is, CPt, ICV, ECV, and Lower Loup phase, the second just comparing CPt phases, and the third just comparing ICV phases. Doing so would have made it easier to see the temporal relationship between and within archaeological cultures. Table 11.3, which is Table 5 in my thesis (Gover 2019:37), demonstrates these relationships much better. However, the table lacks the sequential ordering of start and end times between archaeological cultures demonstrated in the figure.

The Bayesian models showed that there was, in fact, a migration of CPt populations from the Southeast into the Central Plains. It also illustrated cultural continuity between CPt, ICV, ECV, and Lower Loup. These were archaeological cultures in that the Pawnee and Arikara oral traditions demonstrated a relationship. The Bayesian analysis supported all three of my hypotheses:

(1) Northwestward migration of ancestral Caddoans into the Central Plains.
(2) Cultural transformation from Central Plains tradition into Initial Coalescent Variant.
(3) Ethnogenesis of the Chaticks-si-Chaticks (Pawnee) and Sahnish (Arikara) begins by the sixteenth century.

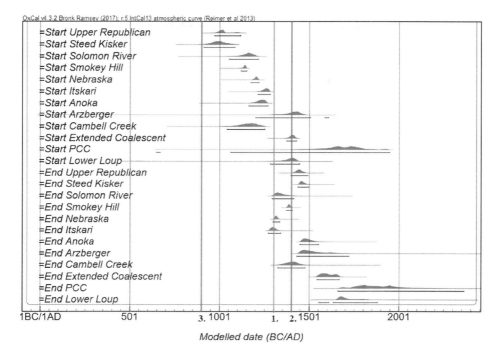

Figure 11.2. "Figure 9. OxCal produced Start and End Boundaries of Central Plains tradition (Upper Republican, Steed-Kisker, Solomon River, Smoky Hill, Nebraska, Itskari), Initial Coalescent Variant (Anoka, Arzberger, Cambell Creek), Extended Coalescent Variant, Post-Contact Coalescent Variant (PCC), and Lower Loup Phases. Indices:Amodel=66.5, Aoverall=96.5. Purple line is 900 AD; the blue line is 1300 AD, and the red line is 1400 AD. Bars below probability distributions indicate 95.4% probability range after the application of Bayesian statistical analysis (Hill et al. 2018). Radiocarbon data for this analysis is listed in Appendix 1, the model used to produce this analysis is shown in Appendix 2, and the model table is shown in Appendix 3." Gover 2019:36.

Conclusion

I demonstrated that Pawnee and Arikara oral traditions were accurate and that they explained the change in the archaeological record that the material culture could not do alone. Using quantitative methods and science, I did *science* with a capital "S."

Oral traditions provided the *why*, whereas archaeology provided the *when* and *how*. Both were equally useful in giving the *where*. I treated the oral traditions like any other historical document, just as Roger advocated for over twenty years ago (Echo-Hawk 2000). The statistical approaches

168 · Carlton Shield Chief Gover

Table 11.3. "Table 5. Posterior density estimates for the chronology of late prehistoric archaeological cultures in the Central Plains." (Gover 2019:37)

Archaeological culture	Phase	Posterior density estimate date range for START BOUNDARY (Cal. A.D. at 95.4% probability)	Posterior density estimate date range for END BOUNDARY (Cal. A.D. at 95.4% probability)
Central Plains tradition	Upper Republican	970–1120	1395–1490
Central Plains tradition	Steed-Kisker	905–1085	1435–1500
Central Plains tradition	Solomon River	1050–1220	1290–1415
Central Plains tradition	Smoky Hill	1115–1155	1370–1410
Central Plains tradition	Nebraska	1170–1220	1295–1380
Central Plains tradition	Itskari	1210–1285	1270–1350
Initial Coalescent Variant	Anoka	1160–1270	1445–1555
Initial Coalescent Variant	Arzberger	1190–1610	1430–1730
Initial Coalescent Variant	Cambell Creek	1035–1250	1320–1480
Extended Coalescent Variant	-	1370–1430	1545–1670
Post-Contact Coalescent Variant	-	645–1950	1655–2625
Lower Loup phase	-	1275–1450	1550–1880

I used, the glottochronology, Summed Probability Distributions, and Bayesian Statistical Analysis, alone could not fully explain the changes and events in the Central Plains over the past one thousand years. But all three approaches, combined with the archaeological data and oral traditions, created a more holistic understanding of the past. One that prioritized Indigenous knowledge of the past.

However, these Bayesian approaches in creating Indigenous chronologies can have a much broader impact than just creating a more holistic understanding of the past. This approach can benefit Tribal governments and Tribal cultural resources divisions in settling land claims and NAGPRA repatriation cases. Through this approach, multiple Nations can demonstrate ties to traditional territories without negating each other's Tribal sovereignty and connections to the land. I see this approach as offering a practical methodology for Indigenous Nations to project their sovereignty over their history, traditional knowledge, and ancestral homelands in deep time.

References

Bronk Ramsey, Christopher

2008 Radiocarbon Dating: Revolutions in Understanding. Archaeometry 50(2):249–275. DOI:10.1111/j.1475-4754.2008.00394.x.

2009 Bayesian Analysis of Radiocarbon Dates. Radiocarbon 51(01):337–360. DOI:10.1017/S0033822200033865.

Buchanan, B., M. Collard, and K. Edinborough

2008 Paleoindian Demography and the Extraterrestrial Impact Hypothesis. Proceedings of the National Academy of Sciences 105(33):11651–11654. DOI:10.1073/pnas.0803762105.

Buck, Caitlin E., and Miguel Juarez

2017 Bayesian Radiocarbon Modelling for Beginners. arXiv:1704.07141 [stat]:1–27.

Buck, Caitlin E., and Bo Meson

2015 On Being a Good Bayesian. World Archaeology 47(4):567–584. DOI:10.1080/00438243.2015.1053977.

Crema, E. R., and A. Bevan

2021 Inference From Large Sets of Radiocarbon Dates: Software and Methods. Radiocarbon 63:23–39. https://dx.doi.org/10.1017/RDC.2020.95.

Echo-Hawk, Roger

2000 Ancient History in the New World: Integrating Oral Traditions and the Archaeological Record in Deep Time. American Antiquity 65(2):267–290.

2018 The Enchanted Mirror: Ancient Pawneeland. CreateSpace Independent Publishing Platform. DOI:10.2307/2694059.

Fiedel, Stuart J, and Yaroslav V Kuzmin

2007 Radiocarbon Date Frequency as an Index of Intensity of Paleolithic Occupation of Siberia: Did Humans React Predictably to Climate Oscillations? Radiocarbon 49(02):741–756. DOI:10.1017/S0033822200042624.

Fox, Greg

1980 A Review of the Initial Coalescent Variant. The Nebraska Anthropologist 5:1–17.

Freeman, Jacob, Jacopo A. Baggio, Erick Robinson, David A. Byers, Eugenia Gayo, Judson Byrd Finley, Jack A. Meyer, Robert L. Kelly, and John M. Anderies

2018 Synchronization of Energy Consumption by Human Societies Throughout the Holocene. Proceedings of the National Academy of Sciences 115(40):9962–9967. DOI:10.1073/pnas.1802859115.

Freeman, Jacob, David A. Byers, Erick Robinson, and Robert L. Kelly

2018 Culture Process and the Interpretation of Radiocarbon Data. Radiocarbon 60(2):453–467. DOI:10.1017/RDC.2017.124.

Gamble, Clive, William Davies, Paul Pettitt, Lee Hazelwood, and Martin Richards

2005 The Archaeological and Genetic Foundations of the European Population during the Late Glacial: Implications for Agricultural Thinking. Cambridge Archaeological Journal 15(02):193–223. DOI:10.1017/S0959774305000107.

Gover, Carlton

2019 Dating Apps in Archaeology: Matching the Archaeological Record with Indigenous Oral Traditions through Glottochronology, Summed Probability Distributions, and Bayesian Statistical Analysis. Laramie, Wyoming: University of Wyoming.

Grange, Roger T.

1968   Pawnee and Lower Loup Pottery. Lincoln, NE: Nebraska State Historical Society.

Hedden, John G.

1994   Riley Cord Roughened Ceramic Variation from Ten Smoky Hill Sites in North-Central Kansas. Central Plains Archaeology 4:27–42.

Hill, Matthew E., Margaret E. Beck, Stacey Lengyel, Sarah J. Trabert, and Mary J. Adair

2018   A Hard Time to Date: The Scott County Pueblo (14SC1) and Puebloan Residents of the High Plains. American Antiquity 83(1):54–74. DOI:10.1017/aaq.2017.60.

Hyde, George

1974   The Pawnee Indians. Norman, OK: University of Oklahoma Press.

Johnson, Craig M.

1998   The Coalescent Tradition. In Archaeology of the Great Plains. W. Raymond Wood, eds. pp. 308–344. Lawrence, KS: University of Kansas Press.

2007   A Chronology of Middle Missouri Plains Village Sites. Smithsonian Contributions to Anthropology 47:1–346. DOI:10.5479/si.00810223.47.1.

Krause, Richard A.

2001   Plains Village Tradition: Coalescent. In Handbook of North American Indians: Plains, vol. 13. William C. Sturtevant, ed. 196–206. Washington, D.C.: Smithsonian Institution.

Kuzmin, Yaroslav V., and Susan G. Keates

2005   Dates Are Not Just Data: Paleolithic Settlements Patterns in Siberia Derived from Radiocarbon Records. American Antiquity 70(4):773–789.

Lees, Robert B.

1953   The Basis of Glottochronology. Language 29(2):113–127. DOI:10.2307/410164.

McKechnie, Iain

2015   Indigenous Oral History and Settlement Archaeology in Barkley Sound, Western Vancouver Island. B.C. Studies 187:193–228.

Page, Michael K.

2009   The High Plains Upper Republican Reconsidered: Stylistic and Petrographic Analyses of Central Plains Tradition Ceramics from the High Plains. Laramie, Wyoming: University of Wyoming.

Parks, Douglas R.

1979   The Northern Caddoan Languages: Their Subgrouping and Time Depths. Nebraska History 18:80–93.

2001a   Pawnee. In Handbook of North American Indians: Plains, vol. 13. William C. Sturtevant, ed. pp. 515–547. Washington, D.C.: Smithsonian Institution.

2001b   Arikara. In Handbook of North American Indians: Plains, vol. 13. William C. Sturtevant, ed. 365–390. Washington, D.C.: Smithsonian Institution.

2001c   Caddoan Languages. In Handbook of North American Indians: Plains, vol. 13. William C. Sturtevant, ed. 80–93. Washington, D.C.: Smithsonian Institution.

Peros, Matthew C., Samuel E. Munoz, Konrad Gajewski, and André E. Viau

2010 Prehistoric Demography of North America Inferred from Radiocarbon Data. Archaeological Science 37(3):656–664. DOI:10.1016/j.jas.2009.10.029.

Reimer, Paula J., William E. N. Austin, Edouard Bard, Alex Bayliss, Paul G. Blackwell, Christopher Bronk Ramsey, Martin Butzin, Hai Cheng, R. Lawrence Edwards, Michael Friedrich, Pieter M. Grootes, Thomas P. Guilderson, Irka Hajdas, Timothy J. Heaton, Alan G. Hogg, Konrad A. Hughen, Bernd Kromer, Sturt W. Manning, Raimund Muscheler, Jonathan G. Palmer, Charlotte Pearson, Johannes van der Plicht, Ron W. Reimer, David A. Richards, E. Marian Scott, John R. Southon, Christian S. M. Turney, Lukas Wacker, Florian Adolphi, Ulf Büntgen, Manuela Capano, Simon M. Fahrni, Alexandra Fogtmann-Schulz, Ronny Friedrich, Peter Köhler, Sabrina Kudsk, Fusa Miyake, Jesper Olsen, Frederick Reinig, Minoru Sakamoto, Adam Sookdeo, and Sahra Talamo

2020 The IntCal20 Northern Hemisphere Radiocarbon Age Calibration Curve (0–55 cal kBP). Radiocarbon 62(4):725–757. DOI:10.1017/RDC.2020.41.

Reimer, Paula J., Edouard Bard, Alex Bayliss, J. Warren Beck, Paul G. Blackwell, Christopher Bronk Ramsey, Caitlin E. Buck, Hai Cheng, R. Lawrence Edwards, Michael Friedrich, Pieter M. Grootes, Thomas P. Guilderson, Haflidi Haflidason, Irka Hajdas, Christine Hatté, Timothy J. Heaton, Dirk L. Hoffmann, Alan G. Hogg, Konrad A. Hughen, K. Felix Kaiser, Bernd Kromer, Sturt W. Manning, Mu Niu, Ron W. Reimer, David A. Richards, E. Marian Scott, John R. Southon, Richard A. Staff, Christian S. M. Turney, and Johannes van der Plicht

2013 IntCal13 and Marine13 Radiocarbon Age Calibration Curves 0–50,000 Years cal BP. Radiocarbon 55(4):1869–1887. DOI:10.2458/azu_js_rc.55.16947.

Roper, Donna C.

2000 Lower Loup Phase Pottery in Great Bend Aspect Sites. Plains Anthropologist 45(172):169–177. DOI:10.1080/2052546.2000.11932001.

2006a The Central Plains Tradition. *In* Kansas Archaeology. Robert J. Hoard and William E. Banks, eds. pp. 105–132. Lawrence, KS: University Press of Kansas.

2006b The Pawnee in Kansas. *In* Kansas Archaeology. Robert J. Hoard and William E. Banks, eds. pp. 233–247. Lawrence, KS: University Press of Kansas.

2014 Assessing the Radiocarbon Age Determinations Dataset and Revising the Chronology for the Central Plains Tradition. Central Plains Archaeology 14(1):17–64.

RStudio Team

2015 RStudio: Integrated Development for R. RStudio, Inc.

Scheiber, Laura L.

2006 The Late Prehistoric on the High Plains of Western Kansas: High Plains Upper Republican and Dismal River. *In* Kansas Archaeology. Robert J. Hoard and William E. Banks, eds. pp. 133–150. Lawrence, KS: University Press of Kansas.

Shennan, Stephen, and Kevan Edinborough

2007 Prehistoric population history: from the Late Glacial to the Late Neolithic in Central and Northern Europe. Archaeological Science 34(8):1339–1345. DOI:10.1016/j.jas.2006.10.031.

Shield Chief Gover, Carlton, Douglas B. Bamforth, and Kristen Carlson

2021   Bayesian Analysis of the Chronology of the Lynch Site (25BD1) and Comparisons to the Central Plains Tradition and Central Plains Oneota. Plains Anthropologist 66(259):1–25. DOI:10.1080/00320447.2021.1895514.

Steinacher, Terry L., and Gayle F. Carlson

1998   The Central Plains Tradition. *In* Archaeology of the Great Plains. W. Raymond Wood, ed. pp. 235–268. Lawrence, KS: University of Kansas Press.

Story, Dee Ann, and S. Valastro

1988   Radiocarbon Dating and the George C. Davis Site, Texas. Field Archaeology 4(1):63–89.

Tiffany, Joseph A., Austin A. Buhta, L. Adrien Hannus, and Jason M. Kruse

2011   New Insights into the Anoka Phase: Initial Results from the Work at the Lynch (25BD1), Anoka (25BD2/201), Hostert (25BD16), and Mohr (25BD139) Sites, Boyd County, Nebraska. Central Plains Archaeology 13(1):1–40.

Wedel, Waldo

2001   Plains Village Tradition: Central. *In* Handbook of North American Indians: Plains, vol. 13. William C. Sturtevant, ed. pp. 173–185. Washington, D.C.: Smithsonian Institution.

2010[1936] An Introduction to Pawnee Archaeology. United States Government Printing Office. Reprint. Whitefish, MT: Kessinger Legacy Reprints, LLC.

Weltfish, Gene

1965   The Lost Universe. Lincoln: University of Nebraska Press.

Williams, Alan N.

2012   The Use of Summed Radiocarbon probability Distributions in Archaeology: A Review of Methods. Archaeological Science 39(3):578–589. DOI:10.1016/j.jas.2011.07.014.

Wood, W. Raymond

1955   Historical and Archeological Evidence: For Arikara Visits to the Central Plains. Plains Anthropologist 2(4):27–40. DOI:10.1080/2052546.1955.11908186.

Zimmerman, Larry J.

1990   Archaeological Evidence for Pawnee Claims for Human Remains and Burial Offerings in the Central Plains. Native American Rights Fund.

Afterword

Archaeology as a Manifestation of Sovereignty, Self-Determination, and Activism

JOE WATKINS

> Knowledge is power.
> Sir Francis Bacon (1561–1626)

> Where there is great power there is great responsibility.
> Winston Churchill (1874–1965)

I chose the two opening quotes to frame my discussion. If knowledge is power, and if with power comes responsibility, then it follows that those with knowledge have a responsibility derived from that knowledge. In archaeology, those with knowledge have a responsibility to teach the generations to follow that they should apply their knowledge in ways that can empower communities whose heritage is studied or investigated. Archaeology, as a branch of social science that is self-described as a quest for knowledge, must also accept the responsibility associated with the knowledge obtained and created.

In the past, archaeology was self-satisfied with its role in creating knowledge about the past. That knowledge rarely benefited anyone beyond the scientific disciplines associated with the mining of archaeological sites for the artifacts held within the ground, the knowledge held within the artifacts, and the ways that the knowledge is (or is not) disseminated. Often it was the archaeologist (and/or the museum or university) that benefited from the research in terms of academic "capital"—publications, tenure, professorships, and promotion. Too often the archaeological site was decimated, the artifacts carted away to a storage facility or perhaps displayed in a museum setting, and the community left wondering what happened to everything that was taken away.

As we continue to move forward, more and more practitioners of archaeology are no longer satisfied with maintaining the status quo, but rather are seeking new ways to integrate western science and traditional sciences in ways that are beneficial to the communities whose heritage is at stake. This volume is a shining example of newer ways that practitioners have and can utilize different experiences in bringing these somewhat disparate sciences together in such a way that others can understand the subtleties of the fields.

When I wrote *Indigenous Archaeology* (Watkins 2000), I was naive enough to think that it was possible to influence the practices of mainstream archaeologists. I recognize that there were many archaeologists who saw some benefit in working with American Indians/Native Americans here in the United States, First Nations in Canada, and other Indigenous peoples throughout the world. I freely took the term *Indigenous Archaeology* from a footnote in George Nicholas and Thomas Andrews's 1997 volume on Canadian archaeology's relationship with First Nations (1997:3, note 5). To me it was the best way forward—to help craft a newer archaeology in such a way that Indigenous people could take advantage of the processes and practices already available to enhance their own self-determination and sovereignty. I can't recall whether I had intended Indigenous Archaeology to be an activist archaeology, for that was not my personality at that time, but it has become more so in recent years.

Today I am more than seventy years old and have been doing archaeology for more than fifty years. Looking backward, I see the stutter-steps in my career. All too often I heard from others about how glad they would be when I would be able to "really open up" on the discipline and tell its practitioners what they were doing wrong in hopes that they would better understand the impacts they have on living people throughout the world. But that person is not me, and it is not within my personality to publicly criticize or to draw negative attention to others. I realize there were probably times when I should have stopped justifying other people's actions or the histories that were being portrayed.

I have been able to write convincingly about the need for Indigenous Archaeology, as well as some of the benefits of it, but I have rarely written about the need for archaeology to be more activist in its focus. I have allowed others to take my words and turn them into pathways forward or to take my words and crafted pathways around the minefield that is archaeology.

As others have noted, perhaps the most encompassing definition of Indigenous Archaeology has been offered (and updated) by George Nicholas as

> an expression of archaeological theory and practice in which the discipline intersects with Indigenous values, knowledge, practices, ethics, and sensibilities, and through collaborative and community-originated or -directed projects, and related critical perspectives. Indigenous archaeology seeks to (1) make archaeology more representative of, responsible to, and relevant for Indigenous communities; (2) redress real and perceived inequalities in the practice of archaeology; and (3) inform and broaden the understanding and interpretation of the archaeological record through the incorporation of Aboriginal worldviews, histories, and science. (Nicholas 2008:1660)

Numerous other authors, including Atalay (2006, 2012), Colwell-Chanthaphonh (2009, 2012), Ferguson (1996), Nicholas (2010, 2014), Silliman (2010), and Wat-kins (2000, 2003) have written about how Indigenous Archaeology can be a way of making archaeology more relevant to contemporary American Indian and other Indigenous communities. Edited volumes approaching the topic include Colwell-Chanthaphonh and Ferguson (2007), Kerber (2006), Silliman (2008), and Smith and Wobst (2005). Colwell-Chanthaphonh et al. (2010, 233), wrote that "Indigenous archaeology is the attempt to introduce and incorporate different perspectives of the past into the study and management of heritage—to accommodate the diverse values for archaeology that exist in our pluralist democracy."

Indigenous Archaeology is great—as far as it goes and so long as its practitioners do not see themselves as the only good practitioners. One doesn't have to be "Indigenous" to be an Indigenous archaeologist, and there is nothing inherently "better" about the archaeology an Indigenous person does as opposed to the work of an archaeologist whose "heart" is in the "right" place (senso Supernant et al. 2020). To think otherwise is to fall victim to the "racialist archaeology" that Roger Echo-Hawk warned us about (Echo-Hawk 2010).

Indigenous Archaeology as Sovereignty

Historically, the relationship between the federal government and the tribes is fraught with legality and uncertainty. Looking at American policies toward tribes, most of them were based on the policies put in place by the British colonial government. At the time of United States victory over Great Britain in the Revolutionary War of 1775–1783, the tribes were much stronger than the fledgling United States of America. Once the federal government took over economic control of the tribes from the various states, the power differential shifted rapidly. In 1803, Thomas Jefferson felt it beneficial for the federal government to encourage various Indian Nations to purchase goods on credit, which would likely lead them to fall into debt. He felt that the tribes could relieve their debt through the sale of lands to the government, and the country could grow in that manner. In 1830, Andrew Jackson signed the Indian Removal Act, thereby initiating removal policies to get the tribes out of the way so that American farmers could take over the land.

John Marshall, in three supreme court cases—Johnson v. McIntosh (1823); Cherokee Nation v. Georgia (1831); and Worcester v. Georgia (1832)—defined the status of American Indians in federal relationships that govern federal interactions with the tribes as one between a guardian and its ward. As such, Indian tribes are recognized by the United States government as "domestic dependent nations," each retaining sovereign powers, except as overtly divested to the United States (see d'Errico 2000, for a more detailed discussion of the history of the concept of Tribal sovereignty in Indian law). In this regard, Indian sovereignty is a key issue defining the interaction between Native Americans and archaeologists on Indian-owned or controlled land. Indian sovereignty means that all archaeological research undertaken on Indian land requires the approval of the Tribal government, and that a tribe retains the right of ownership of all cultural materials found on their land. It also means that tribes may exercise stronger control on what (or if) archaeological research occurs on their lands.

Indigenous communities should take advantage of what archaeology can offer, and Indigenous archaeology can give communities the tools to better integrate local need with regional and national programs. Here in the United States, the heritage preservation program that has the furthest reach is operated under the auspices of the National Historic Preservation Act of 1966 (as amended).

I have written elsewhere about United States historic preservation laws and their impact on American Indian tribes (Watkins 2003; Watkins and Ferguson 2005; Watkins 2009), but I recognize the importance of repeating a bit of it here for newer students of American archaeology. In the

United States, it is the status of land ownership or the involvement of the federal government in a project that determines which (or even whether) cultural resources protection laws apply. Federal laws only apply to projects that occur on federal or Tribal land, if there is federal funding involved in a project, or if a federal permit of any kind is required for the project to occur. The federal government does not have any jurisdiction on privately funded projects on private land unless a federal permit is required; otherwise, project proponents are not required to follow federal laws regarding cultural resources.

As mentioned above, the primary law that relates to the federal historic preservation management is the National Historic Preservation Act (hereafter NHPA) of 1966, as amended. It mandates consultation, which is defined in the federal regulations that govern the NHPA as "the process of seeking, discussing, and considering the views of other participants, and where feasible, seeking agreement with them regarding matters" arising in the compliance process (King 1998:94) at various stages in the historic preservation compliance process. While tribes are not the only communities with which federal agencies must consult, they have stronger voices in the matter because of their special relationship with the federal government.

In 1992, amendments to the NHPA authorized Indian tribes to develop Tribal Historic Preservation Offices (THPOs) and assume the historic preservation functions that are otherwise the responsibility of a State Historic Preservation Office (SHPO) regarding projects on their land. Tribal groups have different reasons for accepting these responsibilities (Anyon et al. 2000; Ferguson 2000), but for many tribes, the assumption of these responsibilities is an issue of Tribal sovereignty since it removes a state official from the decision-making process managing heritage resources on Tribal lands and reinforces the government-to-government relationship between the United States and Indian Nations. As of December 2021, the National Park Service listed 198 THPOs (out of 574 federally recognized tribes as of January 2021). However, because some tribes are not formally a part of the Park Service program, the National Association of Tribal Historic Preservation Officers (NATHPO) reported 207 Indian tribes with THPOs (NATHPO 2022).

Assumption of these historic preservation functions by Tribal programs, however, may prove both detrimental and beneficial. The assumption of such duties does allow the tribe to fully participate within the established federal historic preservation system, but it forces the tribe to adhere to federally defined concepts such as "mitigation," "personnel qualifications," and "significance." Finally, programs for tribes without a large land base (such as tribes in Oklahoma where there are no reservations and only fractionated or minimal amounts of Tribally owned land) are severely underfunded and must try to deal with floods of consultation requests.

In addition to the outside demands placed on the Tribal Historic Preservation Offices, the tribes within the National Park Service program essentially are bound by the disconnect between governmental compliance procedures aimed primarily at physical locations and Tribal concerns for other aspects of their culture that they wish to protect. For example, repatriation actions under the Native American Graves Protection and Repatriation Act (NAGPRA) are entirely separate from and outside of the protection of cultural resources covered by the federal preservation system. Likewise, Tribal concerns about protecting other areas of their heritage (such as languages, Tribal dances, Tribal songs, and so forth) are excluded from the NHPA. Tribes, by virtue of the federal regulations, must organize their preservation program according to western scientific and legal concepts. This format tends to discount Indigenous perspectives of the past rather than foreground it, prevents an equal relationship between preservation "partners," and continues to privilege the archaeologist rather than the cultural practitioner.

One other important point to consider, is that not all "American Indian/Native American" communities are considered by the federal government to be equal. I put the American Indian/Native America in quotes above because there are some groups who do not have the same level of consideration as others—non-federally recognized groups do not have the government-to-government relations that federally recognized groups have.

"Non-federally recognized" means that the group, which identifies itself as a Native American community, is not eligible to receive services from the Bureau of Indian Affairs based on its status as an American Indian tribe. "Federally recognized tribe" is defined as "American Indian and Alaska Native entities legally recognized by the United States Federal government and eligible to receive services from the United States Bureau of Indian Affairs" or "any tribe on the List of Indian Entities Recognized and Eligible to Receive Services from the United States Bureau of Indian Affairs, published annually in the Federal Register" (see https://www.lawinsider.com/dictionary/federally-recognized-tribe). The list published in the Federal Register on January 29, 2021, currently contains the names of 574 federally recognized tribes.

Non-federally recognized groups seeking to gain recognition by the Bureau of Indian Affairs (BIA) must follow a difficult process. The BIA published final rules in 1978 that provided procedures that groups had to meet to secure federal Tribal acknowledgment. There are seven criteria, but four have proven troublesome for most groups to prove. The four require that the group demonstrate long-standing historical community, that outsiders have identified them as Indians, that the group has maintained political authority over its members, and that the members of the groups can demonstrate descent from an historical tribe. While Congress and the federal courts can confer federal recognition, these avenues have been increasingly difficult since 1978. Groups seeking federal recognition are required to submit detailed petitions to the BIA's Office of Federal Acknowledgment (https://www.bia.gov/as-ia/ofa). On average it takes over ten years for a review of petitions, and quite often the petitioners have to make multiple corrections and additions to their petitions in the hopes of gaining federal recognition.

This does not mean that archaeologists should only work with federally recognized tribes. On the contrary, archaeologists should communicate and listen to all communities that wish to be involved in the preservation process. Communities will always be "stakeholders," but some have a different level of recognition within the federal preservation system.

"Sovereignty" does not reside solely with federally recognized tribes. All communities have sovereignty insomuch as they choose the level of interaction it desires to maintain, request, or demand from archaeologists working with them. Often it is a matter of negotiation between the parties involved in working with the heritage under consideration, but it is always a community's right to be involved in the study of its history.

Indigenous Archaeology as Self-Determination

As Sonya Atalay indicated, "[m]anagement of one's own cultural heritage is an important part of self-determination and sovereignty" (2010:48). Archaeology has the possibilities of contributing to the self-determination of Indigenous entities as well as individual Indigenous people. What is "self-determination" and how can archaeology strengthen it? Merriam-Webster's online dictionary defines self-determination as "free choice of one's own acts or states without external compulsion" or "determination by the people of a territorial unit of their own future political status" (Merriam-Webster, n.d.).

Archaeologists—through archaeology's techniques, its ability to flesh out stories derived from material culture, and its possibilities to give voice to past inhabitants—can help breathe life back into materials left behind by past cultures, but archaeology cannot do it without archaeologists who are amenable to doing so. Archaeology without communication or collaboration is sterile and should leave no viable offspring, whereas archaeology conducted with respect for community, trust between all parties involved, and collaborative research designs can lead to an expanded understanding of previous cultural manifestations.

Charles Riggs writes that "What was once an instrument of oppression now seems to me to be an instrument of self-determination" (Riggs 2017). He believes that archaeology can help Indigenous groups protect their cultural heritage so that they do not have to continue to experience "oppression by means of the erasure of cultural heritage" (Riggs 2017).

For Indigenous communities, Indigenous Archaeology, with its community-centered focus, can allow communities to create their own roads forward. The establishment of "deep time" to the satisfaction of others reaffirms the time-depth associated with oral histories, societal culture, and the power of resilience. That is what self-determination is—resilience in the face of dominant cultures that try to minimize, homogenize, and assimilate.

As an example, the Pawnee Nation Oklahoma used archaeology to expand what might be considered its "aboriginal homeland" as well as to extend "Pawnee identity" further back into the archaeological record. Their work to get the Salinas Burial Pit (a "tourist attraction" in Kansas) closed and the human remains and associated funerary artefacts reburied in 1990 (Watkins 2000:105–10) created a precedence establishing their relationships with that geographical area. Furthermore, the Pawnee received human remains and associated funerary objects from the collections of the Colorado Historical Society in 2002 which expanded the Pawnee's reach back in time as human remains associated with the Early Ceramic period or Plains Woodland (ca. AD 100–1000) were repatriated to the tribe. Thus, the Pawnee's use of archaeology was an act of self-determination as they expanded and extended their cultural and geographical boundaries.

More recently, the Confederated Tribes of Grand Ronde in Oregon utilized a collaborative archaeology approach to "strengthen the tribe's capacity to care for cultural resources, to recover histories of survivance on the Grand Ronde Reservation, and to develop a low-impact, Grand Ronde archaeological methodology" (Gonzalez et al. 2018:85). This act of self-determination brings archaeology on the Tribe's lands under a broader umbrella of perspectives and research protocols oriented toward serving the Tribe's needs rather than just the research interests of archaeologists.

Despite the problems involved in trying to integrate American Indian values with the federal regulations and program requirements, participation within the NPS Tribal historic preservation program is an act of self-determination. As I mentioned earlier, by taking over at least some of the responsibilities currently held by the State Historic Preservation Officer on Tribal lands, Tribal groups are exercising their rights of self-governance.

Unfortunately, one of the biggest problems with the federal preservation system is that it was not established to prevent federal projects from going forward, but rather it was designed to require only that federal agencies take the impacts of their decisions into consideration. Basically, a heritage site of utmost importance to a Tribal group or community can be destroyed under federal historic preservation policies so long as the federal agency follows the appropriate procedures.

The National Park Service has repeatedly said it was not trying to force THPOs to be "mini-SHPOs," but its actions speak otherwise. The NPS program has forced tribes to create similar programs as the states within which they live and to "protect" heritage in a manner that they might not naturally use. Federal agencies would better serve Tribal interests and needs if tribes were given latitude to develop procedures that better fit Tribal norms and needs and the funding and authority to manage their heritage resources as they see fit.

Indigenous Archaeology as Activism

Stottman wrote: "As activist archaeologists, we consciously connect the past with the present; and although we may not save the world, in some small way, we can change it" (2010:15). Mickel and Olson write: "archaeology, and its umbrella discipline of anthropology, are, in fact, well-suited to activism" (2021).

I have recently written about activist archaeology (Watkins 2021) and do not intend to go into the topic too deeply here, but I believe that many of us already practice various sorts of "activist" archaeology. Cultural resources/heritage management practitioners recognize that archaeology has impact on and influences the communities within which we work. Jay Stottman's 2010 edited volume *Archaeologists as Activists* and Christopher Barton's more recent 2021 edited book *Trowels in the Trenches* bring the idea of archaeology as social activism to the forefront. While Sarah Cowie, Diane Teeman, and Christopher LeBlanc placed their research at Stewart Indian School in Carson City, Nevada, within the "collaborative" venue, their work is as much an activist project as a collaborative one (Cowie et al. 2019). The editors and the more than twenty authors of the volume demonstrate how a genuine collective effort between a variety of stakeholders can contribute to a fuller presentation of the various stories of the past.

But perhaps the greatest level of activism can be reached through the Tribal heritage preservation programs I have alluded to numerous times above. Archaeologists working for and with Tribal groups have the highest possibility of influencing change, at least on a local level. Thompson and Marek-Martinez write about "a holistic approach in which modern needs are balanced with the protection of cultural resources" (2021:212). In this way, they argue, tribes can actively help their members gain access to social and personal infrastructure needs while at the same time ensuring that cultural resources are not impacted unduly. Involving tribes in this system speeds up local projects, provides culturally based insights into any cultural resources encountered, and makes it easier for local members to get needed work accomplished. If this is not activism, then very little is.

There may be a point where activism becomes too much and can be seen as radicalism, especially now that the discipline is enmeshed in the politics associated with social justice issues and institutionalized racism within contemporary societies. The Society of Black Archaeologists, formed in 2011, uses the archaeology of the African diaspora as a mechanism for increasing social responsibility among archaeologists studying the African diaspora; the Association of Indigenous Anthropologists (AIA) within the American Anthropological Association was established in 2007–2008 with one of its stated purposes to "encourage professional work that will benefit both the discipline of anthropology and Indigenous communities" (statement of purpose at https://aia.americananthro.org/).

While the development of such organizations as the SBA and the AIA can be beneficial networks for incoming students and for emphasizing the

Indigenous Archaeology and Its Future

While creating this chapter, I have been struck with the question of whether Indigenous Archaeology has (or should have) a future. In 2010, George Nicholas wrote "Seeking the End of Indigenous Archaeology." In his article, Nicholas wrote about looking forward to an archaeology that was more inclusive of Indigenous perspectives, one where archaeology would "eliminate Indigenous Archaeology as a creature that resides solely outside of the mainstream" (Nicholas 2010b:233).

Nicholas's reasoning was not the same reasoning that was proposed by archaeologist Robert McGhee, who contends that "proponents of various forms of Indigenous Archaeology base their argument on a paradigm of Aboriginal essentialism ('Aboriginalism') that is derived from the long-discarded concept of Primitive Man" (2008:579). In McGhee's view, those who practice Indigenous Archaeology are not acting "in response to an intellectual problem but, rather, from the emotions and political reactions of scholars to Aboriginal communities that are socially and economically marginal, and that conceive of this situation as the result of historical mistreatment at the hands of western society" (2008:593). That is, the scientific practice of archaeology should be objective and unbiased toward all communities in such a way that archaeologists "cannot be intimidated by those who claim ethnically based special rights of access to archaeological materials, or special historical knowledge and abilities that are not available to those who practice science in the western tradition" (McGhee 2008:595).

Thus is an apparent dichotomy of perspectives on Indigenous Archaeology. McGhee believes "'Indigenous Archaeology' should be considered a branch of 'Aboriginal Studies,' rather than as a component of the academic discipline of archaeology" (McGhee 2008:595), whereas Nicholas believes that, without full integration into mainstream archaeology, it risks becoming "both ghettoized . . . and marginalised [*sic*] . . . thus constraining severely its potential contributions both to the discipline and to Aboriginal communities" (Nicholas 2010b:243). Michael Wilcox wrote that McGhee's solution of "'separate but equal' domains for scientific vs. Indigenous archaeologies misrepresents both science and Indigeneity as homogenous

184 · Joe Watkins

entities, affirms these positions as inherently dichotomized and invites comparison to some of the troubling philosophical legacies of racial segregation" (Wilcox 2010:221).

As we move forward, and as we push the boundaries of archaeology of all forms, we must continue to ask ourselves why we are doing archaeology "with, for, and by Indigenous peoples."

References

Anyon, Roger, T. J. Ferguson, and John R. Welch
2000   Heritage Management by American Indian Tribes in the Southwestern United States. *In* Cultural Resource Management in Contemporary Society, Perspectives on Managing and Presenting the Past. Francis P. McManamon and Alf Halton, eds. pp. 120–141. London: Routledge.

Atalay, Sonya L.
2006   Guest Editor's Remarks: Decolonizing Archaeology. Special Issue "Decolonizing Archaeology," American Indian Quarterly 30(3–4): 269–279.
2010   Chapter Four: Raise Your Head and Be Proud Ojibwekwe. *In* Being and Becoming Indigenous Archaeologists. George Nicholas, ed. pp. 45–54. Walnut Creek: Taylor & Francis.
2012   Community-Based Archaeology: Research With, By and For Indigenous and Local Communities. Berkeley: University of California Press.

Barton, Christopher P., ed.
2021   Trowels in the Trenches: Archaeology as Social Activism. Gainesville: University of Florida Press.

Colwell-Chanthaphonh, Chip
2009   Inheriting the Past: The Making of Arthur C. Parker and Indigenous Archaeology. Tucson: University of Arizona Press.
2012   Archaeology and Indigenous Collaboration. *In* Archaeological Theory Today. 2nd edition. I. Hodder, ed. pp. 267–291. Cambridge, UK: Polity.

Colwell-Chanthaphonh, Chip, and T. J. Ferguson, eds.
2007   Collaboration in Archaeological Practice: Engaging Descendant Communities. Lanham, MD: AltaMira Press.

Colwell-Chanthaphonh, Chip, T. J. Ferguson, Dorothy Lippert, Randall H. McGuire, George P. Nicholas, Joe E. Watkins, and Larry J. Zimmerman
2010   The Premise and Promise of Indigenous Archaeology. American Antiquity 75(2):228–238.

Cowie, Sarah E., Diane L. Teeman, and Christopher C. LeBlanc, eds.
2019   Collaborative Archaeology at Stewart Indian School. Reno: University of Nevada Press.

d'Errico, Peter
2000   Sovereignty: A Brief History in the Context of U.S. "Indian Law." *In* The Encyclopedia of Minorities in American Politics. J. D. Schultz, K. L. Haynie, A. M.

McCulloch and A. L. Aoki, eds. pp. 691–693. Phoenix, AZ: Oryx Press. https://www.umass.edu/legal/derrico/sovereignty.html, accessed December 16, 2021.

Echo-Hawk, Roger

2010   Working Together on Race. The SAA Archaeological Record 10(3):6–9.

Ferguson, T. J.

1996   Native Americans and the Practice of Archaeology. Annual Review of Anthropology 25:63–79.

2000   NHPA: Changing the Role of Native Americans in the Archaeological Study of the Past. *In* Working Together: Native Americans and Archaeologists. Kurt E. Dongoske, Mark Aldenderfer, and Karen Doehner, eds. pp. 25–36. Washington, DC: Society for American Archaeology.

Gonzalez, Sara L., Ian Kretzler, and Briece Edwards

2018   Imagining Indigenous and Archaeological Futures: Building Capacity with the Confederated Tribes of Grand Ronde. Archaeologies: Journal of the World Archaeological Congress 14(1):85–114.

Kerber, Jordan

2006   Cross-Cultural Collaboration: Native Peoples and Archaeology in the Northeastern United States. Lincoln: University of Nebraska.

King, Thomas

1998   Cultural Resource Laws and Practice. New York: Routledge.

McGhee, Robert

2008   "Aboriginalism and the Problems of Indigenous Archaeology. American Antiquity 73(4):579–597.

Merriam-Webster

n.d.   Self-determination. Online document. https://www.merriam-webster.com/dictionary/self-determination, assessed December 13, 2021.

Mickell, Allison, and Kyle Olson

2021   Archaeologists Should be Activists Too. Sapiens. Online document. https://www.sapiens.org/archaeology/archaeology-activists/, accessed December 13, 2021.

National Association of Tribal Historic Preservation Officers

2022   THPO Directory. Online at https://members.nathpo.org/thpodirectory/FindStartsWith?term=%23%21, accessed October 18, 2022.

Nicholas, George P.

2008   Native Peoples and Archaeology. *In* Encyclopedia of Archaeology, vol. 3. D. Pearsall, ed. pp. 1660–1669. New York: Academic Press.

2010a   Being and Becoming Indigenous Archaeologists. Walnut Creek, CA: Left Coast Press.

2010b   Seeking the End of Indigenous Archaeology. *In* Bridging the Divide: Indigenous Communities and Archaeology into the 21st Century. Carolyn Phillips and Harry Allen, eds. pp. 233–252. Walnut Creek: Left Coast Press.

2014   Archaeology, Indigenous. *In* Oxford Bibliography of Anthropology. J. L. Jackson, ed. Oxford: Oxford University Press.

Nicholas, George P., and Thomas D. Andrews

1997   Indigenous Archaeology in the Post-Modern World. *In* At a Crossroads: Archaeology and First Peoples in Canada. Nicholas and Andrews, es. pp. 3–18. Burnaby, BC: Simon Fraser University Department of Anthropology Archaeology Press.

Riggs, Charles R.

2017 Confronting Cultural Imperialism in North American Archaeology. Sapiens. Online document. https://www.sapiens.org/archaeology/native-american-archaeology/, accessed December 13, 2021.

Silliman, Stephen W.

2010. The Value and Diversity of Indigenous Archaeology: A Response to McGhee. American Antiquity 75(2):217–220.

Silliman, Stephen W., ed.

2008 Collaborating at the Trowel's Edge: Teaching and Learning in Indigenous Archaeology. Tucson: University of Arizona Press.

Smith, Claire, and H. Martin Wobst, eds.

2005 Indigenous Archaeologies: Decolonizing Theory. London: Routledge.

Stottman, Jay M., eds.

2010 Archaeologists as Activists: Can Archaeologists Change the World? Tuscaloosa: University of Alabama Press.

Supernant, Kisha, Jane Eva Baxter, Natasha Lyons, and Sonya Atalay, eds.

2020 Archaeologies of the Heart. Cham: Springer International.

Thompson, Kerry F., and Ora V. Marek-Martinez

2021 Engaging Archaeology as Social Justice for Navajo Communities. In Trowels in the Trenches: Archaeology as Social Activism. Christopher P. Barton, ed. pp. 211–222. Gainesville: University of Florida Press.

Watkins, Joe

2000 Indigenous Archaeology: American Indian Values and Scientific Practice. Walnut Creek, CA: AltaMira Press.

2003 Through Wary Eyes: Indigenous Perspectives on Archaeology. Annual Review of Anthropology 34:429–449.

2009. (How) Can Archaeology be Useful to American Indian Groups? Archaeological Dialogues 16(2):149–152.

2021 Conclusion: Beyond Archaeology as Science; Activist Archaeology for Social Action. In Trowels in the Trenches: Archaeology as Social Activism. Christopher P. Barton, ed. pp. 223–244. Gainesville: University of Florida Press.

Watkins, Joe, and T. J. Ferguson

2005 Working with and Working for Indigenous Communities. In Handbook of Archaeological Methods. Herbert D. G. Maschner and Christopher Chippendale, eds. pp. 1371–1405. Walnut Creek: Altamira Press.

Wilcox, Michael V.

2010 Saving Indigenous Peoples from Ourselves: Separate but Equal Archaeology is not Scientific Archaeology. American Antiquity 75(2):221–227.

CONTRIBUTORS

Ash Boydston-Schmidt (Apsáalooke Descendant) is the NAGPRA Coordinator at the Maxwell Museum of Anthropology. She recently graduated with a dual master's in museum studies and law from the University of New Mexico.

Honey Constant-Inglis (Sturgeon Lake First Nation, Saskatchewan) recently completed their master's at the University of Saskatchewan. Previously an interpreter and community coordinator at Wanuskewin Heritage Park, they are now a self-employed artist and heritage educator with Honey Willow nêhiyaw Studio.

Patrick Cruz (Ohkay Owingeh) is currently a PhD student at the University of Colorado, Boulder.

Lydia Curliss (Nipmuc) is currently a PhD student at the University of Maryland, College Park. She received her BA in geology from Oberlin College in 2013 and an MLS/MIS from Indiana University in 2018.

Zoë Antoinette Eddy (Anishinaabe/Wendat) is currently assistant teaching professor at Worcester Polytechnic Institute in the Department of Integrative and Global Studies. She received her BA in 2010 from Bowdoin College and her PhD in social anthropology and archaeology from Harvard University in 2019. Outside of her academic work, she is an advocate and activist for Missing and Murdered Indigenous Women, Girls, and Two-Spirit.

Nicholas C. Laluk (White Mountain Apache Tribe) is currently assistant professor of anthropology at the University of California, Berkeley.

Kay Kakendasotkwe Mattena (Citizen Band Potawatomi Nation) is currently a PhD student in anthropology and archaeology at the University of Massachusetts, Amherst.

Carlton Shield Chief Gover (Cîri–Pâri) is a citizen of the Pawnee Nation of Oklahoma. Carlton received his BS in anthropology from Radford University, his MA in anthropology from the University of Wyoming, and his PhD in anthropology with graduate certificates in museology and Native American and Indigenous studies at the University of Colorado, Boulder. He is currently assistant professor in the Department of Anthropology at The University of Kansas and assistant curator of archaeology at the KU Biodiversity Institute and Natural History Museum. He has conducted archaeological fieldwork in Virginia, Wyoming, Colorado, Nebraska, and across Ukraine. Using Indigenous oral traditions from the Pawnee, Arikara, and Wichita, he uses the radiocarbon record from the Central Plains to date events to identify periods of ethnogenesis and migrations.

S. Margaret Spivey-Faulkner (Pee Dee Indian Nation of Beaver Creek) is currently assistant professor in the Department of Anthropology at the University of Alberta. She received her AB from Harvard College in 2008, and her MA in 2011 and PhD in 2018, both from Washington University in St. Louis.

Ashleigh BigWolf Thompson (Red Lake Ojibwe) is Director of Tribal Collaboration in Research & Education at Archaeology Southwest. She holds BAs in Anthropology, American Indian Studies, English, and Multicultural Studies from the University of Minnesota–Morris and an MA in Anthropology from the University of Arizona.

Emily C. Van Alst (Mackinac Bands of Chippewa and Ottawa Indians) is assistant professor in the Department of Anthropology at Washington State University. She received her BA in Anthropology and Archaeology from Yale University in 2016. She received her MA in 2020 and PhD in 2023 both from Indiana University. Her research is focused on Indigenous women's relationships to rock art in the Northwest Plains.

Joe Watkins, a member of the Choctaw Nation of Oklahoma, is a senior consultant with Archaeological and Cultural Education (ACE) Consultants, LLC, in Tucson, Arizona. He is Visiting Professor in the Global Station for Indigenous Studies and Cultural Diversity, Hokkaido University, Japan (2022–2023), and associate faculty member of the School of Anthropology at the University of Arizona. He is internationally known for his publications on increasing the ethical practice of anthropology and the study of its relationships with descendant communities in the United States, Australia, New Zealand, and in Japan. He was president of the Society for American Archaeology from 2019 to 2021.

INDEX

Page numbers followed by *f* and *t* indicate figures and tables.

Abstraction, 87–88

Adson, Herb, 158

American Anthropological Association (AAA), 182

American Indian Movement (AIM), xxii

American Indian Religious Freedom Act (AIRFA), xxii–xxiii

Ancient History in the New World (Echo-Hawk), 157

The Ancient One, 141

Andersen, Chris, 87

Andrews, Thomas, 54, 174

Animal taxonomies, 34

Anishinaabe: *Deer Clan Story,* 148; epistemology, 139; knowledge (*anishinaabe-gikendaasowin*), 141–42; migration to Great Lakes region, 147; place and, 142; sacred sites of, 133–34; specters and, 4–5; storytelling, xxvii, 139–44, 147–51; theoretical understandings, 145; traditional foodways of, 147–50

Anthropology: colonialism and, xx, 8; concept of race in, xiv; emic perspective in, 33–35, 46; etic perspective in, 33–35; genocidal complicity and, 14–15; Indigenous ontologies, 70–71; Indigenous students in, xxi, 70–71, 155; museums and, 6; relevance to Indigenous communities, 140; spectrality and, 3–4; Western context of, 70–71

Apache, 83–84, 88, 90, 145, 159

Applewhaite, Che, 14–15, 18n9

Apsaalooke people, 96

Archaeological cultures: Arikara and, 160–61, 161*f,* 162, 162*t,* 163–65; Central Plains tradition (CPt), 160–61, 161*f,* 162, 162*t,* 163–66, 168*t;* chronological ordering of, 157,

164–66, 168*t;* descendant cultures, 161*f,* 162*t;* Extended Coalescent Variant, 160–61, 161*f,* 165–66, 168*t;* Initial Coalescent Variant, 160–61, 161*f,* 162*t,* 164–66, 168*t;* language separation, 161; living structures and, 158, 161; Lower Loup Phase, 160–61, 161*f,* 165–66, 168*t;* migration and population trends, 162–66; oral tradition and, 159–60, 162, 162*t,* 166–67; Pawnee and, 160–61, 161*f,* 162, 162*t,* 163–65; Post-Contact Coalescent Variant, 165–66, 167*f,* 168*t;* sequence of, 161, 161*f*

The Archaeological Record in Deep Time (Echo-Hawk), 157

Archaeologies of the Heart (Supernant et al.), xxv, 30

Archaeologists as Activists (Stottman), 182

Archaeology: academic privilege and, 74–75, 173; activism and, 183; activist, 181–82; archives and, 50, 53; artifact typologies in, 35–40; building relationships, 129–30; categorization in, 35; collaboration with Tribal communities, 65–69; colonialism and, xx–xxi, xxv, 82, 130; control of Native American sites, 117–18; decolonizing, xx–xxi, 82, 146–47; defining, xx; destruction and, 27–28; digging instruments, 84; digital technologies and, 57; emic perspective in, 35–40, 46–47; as European folk science, 33; Indigenization of, xxi, 30, 82–85, 92; Indigenous knowledge in, xxiii, 82–85, 116–17; Indigenous perspectives in, 71–72, 115–16; Indigenous theory in, 145; lack of care for artifacts, 25, 27–28; "othering" in, 23, 25; self-determination and, 179–81; social justice approaches, 54; storywork in, 140–41; Tribal self-determination and, 85; Tribal sovereignty and, 176–78; Truth and Reconciliation education, 111, 117–18. *See also* Indigenous archaeologies

190 · Index

Archibald, Jo-Ann, 144
Archives and libraries: absence of lived experience, 15; archaeological artifacts in, 50, 53, 59;
   collaboration in, 58; community-based, 52,
   54–56, 58–60; creation of memory in, 51–52;
   curation crisis in, 53, 59; decolonizing, 50, 58;
   digital technologies and, 57–58; ethical stewardship and, 57, 59–60; Indigenization of, 50,
   58; Indigenous archaeologies and, 7, 50–51,
   54–60; Indigenous Knowledge practices, 50,
   52, 55, 57–58; institutional backlogs in, 52–53;
   More Product, Less Process (MPLP), 53; organizational hierarchies of, 53–54; paradigms
   of, 51–52; Protocols for Native American
   Archival Materials, 55–56, 59; social justice
   approaches, 52, 54; spectrality and, 18n8;
   violence of, 7; Western context of, 51–52
Arikara: ancestry of, 156; archaeological
   cultures of, 160–61, 161f, 162, 162t, 163–66;
   linguistic analysis, 159–60, 160t, 161; migration of, 158–59, 162–66, 167f; oral tradition
   and, xxvii, 155–59, 163, 166–67
Artifacts: archival collections, 53, 57, 59; colonial violence and, 6, 12, 27; cultural heritage
   and, 27–29, 70; experimental archaeology
   and, 27; folk taxonomies and, 42; Indigenous knowledge and, xxiv, 29, 173; lack of
   care for, 25, 27–28; miscategorization of, 28;
   typologies of, 35–40, 42; white supremacist
   interpretation of, 53
Association of Indigenous Anthropologists
   (AIA), 182
Atalay, Sonya, xxiii–xxv, 30, 54, 76, 92, 100, 133,
   141, 146, 175, 178
Autoethnography, 10, 15

Bacon, Francis, 173
Bandelier National Monument, 66
Banks, Dennis, xxii
Barton, Christopher, 182
Basso, Keith, 87–91
Bayesian statistical analysis, 164–66, 168
Beading, 18n5
Bears Ears, 125
Bellecourt, Clyde, xxii
Bender, Barbara, 86
Benjamin, Walter, 25
Benton-Banai, Eddie, xxii

Berlin, Brent, 35, 41
Biidoban (Jackson), 29
Biidoban (Mattena), 1f
Biidoban in the Museum (Mattena), 23f
Binford, Lewis R., 35, 37–38, 85
Black Lives Matter, 119
Blanco, María del Pilar, 10, 18n7
Boas, Franz, xxi
Bowser, Brenda J., 86
Boydston-Schmidt, Ash, xxvii, 96
Bradley, John J., 86
Braided knowledge, 100, 146–48
Breedlove, Dennis E., 35, 41
Bruning, Susan B., 141
Bureau of Indian Affairs (BIA), 178–79
Burnette, Benrita, 84
Bustard, Wendy, 102

Caddoan Language Family, 159–60, 160t,
   162–63
Cajete, Gregory, 105
Canepotatoe, Jim, 115
Casey, Edward, 86
Center for Collaborative Synthesis in Archae-
   ology, 57
Center for Digital Antiquity, 57
Chaco Ancestors, 103
Chaco Culture National Historic Park, 100–103
Cherokee, 40
Cherokee Folk Zoology (Fradkin), 40
Chickasaw Nation, 96
Chippewa, 147
Choctaw, 96
Churchill, Winston, 173
Cibecue Apache, 83
Cipolla, Craig N., 74, 146
Collections: colonial power and, 8, 53; geno-
   cidal complicity and, 14–15; haunted by
   violence, 6–8, 12–13; Indigenous human
   remains and, 17n5; Indigenous materi-
   als in, 8, 18n5, 25, 53; living-ness of, 12–13,
   18n5; museums and, 6, 17n5; spectrality
   and, 10–12. See also Archives and libraries;
   Museums
Colonialism: anthropology and, xx, 8; archaeology and, xx–xxi, xxv, 82, 130; destruction caused by trowels, 84; destruction of
   natural/cultural relationships, 128, 134–35;

destruction of sacred sites, 125; haunting and, 3–4, 10; Indigenous trauma and, 16, 25–26, 29–30; museum collections and, 8, 18n6, 25, 53; in North America, xxi; notions of temporality, 4, 23; repatriation of materials, 5–6, 17n2; spectrality and, 5–6, 9, 15; violence and, 3–5, 12, 15, 104

Colorado Historical Society, 180

Colwell-Chanthaphonh, Chip, 175

Community-based archaeology: archaeology-community partnership, 76, 111–12; building relationships, 129–30; collaboration in, xxiv–xxv, 72–73, 76; defining community, 129–31; Indigenous-oriented, xix–xx, xxiii–xxv, 74–77; IRB approval and, 131; knowledge creation and, 130

Confederated Tribes of Grand Ronde, 181

Constant-Inglis, Honey, xxvii, 109

Cook, Terry, 51–52

Cordova, Viola F., 142

Cowie, Sarah, 182

Crow Canyon Archaeological Center, 73

Crow Tribe, 96

Cruz, Patrick, xxvii, 65–66

Cultural heritage: activist archaeology and, 182; AIM and, xxii; archaeologist control of, 117–18; archives and, 50–51; erasure of, 25–26; experimental archaeology and, 27; Indigenous archaeologies and, xxv–xxvii, 50–51; Indigenous communities and, xxiii–xxv, xxvii, 66, 128; Indigenous knowledge and, xxiii–xxiv, 27; Indigenous ontologies and, 126; Indigenous stories and, xxviii, 132; museum collections and, 25, 27–28; *Ndee* conceptions of, 85; oral tradition in, xxviii, 143, 148–49; preservation programs, 176–78, 181; Pueblo sites, 66–67; reclaiming of, xxvi–xxvii, 115–16, 126, 133–34, 146; self-determination and, 112, 178; transfer from elders to youth, 76–77; Tribal sovereignty and, 112, 140, 176–78

Curliss, Lydia, xxvii, 50

Custer Died for Your Sins (Deloria), 140

Dating Apps in Archaeology (Shield Chief Gover), 155

Deacon, Janette, 134

de Blainville, Henri Marie Ducrotay, 36

Decolonization: of archaeology, xx, 82, 146–47; archives and, 50, 58; braided knowledge and, 146–47; Indigenous archaeologies and, 27, 29; museums and, 28, 107; NAGPRA and, 107; relationship building and, 30; repatriation of land, 134; Truth and Reconciliation education, 117

Decolonization is not a Metaphor (Tuck and Yang), 134

Decolonizing Methodologies (Smith), xxi, 58

Deer Clan Story, 148

Deloria, Ella, xxi

Deloria, Vine, Jr., xxiii, 82, 89, 118, 140, 142

Derrida, Jacques, 4, 18n7

Digital Archeological Record (tDAR), 57–58

Dunnell, Robert C., 38–39

Echo-Hawk, Roger, xxiii, 140–41, 157–58, 167, 175

Eddy, Zoë, xxvi, 3, 118

Eiselt, Sunday, 86

Emic perspective: anthropology and, 33, 35; archaeology and, 46–47; artifact typologies and, 35–40, 42; categorization in, 35; folk taxonomies and, 40, 42, 47; Indigenous archaeologies and, 34, 74

Ethnogenesis, xxvii, 155–56, 166

Ethnography: analogies in, 36–37; collaboration in, 46; complicity in colonial violence, 3; cultural mapping, 132–33; cultural realities and, 46; folk taxonomies and, 40; Indigenous archaeologists and, 131–32; Indigenous marginalization in, 54, 130; oral tradition and, 158; as taxidermy of the past, 22–23, 25; western intellectual tradition and, 130

Etic perspective, 33–35, 40

Excavating Our Braids (Mattena), 123*f*

Experimental archaeology, 27, 29–30

Ferguson, T. J., 175

First Nations, 132, 174

Folk taxonomies: American, English-language, 40–41, 41*f*; benefits of, 45–46; classification of flora and fauna, 40–41, 41*f*, 42; emic perspective in, 40, 42, 47; ethnography and, 40; idealized generic hierarchy in, 42, 42*f*; Indigenous languages and, 42–47; lexical

192 · Index

Folk taxonomies—*continued*
  structures, 43, 43*f*, 44, 44*t*, 45, 45*t*; phyloge-
  netic trees in, 46; principles of, 41–42
Foodways, 147–51
Ford, James A., 33, 35–38
Fradkin, Arlene, 35, 40

Gamble, Philomene, 115
George Gordon First Nation, 114
Glacial Lake Saskatoon, 113
Glottochronology, 159–60, 160*t*, 161, 168
Golledge, R. G., 86
Gone, Joseph P., 16
Gonzalez, Sara, 130
Goodwin, Grenville, 83
Grand Ronde Reservation, 181
Grasslands National Park, 113
Greene, Mark, 53

Haakanson, Sven, Jr., xxiii
Harvard University, 14–15
Haunted by Empire (Stoler), 10
Haunting: anthropology and, 3–4; colonial
  violence and, 3–4, 6–7, 10–15; in cultural
  ghost stories, 4; Indigenous values and, 9;
  memory and, 10; museum collections and,
  5–7, 10–12, 14, 16, 118; past and present in,
  4–6, 9–10; as rupture and fission, 15–16;
  survivance and, 16. *See also* Spectrality
Hauntology, 4–6, 9, 18n7
Hayden, Brian, 35–36
Hidatsa, 159
Hunt, George, xxi

Idle No More, 119
Indian Removal Act, 176
Indian Residential Schools, 114, 118–19
Indigeneity: archaeology and, 33; archives and,
  7; defining, xx; Indigenous archaeologies
  and, 183–84; museum erasure of, 25, 28;
  place-based understandings, 87–92; realism
  and, 85
Indigenous activism, 119–20, 174–75, 181–82
Indigenous archaeologies: activist approach
  to, xx, xxii–xxiii, 174–75, 181–83; archives
  and, xxvii, 50–51, 54–60; assistance to home
  communities, 75, 77; collaboration in,

xxiv–xxv, xxviii, 54, 58, 77, 146; community-
  based, xix–xx, xxiii–xxv, xxvii, 56, 58–60,
  72–80, 111–12, 180; cultural lenses in, 34,
  131; defining, 175; digital technologies and,
  58; in education, 116–17; emic perspective in, 33–35, 47; heritage preservation
  and, 176–77; Indigenous knowledge and
  traditions in, 56–58, 72–73, 84–85, 148;
  Indigenous processes and products in,
  73–74; local contexts, 65–69; ontology and,
  127; perspectives on, 183–84; reconciliation and, 118; redress of inequalities, 73;
  self-determination and, 126, 134, 174, 178;
  social justice approaches, 54; stewardship
  and, 129–30; theory and, xxi, xxiv, 146;
  traditional practitioners and, 47; Tribal
  sovereignty and, 92, 131, 174–79
Indigenous Archaeologies (Bruchac), xxiv
Indigenous archaeologists: advocacy and,
  xxiii–xxiv, 59, 167; archaeological programming and, 116–18; archival materials and,
  54, 59; building relationships, 129–30; decolonizing archaeology, 82; emic perspective
  and, 74; ethnography and, 131–32; identity
  and, 109; Indigenous epistemology and,
  82–83; *Ndee* conceptual tools, 84; work with
  Tribal communities, xxvii, 65–69, 72–80,
  129–31
Indigenous Archaeology (Watkins), xxviii, 174
Indigenous communities: archaeological
  methods and, 91, 129; archives and, 50–51,
  53–54, 56; community-based archaeology
  and, 72–74, 77; dissemination of knowledge, 78, 105; harmful federal policies and,
  175–76; historical trauma and, 14, 16, 118–19;
  Indigenous archaeologies and, xxiv–xxv, 54,
  65–66, 72, 78–80, 129–31; museum practices
  and, 8–9, 69; natural/cultural relationships
  and, 128; non-federally recognized, 178–79;
  police abuse and, 114; repatriation of materials, xxvii, 55; temporality and, 132; Tribal
  IRB and, 131; visiting circles, 132–33
Indigenous historical trauma (IHT) narratives, 16
Indigenous Knowledge: archaeology and,
  82–85, 116–17; archives and, 52, 55, 57–58;
  braided knowledge and, 100, 146–48;

decentering of, 140–41; erasure of, 24–25, 28–29; experimental archaeology and, 27, 29–30; inclusive archaeology and, xx, xxiii, xxvi, 57, 60, 82, 183; information ecologies, 58; material culture and, xxvii, 29; oral tradition in, 142–43, 168; place-based, 83–84, 88–90, 142; rock art and, 125–28, 132–35; as spiritual gift, 141–42; storytelling and, 139–40, 143–44, 150–51; theory and, 145–46; Truth and Reconciliation education, 111; white supremacist interpretation of, 53–54

Indigenous languages: Caddoan Language Family, 159–60, 160*t*, 162–63; contemporary Indigenous lives and, 46–47; emic perspective in, 34–35; folk taxonomies and, 40, 42–47; glottochronology, 159–60, 160*t*, 161; linguistic analysis, 156, 159–61

Indigenous Methodologies (Kovach), 103

Indigenous ontologies: cultural heritage and, 126; emic perspective in, 74; importance of space and place in, 127–28, 133, 135; Indigenous archaeologies and, xxvi–xxvii, 70–71, 80, 126–27; rock art and, 127–28, 133

Indigenous-oriented archaeology, 74, 76

Indigenous peoples: archival documentation of, 53–54; collecting logic, 17n4; colonial violence and, 3–5, 12, 15, 104; embodied knowledge and, xxvi; folk sciences, 33; land-culture interactions, 24, 86; religious rights and protections, xxii–xxiii; self-determination and, 16, 85, 112, 126, 134, 174, 178, 181; seven generations and, 117, 134–35; temporality and, 4, 23; traditional knowledge and, 47; trauma and, 10, 16. *See also* Cultural heritage; Indigenous communities

Indigenous philosophy, 145–47, 150

Indigenous Storywork (Archibald), 144

Institute of American Indian Arts (IAIA), 69

Ioway, 159

Jackson, Andrew, 176
Jackson, Lisa, 29
Jefferson, Thomas, 176
Jicarilla Apache, 86–87

Kashia Band, 130
Kearney, Amanda, 86

Kelly, Robert, 155–56
Kerber, Jordan E., 175
Knife Chief, John Michael, 158
Kovach, Margaret, 103
Krieger, Alex D., 36–37

Laluk, Nicholas C., xxvii, 82, 91, 145
Land: Indigenous values and, 71; more-than-human relatives on, 142–43, 148; natural/cultural relationship, 86–87, 127–28, 132–33, 149; place-based understandings, 87, 90–91, 109, 113, 116, 142; preservation of sacred spaces, 68, 115; reclamation of, 134; rock art sites, 125, 127, 132–33; stewardship of, 113–14, 149; Traditional Ecological Knowledge (TEK) and, 24; western gaze and, 86. *See also* Place

LeBlanc, Christopher, 182
Lee, Mary, 115
Lekson, Steve, 67
Libraries. *See* Archives and libraries
Linguistic analysis. *See* Indigenous languages
Lippert, Dorothy, xxiii
Lithic materials, 5–6, 17n2
Lorna J. and Laurence K. Marshall Archive, 14

Mackie, Madeline E., 128
Mandan, 159
Manidoomin, 18n5
Marek-Martinez, Ora V., 182
Markey, Nola, 141
Marshall, John, 176
Martin, Jack B., 43
Martinez, Desiree, xxiii
Material culture: archaeology and, xxvi; ceramic analysis, 156; experimental archaeology and, 27, 30; folk taxonomies and, 33–34, 39; Indigenous knowledge and, xxvii–xxviii, 131, 135; Indigenous ontologies and, 127; misinterpretation by museums, xxvi; oral tradition and, 167; reclaiming heritage, xxvii, 134; Traditional Ecological Knowledge and, xxvi–xxvii, 27–28. *See also* Artifacts
Mattena, Kay Kakendasotkwe, xxvi, 1*f,* 22, 23*f,* 63*f,* 123*f*
Mauldin, Margaret McKane, 43
Mbembe, Achille, 12

194 · Index

McDonald, Jo, 133
McGhee, Robert, 183
McNab, Hilliard, 112, 114–15
Medicine, Beatrice, xxiii, 143
Meissner, Dennis, 53
Memory, 10, 51–52
Mickel, Allison, 181
Mike, Ernie, 115
Milholland, Sharon, 73–74
Mitchell, George, xxii
Mitsch, R. H., 12
Mohegans, 146
Mukii, Ng'endo, 22
Muscogee (Creek) Nation, 43
Museums: collaboration in, 25–26, 69–70; collections in, 6, 17n4, 70; colonial power and, 8, 18n6, 25–26; decolonizing, 28, 107; erasure of Indigeneity, 25, 28; haunted by violence, 6–8, 10, 12–14, 16, 18n6, 118; Indigenization of, xxvii, 8–9, 18n6; Indigenous materials in, 8, 18n5, 25, 53; Indigenous professionals in, 69; linear progression in, 25; misinterpretation of material culture, xxvi, 25; repatriation of materials, 5–6, 8, 17n2, 56, 59, 101, 140–41, 180; as sites of trauma, xxvi, 6, 9–14, 17, 26; social lives of Indigenous objects, 70; spectrality and, 3, 6, 9–14, 16–17, 18n7, 18n8; temporality and, 25, 29; Tribal, 8, 69. *See also* Collections
Mvskoke language, 43–44, 44*t*, 45, 45*t*

National Association of Tribal Historic Preservation Officers (NATHPO), 177
National Historic Preservation Act (NHPA), 176–77
National Park Service (NPS), 66–69, 100–101, 177–78, 181
Native American Graves Protection and Repatriation Act (NAGPRA): AIRFA and, xxii; archives and, 54; Chaco Canyon compliance, 100–103; DOI rulemaking process, 99–100; expansion of inventories, 104–5; GAO review of, 98–99; Indigenous responsibilities, 106–7; linkages of affiliation, 68; as living relationship, 96–100, 103–7; museum practices and, xxiii; National Park Service and, 101–3; process and compliance, 98–100, 104–7; repatriation of materials, xxvii,

8, 17n2, 55, 104, 107, 140–41, 168, 178; tDAR and, 58; Tribal participation and, 67, 75, 103–5; western scientific control in, 140–41
Native American Rights Fund (NARF), xxii
Native Science (Cajete), 106
Ndee: conceptions of place, 83, 86–91; contemporary western placenames, 88–90; cultural heritage management and, 85; *Gozhǫǫ* and, 85, 90; Indigenized wisdom and, 89–91; knowledge and, 84; moral responsibility and, 87
A New England Document, 14
New Systematics, 35, 38–39
Nicholas, George P., xxi, xxv, 54, 73, 141, 174–75, 183
94 Calls to Action, 118–19
Nokomis and Mishomis at the Precipice (Mattena), 63*f*
Northern Plains peoples, 110–11, 113, 115–16, 119, 125, 128
Northern Tonto Apache, 83

Oak Flat, 125
Ohkay Owingeh, 66
Ojibwe, 139, 141, 143, 147–51. *See also* Red Lake Ojibwe
Oka Crisis, 119
Olson, Kyle, 181
Omaha, 159
Only-A-Chief, Marti, 158
Opimihaw Valley, 109–13, 116, 119
Oral tradition: archaeological cultures and, 161–62, 162*t*, 166–67; archaeology and, xii, xiii, 140; Arikara, 155, 157–59, 163, 166–67; Bayesian statistical analysis, 164; chronology of migration in, 158–59; cultural heritage and, xxviii, 143, 148–49; ethnography and, 158; folk taxonomies and, 40; Indigenous knowledge and, xxvii, 142–43, 168; living structures in, 158–59, 161; Pawnee, xxvii, 155, 157–59, 163, 166–67; radiocarbon dating and, 155–57, 161, 163–64; Wichita, 157–58. *See also* Storytelling

Parker, Arthur C., xxi
Parker, Bertha, xxii
Pascua Yaqui, 139
Pawnee: aboriginal homeland, 180; ancestry

of, 156; archaeological cultures of, 160–61, 161f, 162, 162t, 163–66; identity and, 180; linguistic analysis, 159–60, 160t, 161; migration of, 155, 158–59, 162–66, 167f; oral tradition and, xi, xxvii, 155–59, 163, 166–67

Peabody Museum of Archaeology and Ethnology, 14–15

Peacock, Thomas, 143

Peeren, Esther, 10, 18n7

Perry, Richard, 84

Pike, Kenneth L., 34

Place: archaeological approach to, 85–87, 89–91; Indigeneity and, 87–92; Indigenous knowledge and, 142; Indigenous ontologies and, 127–28, 133; Jicarilla cosmogeography and, 86–87; meaning in placenames, 89–91; *Ndee* conceptions of, 83, 86–91; rock art and, 127–28, 135; self-reflection and, 88; storytelling and, 89; western gaze and, 86; White Mountain Apache and, 84; wisdom and, 89–91

Plains Cree, 109, 114, 116

Poarch Band of Creek Indians, 43

Pomo Indians, 130

Ponca, 159

Preucel, Robert W., 74

Protocols for Native American Archival Materials, 55–56, 59

Public archaeology, xxiii, 112

Pueblo peoples, 66–68, 75, 77

Radiocarbon data: Bayesian statistical analysis, 164–66, 168; Indigenous chronologies and, 157, 166–68, 168t; migration and population trends, 162–66, 167f; oral tradition and, 155–57, 161, 163–64; summed probability distributions (SPDs), 162–65, 168

Rainbow Fire, 88–89

Raven, Peter H., 35, 41

Red Lake Indian Reservation, 149

Red Lake Ojibwe, 139, 147–51

Red Lake Tribal Historic Preservation Office (THPO), 147–49

Reed, Matt, 158

Repatriation: archives and, 56, 59; Chaco Culture National Historic Park, 101; ethical and radical, 8; human remains and, 140,

180; Indigenous archaeologies and, 104; of the land, 134; lithic materials and, 5–6, 17n2; museums and, 5–6, 8, 17n2, 56, 59, 101, 140–41, 180; NAGPRA and, 8, 17n2, 55, 104, 107, 140–41, 168, 178; opposition to, 8; plains bison, 112; sacred objects and, 104–6, 140

Research is Ceremony (Wilson), 103

Riggs, Charles, 180

Rock art sites: community of artists in, 128; cultural knowledge and, 133–34; Indigenous-based preservation, 125–26, 128, 130–31, 133–35; Indigenous knowledge and, xxvii, 125–28, 132–35; Indigenous ontologies and, 127–28, 135; reclaiming heritage, 133; research methodology, 126–27; sacred sites of, 125; ties to place and land, 127–28, 132–33, 135; Western perspectives on, 125–26

Rouse, Irving, 37

Rutherford Falls, 134

Sacred objects: NAGPRA and, xxiii, 54, 99, 105; photography of, 105; protection of, xxii–xxiii; repatriation of, 104–6, 140, 180

Sacred sites: archaeological desecration of, 60, 97; colonial destruction of, 125; displacement of Indigenous from, 68, 125, 127; rock art and, 125–26, 133

Saginaw Chippewa peoples, 133

Salinas Burial Pit, 180

San Carlos Apache Tribe, 83

Sanilac, 133

Saskatchewan: education in Indigenous ways of knowing, 111–12; Glacial Lake Saskatoon, 113; Indian Residential Schools, 114, 118–19; Indigenous communities in, 110–11, 114–16; Opimihaw Valley, 109–13, 116, 119; Truth and Reconciliation education, 113, 117–18. *See also* Wanuskewin Heritage Park

Schillaci, Michael, 102

Scientific analysis: colonialism and, 130; cultural classifications and, 39; cultural lenses in, 34–35; etic perspective in, 33, 35; Euro-American ideals, 15, 178; folk taxonomies and, 40–41, 41f, 42, 42f, 43, 43f, 44–46; Indigenous perspectives and, 71–72, 183; IRB approval and, 131; objectivity and, 38, 46; phylogeny, 34, 40, 46; typologies and, 36–40

196 · Index

Self-determination: archaeology and, 179–81; cultural heritage and, 112, 178; defining, 179–80; Indigenous peoples and, 16, 85, 112, 126, 134, 174, 179–81
Seminole Nation of Oklahoma, 43
Seminole Tribe of Florida, 43
Shield Chief Gover, Carlton xix, xxvii, 155
Silliman, Stephen W., 175
Simpson, Leanne Betasamosake, 145
Skiri Band of Pawnee, 156, 158
Smith, Claire, 175
Smith, Linda Tuhiwai, xxi, 58, 145
Social Networks and Archival Context (SNAC) Platform, 57–58
Society of American Archaeology (SAA), xxi, 129
Society of American Archivists (SAA), 51
Society of American Indians, xxii
Society of Black Archaeologists, 182
Southern Apache, 83
Southwest, 36, 66, 69, 83, 87
Spaulding, Albert C., 33, 35–37
The Spectralities Reader (Blanco and Peeren), 10, 18n7
Spectrality: cultural theories of, 3–4; Indigenous knowing and, 8; Indigenous trauma and, 10, 14; museums and, 3, 6, 9–14, 16–17, 18n7, 18n8; real/unreal ghosts, 9, 12, 14; as rupture and fission, 16; settler colonialism and, 5–6, 9, 15; subjugation and, 5–6; trauma and, 10. *See also* Haunting
Spivey-Faulkner, Margaret, xxvii, 33, 127
Standing Rock, 125
Starlight Tours, 114
State Historic Preservation Office (SHPO), 177, 181
Steward, Julian H., 33, 36–37
Stewart Indian School, 182
Stimson, R. J., 86
Stoler, Anne, 10
Stop Asian Hate, 119
Stop Line Three, 119
Storytelling: *aandisokaana* (sacred stories), 143–44; Anishinaabe, 139–44, 147–51; in archaeology, xxvii, 140–41; cultural heritage and, xxviii; *dibajimowinan* (personal stories), 143–44; Elders' knowledge and, 141, 143, 147; Indigenous knowledge and, 143–44, 150–51; information through, 144; oral histories in, 142, 146; principles of, 144; sacred stories, 143–44; as spiritual gift, 141–42; as theory and method, 144–46, 150–51; traditional foodways in, 147–51. *See also* Oral tradition
Stottman, Jay M., 181–82
Strand, Kerry J., 76
Sturgeon Lake First Nation, 109
Sundstrom, Linea, 125
Survivance, 16, 150

Taçon, Paul, 128
Tantaquidgeon, Gladys, xxi
tDAR. *See* Digital Archeological Record (tDAR)
Teeman, Diane, 182
Temporality, 4, 23, 25, 29, 132
Temporal sovereignty, 23
Tewa peoples, 67, 77
Thomas, Terry, 134
Thompson, Ashleigh Big Wolf, xxvii, 139
Thompson, Kerry F., 182
Tipi Teachings (Lee), 115
Tobacco, Lawrence, 115, 120
Tohono O'odham, 139
Traditional Ecological Knowledge (TEK), xxvi–xxvii, 24, 27–29
Transforming Archaeology (Atalay), xxiv, 129
Trauma: colonial encounter and, 6, 25–26, 29–30; descendant community, 14; ghosts and, 10; Indian Residential Schools and, 114; Indigenous narratives, 16; museums as sites of, xxvi, 6, 9–14; spectrality and, 10
Travis, Rebecca Hatcher, 97, 107
Tribal archaeology, 74
Tribal Historic Preservation Officers (THPOs), 60, 129, 177–78, 181
Tribal museums, 8, 69
Tribal Preservation Officers/Tribal Historic Preservation Officers (TPOs/THPOs), 100
Tribal sovereignty: activist archaeology and, 182; archival documentation and, 54; cultural heritage management and, 112, 140, 176–78; federal recognition and, 176–77; Indigenous archaeologies and, 92, 131, 174–79; *Ndee* concepts and, 84–85; traditional territories and, 168

Trowels in the Trenches (Barton), 182
Truth and Reconciliation Commission (TRC), 117–19
Truth and Reconciliation education, 111, 113, 117–18
Tuck, Eve, 134
Two Bears, Davina, xxiii
Typologies: archaeological inquiry and, 35–40; artifacts and, 35–40; emic perspective in, 34–40, 42; etic perspective in, 34, 40; folk taxonomies and, 42; historical meaning and, 37–38; New Systematics and, 35, 38–39; normative stance, 37–38; pottery, 165; relative chronologies and, 36; scientific analysis and, 38–39; seriation and, 36; statistical analysis and, 36–37

Umatilla Tribe, 141
UNESCO World Heritage Site, 110, 113, 120
United Nations Declaration on the Rights of Indigenous Peoples (UNDRIP), 119
"Upright" (Travis), 106–7
US Department of the Interior, xxiii
US Forest Service, xxiii

Van Alst, Emily C., xix, xxvii, 125
Violence: archives as co-conspirators in, 52; colonialism and, 3–5, 12, 15, 104; haunting of museum collections, 6–7, 11–14, 16, 18n6; museum practices and, 14, 17n4, 18n6, 25. *See also* Trauma
Vitkowski, Mike, 113–14
Vizenor, Gerald, 150

Walker, E., 112, 114, 118, 120
Walter, Maggie, 87
Wanuskewin Heritage Park: archaeological research and, 113–14, 119; community-based archaeology and, 112; Elder's Council and, 110–12, 115; founding of, 110, 114–15; grasslands restoration efforts, 113, 120; Indigenous archaeologies and, 112, 120; Indigenous perspectives for, 109–10, 115; interpretive guides, 116; as National Historic site, 110, 119; *nehiyaw* worldviews in, 116–17; Northern Plains Indigenous peoples and, 110–11, 115–16, 119; reclaiming of cultural site, xxvii, 110, 113; Thundering Ahead fundraising campaign, 112–13; Truth and Reconciliation education, 111, 113, 117–18; as UNESCO World Heritage Site, 110, 113, 120
Wanuskewin Heritage Park Act (1997), 110
Wanuskewin Heritage Park Authority (WHPA), 110–11
Watkins, Joe, xxiii, xxv, xxviii, 99, 173, 175
Western Apache, 83–84
Whiteley, Peter M., 71
White Mountain Apache Tribe, 83–84
Whitridge, Peter, 86
Wichita, 156–57, 159, 160t
Wilcox, Michael, xxiii, 183
Wildcat, Daniel R., 85, 89–90
Willey, Gordon, xx
Wilson, Shawn, 103, 132
Wisuri, Marlene, 143
Wobst, H. Martin, 175
Wolfe, Patrick, xx

Yang, K. Wayne, 134
Yellow cattail pollen, 84
Yellowhorn, Eldon, xxiii
Yellowstone National Park, 113
"Young Bones" (Travis), 97

Printed in the United States
by Baker & Taylor Publisher Services